PASCUA

A Yaqui Village in Arizona

PLATE I
Matachín Musicians

PASCUA

A Yaqui Village in Arizona

EDWARD H. SPICER

THE UNIVERSITY OF ARIZONA PRESS
Tucson, Arizona

About the Author

EDWARD H. SPICER (1906–1983) spent much of a distinguished career in anthropology teaching and writing about American Indians. In terms of a lifelong conviction that "one goes to ordinary people for cultural essentials," Spicer learned about Indian peoples by living among them, residing at various times in two different Yaqui villages: old Pascua in Tucson, Arizona, and Potám in Sonora, Mexico. The present volume, first in a renowned series of village studies, offers the pioneer discussion of ritual kinship, a focal point for modern anthropologists' thinking about social organization. Spicer, who joined the University of Arizona faculty in 1946, became editor of the *American Anthropologist* and president of the American Anthropological Association. Author of nine books and countless essays and articles, Spicer was perhaps best known for *Cycles of Conquest* (1962) and *The Yaquis: A Cultural History* (1980), both published by the University of Arizona Press.

THE UNIVERSITY OF ARIZONA PRESS
First Printing 1984
Manufactured in the U.S.A.

Library of Congress Cataloging in Publication Data

Spicer, Edward Holland, 1906–
Pascua, a Yaqui village in Arizona.

Reprint. Originally published: Chicago: University of Chicago Press, 1940.
Bibliography: p.
Includes index.
1. Yaqui Indians. 2. Pascua Village (Ariz.)—Social life and customs. 3. Yaqui Indians—Rites and ceremonies. 4. Indians of North America—Arizona—Rites and ceremonies. I. Title.
F1221.Y3S65 1984 306'.08997 83-18312
ISBN 0-8165-0845-3

TABLE OF CONTENTS

LIST OF ILLUSTRATIONS

PLATES

FIGURES

LIST OF TABLES

FOREWORD

RECENTLY Alexander Lesser has argued, for the benefit of anthropologists, the wisdom of defining research enterprises in terms of problems rather than of mere subject matter.[1] The present volume is evidence to the point. Before he began his field investigation, Dr. Spicer had learned enough about the Pascua community to make it seem probable that it held facts bearing on a problem of general importance. Preliminary information indicated that the people of that Arizona village constituted a well-integrated society, although their religious and ritual activities were unrelated to their ways of maintenance. These Indians, he knew, had become day laborers on cotton ranches or employees on casual jobs, and with these activities their ceremonial life and religious conceptions, known to have been imported from Mexico, where they had been hunters and independent farmers, could have little to do. If, indeed, the Pascua society should nevertheless be found to be in relatively stable adjustment, then it would present an exception to an (approximate) generalization, for we are used to finding in simple societies that the ritual and religious life centers around the supply of food or other objects of economic value. We have many cases (furthermore, thought Dr. Spicer) of primitive societies whose entire social life has been disorganized by a change of circumstances destroying the old ways of making a living, the religion and the social

[1] "Problems versus Subject Matter as Directives of Research," *American Anthropologist*, XLI, No. 4 (new ser.; October–December, 1939), 574–82.

organization which depended on the maintenance customs disintegrating as a result. If Pascua should present a case where this did not happen, it would be a strategic place for research. So he set himself the task of determining the relations now existing between the economic life of that community, on the one hand, and the social organization and religion, on the other.

If Dr. Spicer's report does not quite prove that a simple society may long endure with a social organization and a moral and religious life which take little account of the ways of making a living, it does at least indicate that such a society might indeed persist. The reader, before he finishes the book, will think of ways these Yaquis could develop in which to support the ceremonial leaders so that no man need give up his ritual responsibilities in order to make a living. If they did develop such a solution and nothing else happened to disturb them, the society might go on for a long time as it is. It appears from this account that it is not so necessary as might have been supposed that ritual values of a simple society center about the necessities of economic life.

A striking fact about the people of Pascua is, then, that their working lives form a separate compartment of their existence. They work outside the system of values which characterize Pascua as a distinct culture group, but they pray, cure, and associate with one another within that system. With the exception noted, Pascua turns out to be like most folk or primitive societies in that it is a society of kinship, in that the social organization is, so to speak, extended into and supported by the religious conceptions, and in that much of conduct rests under sacred sanctions. The degree to which integration does exist—setting aside the work customs—is impressive. Did the immigrants from Mexico bring the present organization with them, developed as we now find it? This may be doubted when it is remembered that they came from different Yaqui communities in Mexico and at different times.

Dr. Spicer's materials give strong suggestion that adjustment of religion and social organization to each other, and of parts of each to other parts, has taken place in response to the changed conditions. The reinterpretation of the *pascolas* and the divergent efforts at such reinterpretation by individual Yaquis are evident instances of that process whereby consistency among elements of a culture comes about through the persisting living-together of communicating individuals. One wonders if the interesting, threefold system (kinship, sponsorship, and ceremonial societies) by which relations among members of the society are established and regulated fully developed only after settlement in Arizona. The hypothesis may be entertained that the extension of the sponsor system to include all the community may have been a response to a need for solidarity in a new and alien world—a speculation with which Dr. Spicer may not agree. It strikes at least this reader that the present form of social organization is well adapted to the situation in which the Yaqui now find themselves—in that, while security and status are provided for everyone, the kinship relations are, as Dr. Spicer puts it, "generalized," so as to make it possible for individuals to drop out and the composition of groups frequently to change, as must be the case where men leave to work in other fields or on other outside jobs. The looseness of the household groups is another corresponding feature. Pascua social structure preserves the solidarity of the whole society while it is so flexible as to allow for frequent changes in its personnel.

Thus the work, guided by a sense of specific problem, gives rise to new hypotheses as to the course of change in Pascua. It is suggested that this society, at least as represented in its ceremonies, "is moving from a former system based on intimate connection with the natural environment . . . . to a pattern which is not closely related to the natural environment." In this new system curing plays a central role, instead of interest in assuring the food supply, as must have been true in earlier days in Mexico. It is shown that one ceremonial institution, the deer-dancer, having no meaning except the old connection with hunting, is becoming simply secular entertainment, and thus, inadequately supported by functional value, tends to disappear altogether. In contrast the religious dancers known as *pascolas* seem to be developing firmer connections with the funeral cult and the sacred beings of Catholic origin; they are entering into the newer system of values. Dr. Spicer properly recognizes that these hypotheses call for historical research and will also receive support or confutation from study, such as Dr. Ralph Beals has made and will make known to us, of other Yaqui groups.

There are other aspects of this book which deserve comment and approbation. The student of kinship systems will welcome in the chapter "Ceremonial Sponsorship" a detailed account of what is perhaps the most extensive instance of ritual kinship that we have. The author is to be applauded for the recognition he has given to the fact that the conflicts arising in a situation of social change are to be studied not simply in the changing forms of customs but as "a collection of conflicts of varying intensity in the daily activities of specific persons." The distinction with which the volume concludes between that solution whereby conflicting ideas are adjusted by modification so that a system of conventional understandings is preserved and that solution whereby an individual ceases to live in terms of the entire system, but only of a part of it, is suggestive in the study of social process. The latter outcome, illustrated by those Yaqui who give up the ceremonial life because they cannot maintain it and make a satisfactory living, brings about that compartmental or fragmented sort of living which is characteristic of the civilized societies as contrasted with those characterized by well-integrated cultures. In this connection the attempt to clarify the distinction between "culture" and "society" is noteworthy. And—to mention a very different reason for praising this work—we must welcome a study of an Indian group in the Southwest which does not make out that the Indians exist without relations with other people but which realistically reports the society as composed of both Indians and non-Indians.

The work is another evidence of the existence in that miscellany called "social science" of orderly study of social phenomena without reference to immediate action and with guidance from a well-defined problem of general theoretical interest.

ROBERT REDFIELD

UNIVERSITY OF CHICAGO
February 1940

PREFACE

THE Yaquis of Arizona differ from those in Mexico in that they are undergoing contact with a culture which is non-Spanish in origin. Mexican Yaquis have been experiencing an acculturation process, ever since the early 1600's, which has resulted in an intricate interpenetration of aboriginal and Spanish cultural elements. There seems to be good evidence that Yaqui culture in about 1880, when Yaquis first began coming to the United States, was greatly hispanicized, although it could be regarded as showing less Spanish influence than the cultures of the central Mexican plateau. The Yaquis of Arizona, in making their adjustment to the cultural milieu of the United States, have preserved in striking fashion the Spanish-Indian forms of social and ceremonial organization which had been developed in Sonora by the 1880's. They are, nevertheless, subject to a new set of influences which is certain to give a different direction to their cultural development. The effects of the new contact will be more apparent twenty years from now, but what is taking place at present may, nevertheless, be studied as it happens. The present volume is a result of an attempt to carry out such a study. It seeks to examine one village of Yaqui Indians in southern Arizona in an effort to isolate, on the one hand, some of the factors which are making for cultural stability and, on the other, some of those which are bringing about change.

THE PROBLEM

Pascua Village is a settlement of Yaqui Indians on the outskirts of the city of Tucson. Its inhabitants are either immigrants from Mexico or descendants of those immigrants, the former having entered the United States at various times from 1882 to the present. In 1934 Dr. John H. Provinse of the University of Arizona became interested in the fact that the village maintained an elaborate set of ceremonies annually at Easter and in other ways remained distinct from the surrounding Mexican population, despite apparent assimilation into American economic life. It seemed to him that some explanation was required for this maintenance of cultural integrity. In the spring of 1936 he suggested to the writer that a study of the village be made. A plan of research was formulated with the assistance and ultimate approval of Dr. Robert Redfield of the University of Chicago, and field work was begun under the auspices of the latter institution in July, 1936.

As originally formulated, the problem guiding the field research was as follows:

> Pascua may be classified as an immigrant "peasant" group which has voluntarily come into contact with an urban environment. The village presents an instance of culture contact between friendly groups of markedly different size and of unequal degrees of complexity in material and nonmaterial culture. . . . . It appears that the sort of acculturation with which we are dealing in the case of Pascua is adaptation. That is, the community at the present stage of its development is maintaining most of the institutions and customs with which its members entered the United States; yet at the same time it has taken over, and is participating in, many aspects of the surrounding culture. This participation is most marked in the case of economic life and material culture. To all outward appearances, however, this fusion of traits has not resulted in any breakdown of the cultural organization of the group. . . . . In general, the village presents the appearance, at least from a superficial view, of a well-integrated community, exhibiting a minimum of culture conflict. . . . . In view of this apparent satisfactory integration of new traits with old, the village provides an opportunity for the study of the nature and the processes of adaptation under conditions of acculturation. A specific problem in this connection may be stated as follows: What is the nature of the relationship that exists

at present between the economic aspects of Pascua culture and the social organization, the system of social control, and the religious ritual and concepts?[1]

Implicit in this statement of the problem was the belief that Pascua provided a very simple situation for the study of "culture contact." The situation was conceived of in somewhat the following manner. A culture, that of Sonora Yaquis, had been lifted bodily, as it were, and placed in contact with American culture. A proof of the bodily lifting was seen to lie in the continued existence of the elaborate Easter and other ceremonies. The general nature of the contact also appeared fairly clear. It consisted in the daily participation of the bearers of Yaqui culture in the economic system of the Americans, a participation demanded by the necessities of physical existence. Here, then, was a sort of splicing of cultures: the combination of an economic system developed in one culture with a social and ceremonial system developed in another. The question immediately arose: How do they fit together? If they fit harmoniously, how is that to be explained? If there is conflict, what is its nature? The answers which were obtained to these questions are detailed in the following pages.

However, a large part of the present study is devoted merely to stating the problem with more precision. For instance, on closer examination it became apparent that the culture was not "lifted bodily," that it had suffered a ten- to twenty-year interval of suppression during which time its main features lived only in the memories of its bearers. It was revived in the form of overt behavior only some time after the Yaquis arrived in the United States.

[1] E. H. Spicer, "A Problem in Acculturation To Be Attacked through Field Investigation" (manuscript in Department of Anthropology, University of Chicago).

Again, the "economic assimilation" has had to be defined in the light of the actual situation in the village. Economic assimilation consists in a great deal more than the taking-over of techniques and the acceptance of wage labor, for example, as a means of subsistence. In the light of closer study it became apparent that these acceptances did not involve the acceptance of the values of the economic system from which they were taken. It became necessary to define just what economic assimilation meant in this particular case and what it did not mean. Accordingly, much of what follows is concerned with a restatement of the assumptions which influenced the formulation of the problem.

The original statement of the specific problem avoided the difficulties involved in the approach just discussed, but it is clear that the assumptions mentioned played a part in the formulation of the problem. As it was first stated, the task was seen as primarily the determination of the functional interrelations of the different aspects of the culture of the village. The preliminary statement went on to say:

> The problem is not of the from-when to-when type. It is not proposed that the present study of Pascua concern itself with comparisons with Yaqui . . . . culture in Mexico. Such considerations will be in order only after the present study is completed. Even if the results of recent studies of Yaqui culture in Mexico were available, it is not likely that their conclusions could be used as a datum plane for comparison. The members of the present group originated in different parts of the Yaqui country. They did not come from the same, nor so far as we know, identically constituted communities. They probably represent communities in which the processes of acculturation had already taken diverse directions. A generalized description of Yaqui-Mexican culture could hardly, therefore, serve as a base from which we could deduce the culture of our particular group.
>
> The problem is one of determining the character of the present integration between economic and other aspects of the culture. It is pro-

posed that this can be got at through the analysis of three types of facts:

1. The deliberate adjustments which the group, as a group, is making (or has made in the recent past) to the new economic adaptation, e.g., modification of ceremonial schedules to fit the exigencies of holding jobs.
2. The modification of Western concepts of economic life, e.g., the expansion of the idea of individual ownership of land to that of family or kin group ownership of land although the land is held by Western deed.
3. Individual conflicts that center about or are connected with the economic life, e.g., conflicts between the necessities of holding a job and the demands of a kinship behavior pattern.[2]

All three of these lines of approach were pursued, the last being the most fruitful. But the greater part of the field work was devoted to determining the outlines of the unfamiliar social institutions which were found to exist in the village. A discussion of the manner in which they were studied is now in order.

THE FIELD PROCEDURE

The writer and an assistant, his wife, began work in July, 1936, maintaining residence in the village through June, 1937. The whole of this time was spent in the village, except for three weeks in November, when a brief survey of other Yaqui settlements in Arizona was carried out. The investigators lived not with a Yaqui family but in a building in the village which had formerly been used as a hospital.

The conditions under which the investigators worked may best be summarized by indicating the general nature of the contacts with villagers during the course of the year. For the first two months no systematic research into village affairs was carried out. Two students of Dr. Prov-

[2] *Ibid.*

inse had been living in the village during the preceding year, and the newcomers were known simply as friends of these men. They established themselves in their house, made casual acquaintances in the village, attended all public ceremonies, and let it be known only that they were interested in the language. During this period the most intimate contacts were with children from the neighboring families and young boys who gathered at the house to play the musical instruments possessed by the investigators. Efforts were concentrated chiefly on mastering conversational Spanish and gathering material for the study of the Yaqui language.

At the beginning of the third month a village official, the third *maestro* in the church, began coming to the house. He proved willing to talk at length about the history of the village and of Yaquis in Mexico. For the next two months almost daily conversations were held with this man, and during this time the objectives of the study were made known to him. He became a conscious informant, much of the material gained from him being recorded in his presence. He remained throughout the year very intimate with the investigators, and they came to rely on him greatly. Still, although ceremonies were attended and acquaintance throughout the village was widened, there were no other intimate contacts except with the children who continued to come to the house.

The greater part of the fifth month was spent in a survey of other Yaqui villages in Arizona and of the few isolated families scattered over the state. Acquaintances were made in all but one of the other villages, and interviews were conducted in each. Pascua families who were employed at various ranches picking cotton were visited, and some study of their life under these conditions was carried out.

Shortly after the investigators' return to Pascua a lonely

bachelor committed suicide, and they were called in by his neighbors to deal with the county authorities who concerned themselves in the case. From this time on, the beginning of the sixth month, the investigators were called with increasing frequency to act as go-betweens in matters involving the relations of Pascuans with city and county officials. They continued for the next seven months to arrange funerals and to call the county doctor whenever such actions were desired by any Pascuans. During the period some form of this service was rendered for all but one or two Pascua families. The investigators began to have a definite function in the village. All houses were open to them, and no excuses were necessary for their increasingly obvious interest in village affairs.

With the development of this social function, the leaders of the village began to establish increasingly intimate contacts with the investigators. One of them in particular, the leader of a dance society, began making almost daily visits to their house, and through him they were enabled to keep in touch with most of the happenings not only of a public but also of a private character. Through him they began to eat regularly at *fiestas* at the special table for the dance society of which he was leader. In this and other ways he brought them into close contact with the details of the ceremonial organization.

At the same time that contacts with village leaders were being developed, intimacy with neighbors was being cultivated. This intimacy culminated at Easter in the investigators' becoming godparents of one of the children of a neighboring family. The godparent relation established social bonds not only with this family but also with three others, the families of previously established godparents of the child. During the remaining three months contacts with these families became so intimate as to hinder, at times, the more systematic work which the investigators were attempting to carry on. The end of the year's stay found the investigators so involved in village affairs that proper recording of happenings and their interpretation was seriously interfered with.

In general, the program followed was to observe and record whatever events came to notice in the village and then to examine these in the context of the personalities who participated in them. In so far as possible reliance on one or a few individuals for supplementary data was avoided. Efforts were made to extend contacts as widely as possible. Naturally, village-wide contacts of which use could be made in the investigation of each event could not be established in even such a small community. The investigators became especially friendly with six or seven individuals and came to rely on them more than on others for information and interpretations. No regular paid informants were employed, although many gifts were made to individuals who were especially helpful.

The techniques of observation and record-making cannot be said to have been reduced to highly systematic or efficient form. In the first place, the fact that the Spanish language had to be mastered during the course of the year and that Yaqui never was mastered reduced the efficiency of all observations. With all but two of the most frequently used informants, conversations and interviews were carried on in Spanish. With the two exceptions English was used. The investigators ultimately became able to get the drift, but only the drift, of public speeches and conversations in Yaqui. A few interviews in Yaqui were conducted with children toward the end of the period of residence. Interpreters were not used at any time.

The immediate objectives of the field work were to obtain a complete record of the events which took place in the village during the year and to obtain life-histories of each individual. Neither objective was realized. The first was pursued by means of keeping diaries in which all events which came to the observers' notice were recorded. "Events" included the daily round of life in households with which the observers were most intimate, ceremonial occasions, extra-village activities of Pascuans, and conversations overheard or participated in by the observers. Little conscious selection of events was made until well along in the study when the main outlines of the culture were beginning to be understood. Ultimately a greater or less amount of information was obtained either directly or indirectly concerning the past history and present views and activities of every individual living in Pascua. This information was recorded and filed under each person's name.

The greater part of the material collected is contained in the two chronological accounts of village affairs during 1936–37, the diaries of the investigators. In these are records of daily happenings which came to their attention along with any village comment which could be gathered. There are detailed accounts of marriages, baptisms, wife-beatings and their aftermaths, ceremonies of all kinds, passive non-co-operation with the city dogcatcher, opinions of one villager concerning another, witchcraft cases, domestic techniques, etc.

Interview was the technique ranking next in importance to observation of behavior. Interviews were conducted for the most part as efforts to obtain interpretations of events as they happened. The method of intensive interview of specific individuals for the purpose of obtaining a detailed knowledge of their personal organizations of the culture was not pursued. Interviews were frequently conducted during *fiestas*, as the observers stood about with the crowd or assisted in the ceremonies. More extended interviews were, however, conducted in other ways, in the homes of the villagers or of the investigators. Chiefly the objective was to get the person interviewed to talk about anything in which he was interested. At first anything whatever was considered relevant, and the interviews took the form of casual conversations. Later, as the observers were beginning to be able to find their way around in the culture, the interviews had more specific direction. Several consecutive days, for example, would be devoted to aspects of kinship, an investigator remaining in a single household talking with individuals in the family as he noted behavior and attitudes. Toward the last, but never at first, notes were sometimes taken during the course of such interviews. The great majority of interviews were recorded only after they had taken place.

ORTHOGRAPHY

All Spanish words have been transcribed according to conventional Spanish orthography.

With certain exceptions, Yaqui words have been transcribed in the International Phonetic Alphabet. For the benefit of those not familiar with this system of transcription, attention is called to the following symbols which are of frequent occurrence in Yaqui words:

ʧ has the sound of *ch* in English *choose.*

ʾ (the glottal stop) has no English equivalent but consists in a sudden stoppage of the voice by a contraction of the throat.

j has the sound of *y* in English *yes.*

χ has the sound of *ch* in German *nacht.*

ˈ is the stress accent symbol and always *precedes* the accented syllable.

Vowels are, in general, like those of Spanish and may be so pronounced without fear of misunderstanding.

Other consonants are, in general, like those of English.

Yaqui plurals end in *m.*

There seems to be no traditional usage as regards the word *matachín;* it occurs in the literature in different forms, such as *matachine*, *matachin*, and *matachina*, various observers recording it in accordance with local usages. It is recorded here in Spanish orthography, but as the Yaquis pronounce it, that is, as *matachini*. It has also been given the Spanish plural. It should be borne in mind that this word and others frequently used in the text, such as *maestro* and *cantora*, have accepted Yaqui forms. The Spanish forms are used in what follows merely to facilitate reading.

ACKNOWLEDGMENT

The field work on which this study is based was financed by the Department of Anthropology of the University of Chicago. The writer takes this opportunity to express his thanks to the members of the department for this assistance. He is also greatly in debt to Dr. John H. Provinse of the United States Soil Conservation Service for the original suggestion that Pascua Village be studied and for invaluable counsel during the course of the field work. At the beginning of the investigation much help was received from Mr. Philip Welles and Mr. David J. Jones, Jr., students of Dr. Provinse who were already resident in Pascua. Assistance in the linguistic aspects of the work was rendered by Dr. George Herzog of Columbia University, and a very pleasant and fruitful contact was enjoyed in the field with Dr. Ralph L. Beals of the University of California at Los Angeles. Dr. Beals also placed at the disposal of the writer his unpublished manuscripts on the Yaquis and Mayos of Sonora. Miss Thamar Richey and Miss Doris Weston of Tucson were helpful in many practical ways during the whole year of residence in the village. In the preparation of the manuscript Dr. Robert Redfield and

Dr. Fred Eggan of the University of Chicago gave much valuable assistance. Both the field work and the writing-up of the material were carried on at all times in collaboration with Rosamond B. Spicer. To all these persons the writer is extremely grateful.

Grateful acknowledgment is made to Edwin F. Embree of the Rosenwald Fund for the interest and support he has extended to this and other University of Chicago projects in the field of race relations and minority groups.

To indicate the full extent of the collaboration in the work, it would be necessary to mention all of the four hundred and twenty-nine individuals in Pascua Village, but it is possible to name some as having contributed more than others. The writer recalls with especial pleasure and gratitude his association with Sra. Juana de Amarillas, Sr. Frank Acuña, Sr. Ignacio Alvarez, Sr. Tomás Alvarez, Sr. Guadalupe Balthazar, Sr. Lucas Chavez, Sr. José María Casillas, Sr. Jesús Garcia, Mr. Cayetano Lopez, Sr. and Sra. Luís Martinez, Sr. Sixto Matus, Mr. Joe D. Romero, Mr. Refugio Savala, Mr. Juan Silvas, Mr. Dolores Valenzuela, Miss Salamina Valenzuela, and Sra. Micaela Vasquez. Without their constant co-operation no progress could have been made in the study.

Plates II, III, and IX are from photographs made by Mr. David J. Jones, Jr.; Figures 1 through 9 are from drawings made by Rosamond B. Spicer.

Fictitious personal names have been used in most instances throughout the text.

E. H. Spicer

University of Arizona
September 1939

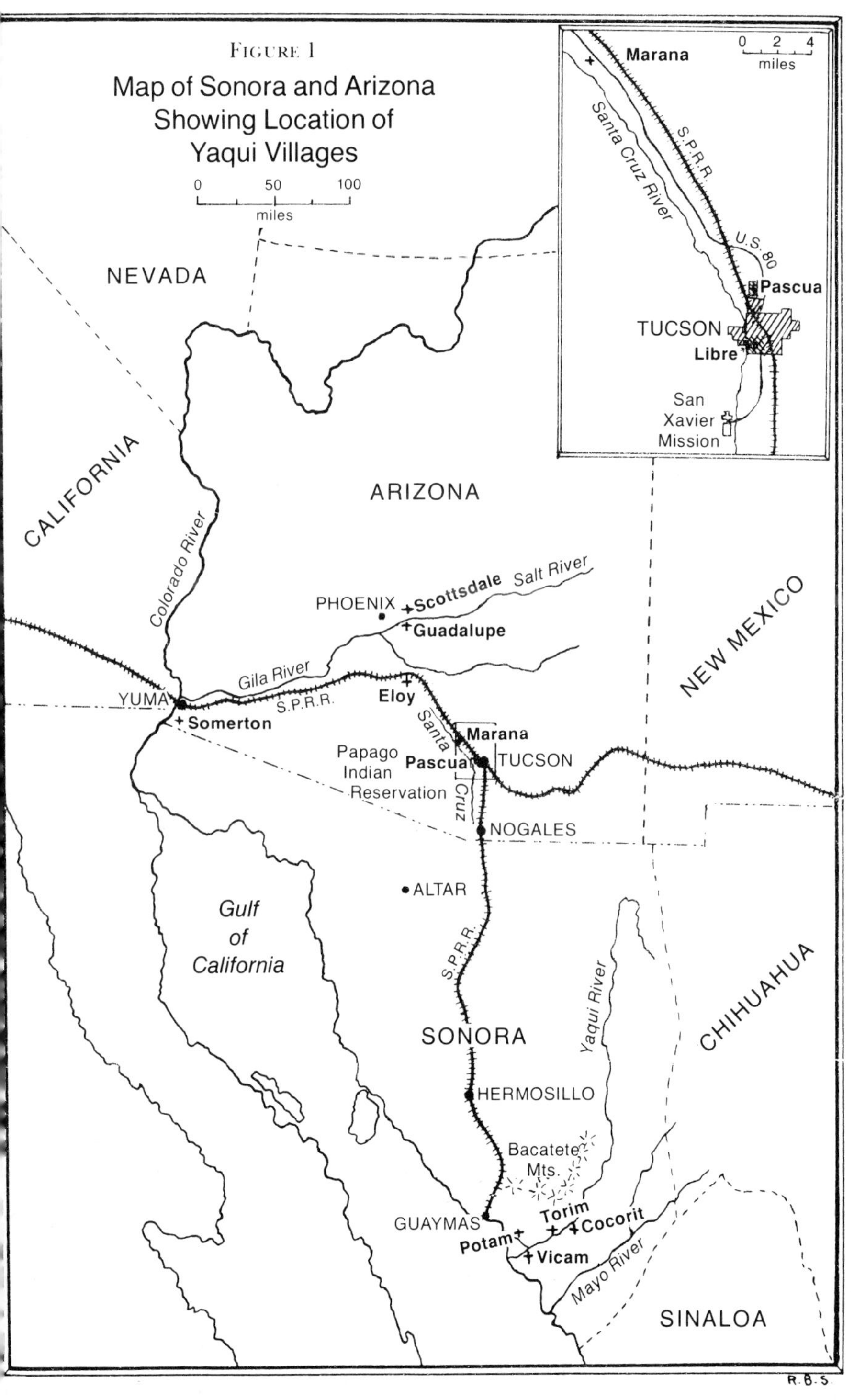
Figure 1
Map of Sonora and Arizona
Showing Location of
Yaqui Villages
0
50
100
miles
NEVADA
CALIFORNIA
ARIZONA
NEW MEXICO
CHIHUAHUA
SONORA
SINALOA
Colorado River
Salt River
Gila River
PHOENIX
Scottsdale
Guadalupe
YUMA
Somerton
S.P.R.R.
Eloy
Santa
Cruz
Marana
Pascua
TUCSON
Papago
Indian
Reservation
NOGALES
ALTAR
Gulf
of
California
Yaqui River
HERMOSILLO
Bacatete
Mts.
GUAYMAS
Torim
Cocorit
Potam
Vicam
Mayo River
0
2
4
miles
Santa Cruz River
U.S. 80
Libre
San
Xavier
Mission
R.B.S.

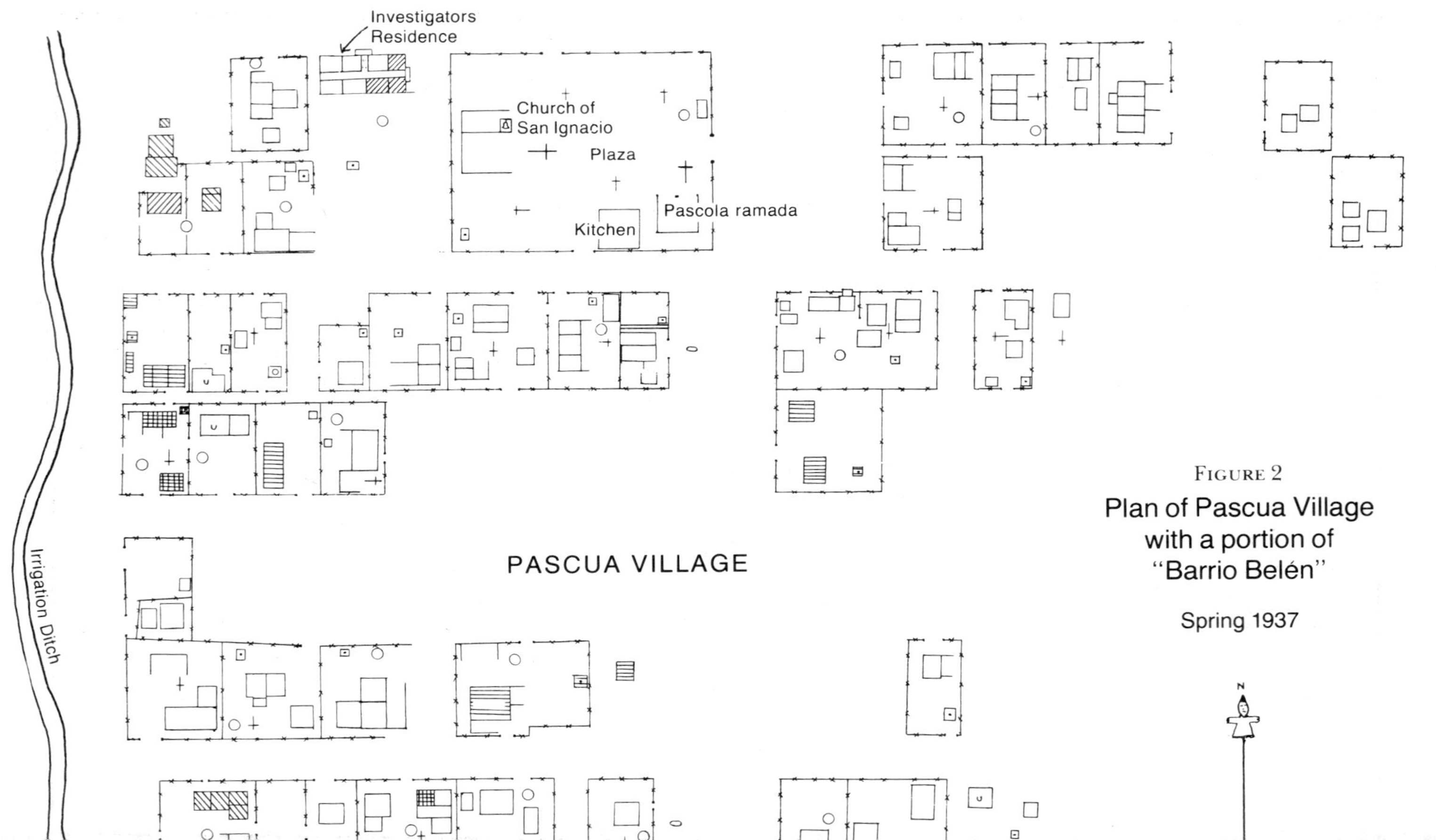

FIGURE 2
Plan of Pascua Village
with a portion of
"Barrio Belén"

Spring 1937

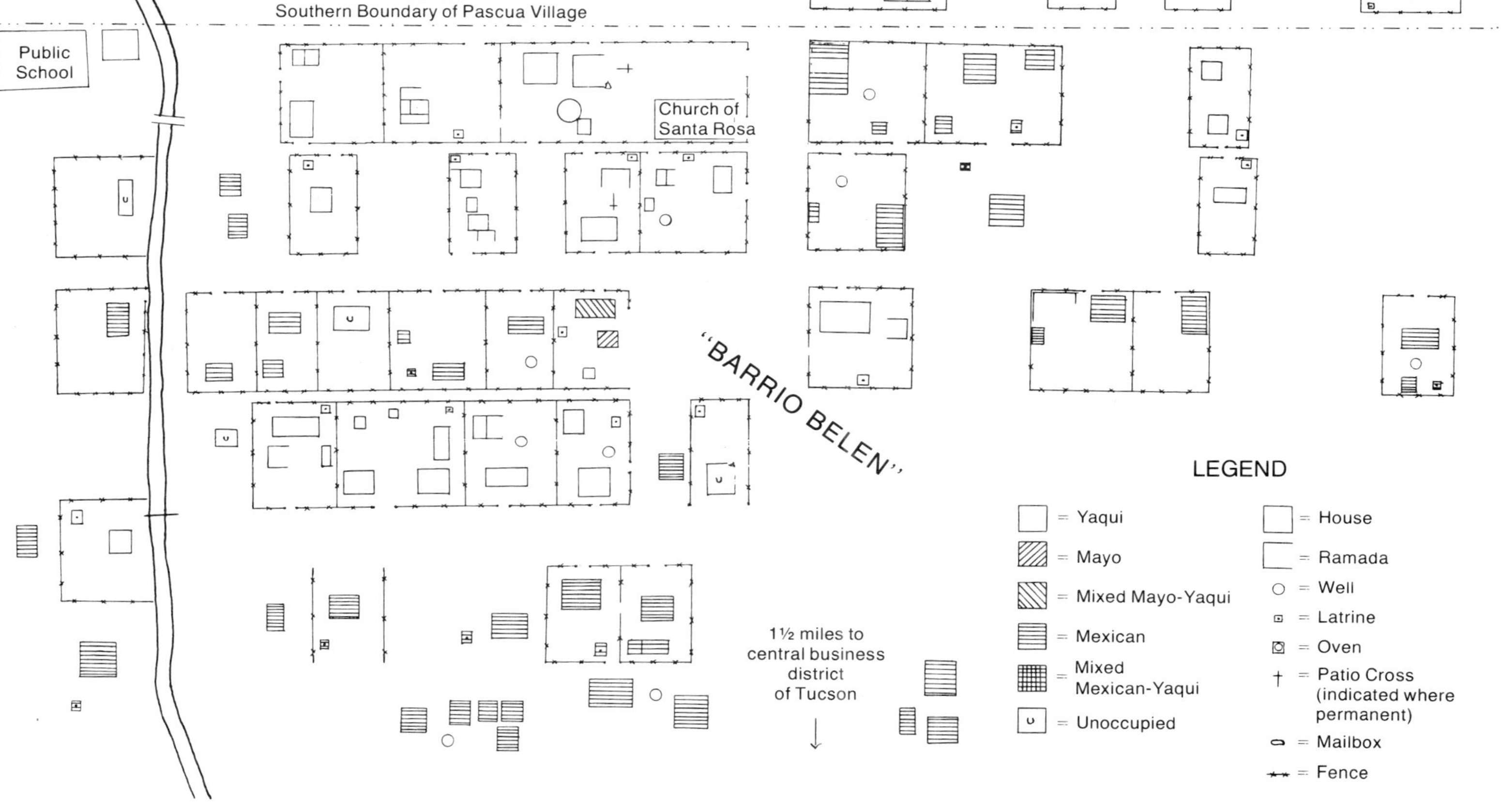
Southern Boundary of Pascua Village
Public School
Church of Santa Rosa
"BARRIO BELEN"
1½ miles to central business district of Tucson
LEGEND
= Yaqui
= Mayo
= Mixed Mayo-Yaqui
= Mexican
= Mixed Mexican-Yaqui
= Unoccupied
= House
= Ramada
= Well
= Latrine
= Oven
= Patio Cross (indicated where permanent)
= Mailbox
= Fence

CHAPTER I

PASCUA VILLAGE

A CASUAL inspection of the cluster of nondescript shacks at the northwest corner of the city of Tucson, Arizona, gives little indication of the cultural gulf which separates the inhabitants of the area from the rest of the people of Tucson. The houses are made of crumbling adobe bricks, wattle and daub, or odds and ends of old sheet metal and wood from the city dumps. They do not depart noticeably from the pattern of house construction that one may see in other parts of Tucson inhabited by families of the lowest-income level. The area is laid out in streets, and there is an approximation to the city-block arrangement of houses. Only a keen observer might note that the houses here are different from those closer to the center of the city in that they are more consistently surrounded by fences and that nearly everyone has a yard in which is to be seen a rough wooden cross a few paces from the house. Such an observer would have already noted that the bulky crosses of dry willow branches, hanging on the walls of the houses, were no more characteristic of these than of many of the Mexican shacks in the city. This hypothetical keen observer would eventually discover, at the edge of a fenced area, a tiny board building, obviously not a dwelling. Painted in faltering white letters on this most nondescript shack of all he would read: "Pascua Village, S.Y." It would probably be some time before he could find anyone who would be willing to explain to him in English that "S.Y." stands for St. Ignatius of Loyola (San Ygnacio) and that the open-front building made of railroad ties at the other end of the plaza is the "Yaqui church" dedicated to that saint.

THE SETTING OF THE VILLAGE

The southwestern third of the state of Arizona is spoken of by geographers as a desert. It is one of the most arid regions of the United States, embracing as it does a portion of the Sonoran Desert bordering the Lower Colorado River, where rainfall averages less than four inches annually. It is a country of many, rugged, and brief mountain ranges, all with a northwest-southeast trend, which rise sharply one after another out of nearly level-floored valleys. The vegetation varies with altitude, but that which is characteristic of the inhabited portions of the region is sparse and consists mainly of highly specialized desert flora, such as creosote and saltbush and a great variety of cacti, including the picturesque giant cactus.

From the point of view of human life, the significant characteristic of the region is the scarcity of water. Both prehistorically and at present men have been concentrated in the valleys of the Gila, Colorado, Santa Cruz, and other lesser rivers. In these valleys irrigation has been practiced since prehistoric times, and here the limited population has always dwelt. Now, as formerly, the chief source of subsistence is agriculture, and now, just as in the past, vast reaches of the territory, where water from the rivers is not available, remain uninhabited. Nevertheless, the greater part—three-fourths—of the total population of the state occupy the seven "desert" counties. It is only here that we find a concentration of population into cities of any size. The two major cities of the state—Phoenix, with a population of 48,000, and Tucson, with 32,000—are situated in the desert in the valleys of the Gila and the Santa Cruz, respectively. It is these concentrations of people which raise the population density of this comparatively uninhabited region to slightly less than six persons per square mile.

The urban centers, if they may be called such, of southern Arizona have experienced extremely rapid growth in the last fifty years, an increase in population which amounted in the years between 1920 and 1930 to more than 60 per cent in each. Correlated with this has been a spectacular tapping of water resources which has placed large acreages of former desert land under cultivation. Citrus fruits have been developed in some quantity, but the greater part of the new agricultural development has been devoted to cotton. The development of cotton cultivation, together with copper mining, has attracted large numbers of Mexicans into the state as laborers. This influx of immigrant labor has been an important factor in the steady increase in the population of the region.

Tucson is one of the oldest continuously inhabited towns in Arizona. In 1840, under Mexican rule, it was a place of several thousand inhabitants. After coming under American control, it developed as a base of supplies for gold and copper miners, as a center of the cattle industry, and as a division point on the Southern Pacific Railroad. Although it has not been so much affected by the recent agricultural developments in the state, its growth in the last fifteen years has proceeded nearly as rapidly as that of Phoenix, which is in the heart of the new irrigated districts. In no sense an industrial center, Tucson subsists ultimately and chiefly from the agricultural developments of the Santa Cruz Valley.

The present 32,000 inhabitants of Tucson are at least

one-third foreign born, mainly Mexican. There are besides the Mexicans some Chinese, Japanese, Filipinos, Negroes, and Indians (chiefly Papago). In this mixed population Yaqui Indians constitute a minute minority—an estimated 1,200.

YAQUI VILLAGES IN ARIZONA

Tucson contains nearly half of all the Yaqui Indians in the state, the majority of the others living near Phoenix. There are not less than 2,500 Yaquis in Arizona. A survey of the southern part of the state indicates that there are at least ten more or less permanent points of concentration for Yaquis, seven of which might be spoken of as villages or towns. The seven villages are to be found scattered from Tucson westward to Yuma, always in close proximity to larger towns, that is, to Phoenix, Tucson, and Yuma. In addition, there are Yaqui families here and there over the region, living in the Mexican areas of the towns, at the railroad section houses, at the labor camps of irrigation companies, or on isolated ranches. Nowhere is there to be found a Yaqui who owns agricultural land or who is in any way independent of American or Mexican employers.

The Yaqui population of Arizona consists of immigrants from the Mexican state of Sonora and their descendants. Other than those born in the United States, there are few, if any, citizens of the United States. The immigrant basis of the population has entered this country at various times from 1882 to the present. As early as 1904 there was a settlement of Yaquis at a place called Guadalupe, about seven miles east of Phoenix. This settlement has continued to grow and at present has a population of more than a thousand persons, some half of whom are Yaquis, the others being chiefly Mexican. In recent years the Guadalupe colony has contributed to the development of another Yaqui village a few miles to the north, near Scottsdale, which now has a population of about 400 persons, almost all of whom are Yaqui. These two villages are the major centers of Yaqui settlement in the vicinity of Phoenix.

South of Yuma, near Somerton, there is a village of about 100 Yaquis, which constitutes the largest settlement of Yaquis in the Yuma Valley, although there are others living in the town of Yuma itself. The Somerton village is probably the most isolated of any of the Yaqui villages in Arizona.

At the time of the founding of Guadalupe, about 1904, there were several hundred Yaquis living in the vicinity of Tucson. At present there are two principal centers of Yaqui population in Tucson—one in the southwest portion of the city and one in the northwest. The former is commonly referred to by Yaquis as "Barrio Libre." It is an integral part of the separately incorporated city of South Tucson. In Libre there is no distinctly demarcated Yaqui settlement. Yaquis, Papagos, and Mexicans live side by side. There are perhaps 500 Yaquis in this part of Tucson.

The Yaqui settlement in the northwest corner of Tucson is Pascua Village. It is more sharply marked off from the surrounding Mexican section than is Libre and was originally designed to be exclusively for Yaquis. In recent years, however, its expanding population has begun to move into the neighboring "Barrio Belén," where the inhabitants are chiefly Mexican and an occasional Chinese. Also in recent years some families of Pascua have moved, along with others from Libre and the Phoenix settlements, to two new Yaqui villages to the north. One of these is Marana, in a cotton irrigation district twenty miles north of Tucson, and the other is Eloy, also connected with a new agricultural development, about forty miles north of Tucson. Marana and Eloy each have a population of about 100 persons.

Pascua is geographically a part of the city of Tucson. Its south edge borders directly on the Mexican Barrio Belén, and the latter merges imperceptibly into the city, being in fact within the city limits. The central unpaved street of Pascua continues as an automobile road into Tucson. The Pascua church is less than two miles from the central business district. On the west side of the village, a quarter of a mile away, runs the Southern Pacific Railroad, and on the east side, a half-mile away, lies U.S. Highway 80, a major transcontinental automobile route. The neon signs of the restaurants, saloons, and stores which line the highway are clearly visible from the village every night. There are no electric lights, running water, sewer system, or telephones in Pascua, but these utilities are available within a quarter of a mile of the village. A rural free delivery route passes through the chief thoroughfare, and Pascuans have mailboxes. Hucksters and butchers visit the village daily. The city has established a school at the edge of the village, and the Catholics of Tucson have built a church near by. Missionaries of various denominations are constantly giving out literature, holding meetings in or near the village, and utilizing phonographs and loud-speakers at private houses or on the streets for purposes of evangelization.

Pascua is thus far from being an isolated settlement. It is, on the contrary, very much within the urban atmosphere of Tucson. Its isolation is of a cultural, not of a physical, kind. It is less isolated than Guadalupe, Scottsdale, Somerton, Marana, or Eloy, but somewhat more isolated perhaps than Libre, where electric lights and running water are common and geographical unity is less preserved.

THE POPULATION OF PASCUA

In May, 1937, there were sixty households in Pascua and Barrio Belén, the heads of which claimed Yaqui or Mayo blood. Within these sixty households lived 429 persons. The activities and ideas of these 429 individuals constitute the basic data of the present study. Henceforth, except where otherwise stated, these persons in their interrelations will be considered to make up the "society" under observation, and the society will be spoken of as Pascua or Pascua Village, regardless of the fact that some of the persons live not in the geographical area officially designated as Pascua but in the adjoining area called "Barrio Belén."

Race and nationality.—Racially, the village of Pascua is about 90 per cent Yaqui, the definition of "Yaqui" being dependent on claims of individuals rather than on any precise physical classification. Ninety per cent of the village claim to be "pure-blood" Yaquis, and nothing has been found in the case of this number to discount their statements. The rest of the population is divided between persons who claim to be pure-blood Mayo Indians, mixed Mayo-Yaqui, mixed Mexican-Yaqui, or Mexican.

The Mayos of Mexico are neighbors of the Yaquis and, aboriginally, were almost indistinguishable from the latter racially, linguistically, and culturally. In the nineteenth century, however, the Mayos mingled more extensively with Mexicans, and they are thought of now by the Yaquis as being more similar to the Mexicans both physically and culturally. A light-colored Yaqui of mixed blood is often referred to in Pascua as a "Mayo," and it is believed that "pure-blood" Mayos may have blue eyes and white skin. There are three men and one woman who claim to be Mayos; they and their descendants are here classified as Mayos.

The Mexicans who are included in the sixty households of Pascua are three women who have married Yaquis. The definition of "Mexican" is necessarily somewhat vague. It will be taken here to be applicable to persons who lay claim to the blood of no specific Indian group, but who would be *mestizos* in Mexico.

The social aspects of intermarriage and the mixed-bloods will be discussed below. At present it is our purpose only to point out that there are no sharp contrasts in physical characteristics in the village. Skin color, hair form, and facial and bodily features present considerable uniformity throughout the village. Yaquis are, moreover, not strongly contrasted with the surrounding Mexicans and Papagos. They are possibly, on the average, a little darker in color than Mexicans, but the color variation of the latter is great. No one attempts to tell, except in the case of very light-skinned persons who are generally classed as Mayos, the "racial" affiliations of a person by means of his physical characteristics.

With a few exceptions, persons in the village under the age of thirty are United States born. Those over thirty are almost all Sonora born. Persons of the first kind, that is, United States born, are in the majority by about two to one.

Language and literacy.—There are three languages in use in Pascua—Yaqui, Spanish, and English. The people themselves say that there is a fourth—Mayo—but the language spoken by the few Mayos in the village shows only minute differences of phonetics and vocabulary from

Yaqui. Everyone in the village is bilingual, making use of Yaqui or Spanish according to circumstances. Most of those between the ages of ten and twenty, that is, those who have attended school in the United States, are trilingual, speaking English as well as Yaqui and Spanish.

The Yaqui, which is the language of home life of the families which have not intermarried with Mexicans, is a Uto-Aztekan language in its grammatical structure but in vocabulary might be classed as largely Indo-European. In the first place, a major part of the words designating the tools and material articles in use are Spanish in origin. An inventory of a typical household reveals the fact that nearly two-thirds of the names of articles in everyday use are either Spanish or variations of Spanish words. Some are unmodified; a majority are incorporated into the language simply by means of the suffix *-um* and remain readily identifiable as Spanish.

The penetration of Spanish into the culture is not confined to material aspects. It extends also into the terminology of social life and ritual. Thus two of the fundamental social groupings, the elementary family and the village, have no designations except the Spanish-derived words *'familum* and *'pweplum* (*familia* and *pueblo*). The kinship terminology, as will be pointed out more fully below, is predominantly Spanish when we consider the terms in actual use. The godparent system, which is important in the social organization, also has a terminology of Spanish words which are more often used than the Yaqui equivalents and for some of which there are no Yaqui equivalents. Similarly, ceremonial societies go by Spanish names, and their officers are called by Spanish titles more frequently than by Yaqui. In addition, the important deities as well as the major religious concepts, such as "soul of the dead," "penitence," "saint," "sacred," etc., are all expressed in Spanish, and for most of them there is not even a remembered Yaqui term. The substance of life, therefore, is dealt with and thought about mainly in Spanish terms, even by persons who lay no claim to much knowledge of Spanish. The verbs and the grammatical structure alone remain Yaqui.

Yaqui is still the language of the home and of ordinary intercourse between Pascuans, but Spanish is the language of intercourse with the surrounding world. Most jobs are obtained through the medium of Spanish, and it is the language used on the job and in procuring food and other necessities of life. Yaquis thus identify themselves, in the eyes of the outside world, with the Mexicans. In some of the households headed by younger men who are American born there is a tendency to adopt Spanish as the language of the home. One such family is even discouraging its youngest child from learning Yaqui. In mixed households of Mexican women and Yaqui men both languages are used constantly, children speaking Spanish with their mothers and Yaqui with their fathers. In almost all households a child learns Spanish nearly as quickly as he does Yaqui and uses both before his contacts with the outside world have become very extensive. No one is without a knowledge of Spanish, although the older women generally prefer not to use it except when there is no other course.

English remains the distinctive characteristic of those who have gone to school in the United States. Many men about twenty years old or under can use it fluently, but there is no one who prefers it to Spanish. Very few men will use even a few words of English when they are sober, but a number speak it fairly well when drunk. English expressions like "Hurry up!" "Come on, boys!" and "What's the matter?" are in daily use by individuals who use no other English.

A few persons in the village have a smattering of knowledge of Papago-Pima which they have picked up through work contacts or as a result of intermarriage of a relative with a Papago or a Pima. No one is fluent in any other Indian language.

Two-thirds of the males over ten years of age can write their names, and the majority of these are able to read simple sentences in Spanish or English, only one-third of them in the latter language. All who are literate in English are also literate in Spanish. Of the women over ten, only one-third are able to read and write, and all but three or four of these do either with difficulty.

The quality of the literacy is, of course, more significant than the quantity. Attendance at the Pascua school for the last four years has averaged about fifty Yaqui children, who attend together with Mexicans from Barrio Belén. The school has been in existence since 1923. Attendance has never been strictly enforced. Only a half-dozen Yaqui children attend it during the fall term when most families are away on ranches picking cotton. The school is designed primarily to teach English and to prepare pupils for entrance to the elementary schools of Tucson. In 1936–37 there were thirty children in attendance from Pascua at the latter institutions. Only one person now resident in Pascua, a woman of about twenty, reports remaining in school as far as the sixth grade. All others dropped out after the second or third. There is no one in the village now attending high school.

Only about twelve men and two women spend any time reading. Some fifteen households receive regularly the Spanish-language newspaper of Tucson, *El Tucsonense*, and there are two which take an English-language newspaper. *El Tucsonense* is a weekly; the English-language papers, daily. All those persons who do any reading at all read *El Tucsonense* more or less regularly. Some of these persons are the leaders of the village religious services who also spend a good deal of time pouring over paper-bound books of Spanish prayers, various volumes of Catholic ritual, and their own notebooks of prayers and chants, written in Spanish, Yaqui, and Latin. No one understands the Latin of the ritual, although they read and recite it. The greater part of the reading that goes on in the village is confined to these two fields—the Spanish newspapers and Catholic ritual.

Books owned by individuals, besides the religious ones, are very few—only a popular Spanish "encyclopedia," some books in English on electricity, a number of volumes on law owned by a man who once had aspirations to become "chief of all the Yaquis in Arizona," and tracts in Spanish issued by Judge Rutherford, the anti-Catholic radio preacher. A few persons read an occasional magazine. Those which were read in 1936–37 include a Mexican illustrated news weekly which contained photographs of Yaqui dancers in Sonora, *Startling Detective Stories*, *Life*, *National Geographic*, *Collier's*, and *True Confessions*, the last three being gifts from white employers. All the magazines were read only casually and occasionally. The twelve habitual readers were persons of different ages, ranging from twenty to seventy.

Two young men, one about twenty and one about thirty, have written original poetry, the former in Spanish and the latter in English. The single production in Spanish deals with a beautiful horse; the English poems, with Christian religious themes.

MATERIAL CULTURE

It is not in the material culture that we can look for marks of the separateness of Pascua from the rest of Tucson. Except for a few things associated in one way or another with the ritual life, the articles of which Pascuans make use are identical with those of the surrounding Mexicans. Houses, clothing, kitchen utensils, even food differ hardly at all from the general Mexican-Indian pattern, with some American introductions, which obtains among Tucson Mexicans.

The village of Pascua proper is laid out regularly in streets, having been originally surveyed and divided up into building lots by a Tucson real estate company. There is a large plaza, surrounded by a wire fence, in which are the three buildings necessary to a Yaqui *fiesta*—the church (constructed of discarded railroad ties), the common kitchen (made of remnants of tin and metal roofing from the city dump), and the dancing *ramada* (of adobe bricks). The church and the dancing *ramada* both have open fronts to permit religious processions and dancing groups to pass in and out. Beside the church rises a wooden tower surmounted by a large bell which is rung before every ceremony and at the time of every death.

As has been indicated, the dwelling houses are made of adobe, sometimes of wattle and daub in the manner of the Papagos, and frequently of old lumber or flattened-out tin cans from dumps or other sources. The architecture seems to have no features distinguishing it from that of poorer Mexicans in Tucson. The houses are simply constructed, usually single-room affairs. The floors of all but one house are of dirt. Nearly every Yaqui house is surrounded by a fence, and somewhere within the inclosure, often to the east of the house, is the simple wooden cross already mentioned. Except during the few colder winter months, not much time is spent within the houses. Every house has in conjunction with it one or more *ramadas*, a *ramada* being simply a thatched roof supported on four posts or, in other words, a room without walls.

The important domestic utensils are metal pots and pans, the metal food-grinder, the sewing machine, and the stone *metate*. Most houses possess both the metal food-grinder and the *metate;* the former is used for grinding meat, cheese, and whole corn, the latter for corn or chile. Young women make little use of the *metate*, although older ones still cling to it. It is a notable fact that men may sometimes be seen grinding food in the metal grinder, but none ever uses the *metate*. Few households are without sewing machines. Some of the cooking is done inside the house on cast-iron cookstoves, only two houses being without them, but perhaps the greater part of the cooking is carried on outside the house, under the *ramadas*, on an open fire. Eating utensils are conventionally limited to crockery or china bowls and metal spoons. Plates are very rarely used, and forks and table knives are extremely scarce. Beds and chairs are like those to be found in any poorer American household. Nearly every house has a phonograph and a clock. There are a few iceboxes, and one radio was installed in 1936–37—a battery set. The automobile is in common use, about three-quarters of the families having some sort of car, usually an old-model Ford or Chevrolet.

A majority of houses have a household shrine consisting of anything from a simple crucifix on a shelf to a table, covered with a white-cloth canopy, on which rest images of the Virgin Mary, the Virgin of Guadalupe, crucifixes, or pictures of the saints. The ceremonial paraphernalia belonging to members of the household is sometimes kept on the shrine but may as often be seen hanging in various places about the house.

The food in general use in the village consists of wheat-flour *tortillas*, boiled beans, dried beef, white potatoes, Mexican brown sugar, white sugar, coffee, lard, and a few vegetables such as chick-peas, cabbage, melons, and turnips. The familiar Mexican dishes involving corn meal in some form, such as *tamales*, *enchiladas*, *atole*, and *pinole* are in regular use. *Tamales* are used chiefly on some ceremonial occasions, such as All Souls' Day, Christmas, or a saint's day, but they are not strictly confined to such dates. The only distinctive *fiesta* food is a mixture called *'wakavaki*, which consists of a stew of beef, lard, and a vegetable. This is regarded as an essential delicacy at every *fiesta*.

Men wear the ordinary cotton clothing of the American laborer of the Southwest, usually blue-denim pants and shirt, heavy work shoes, and a broad-brimmed felt hat. Only one man affects the large straw hat of the Sonora Mexican, and he wears this only on dress occasions. A distinctive Yaqui type of sandal consisting simply of a leather sole tied on the foot with leather thongs in a special way is worn by the men only on ceremonial occasions at Easter time.

There are two modes of dress distinguishable among the women, one characterizing those over and the other those under thirty. The old-style clothing consists of a voluminous, ankle-length skirt and loose blouse. Ordinarily nothing is worn on the feet, either stockings or shoes; but, when footwear is used, as for a trip to town, it consists of a pair of American shoes. Beneath the blouse is worn an elaborately embroidered waist, which remains invisible. The younger women wear short dresses often bought in the city stores, shoes, stockings, and considerably more cheap jewelry than the older women. The older women, like the Mexicans, always wear a head-covering consisting of a simple cloth, the *rebozo*. The younger women, like the younger Mexican women, rarely wear any head-covering except in church.

The distinctive arts of the village are not of much importance. Pottery is made very occasionally by some of the old women. It is a simple, undecorated brown ware and is made only in the form of shallow bowls. There are not more than a dozen such pieces in the village. They are used mainly in the ceremony of mourning which occurs one year after the death of a person. Pottery bowls for such occasions, however, are often obtained from Papagos and Maricopas. Water for household use is usually kept in buckets or earthenware crocks bought in the city rather than in *ollas*.

One man and his son make a living during a part of the year by the manufacture of baskets. The type of basket is a deep, straight-sided kind with a lid, made of willow twigs in wicker weave. It is probably not aboriginal.

There is one old man and a woman who are professional makers of fireworks. They work together, manufacturing perhaps half the fireworks used by the village on ceremonial occasions. Their product is a simple type of skyrocket, called *cohete*, made by a rather complicated process. They are sold only in the village, for fifty cents a dozen. At present Chinese firecrackers obtained in the city seem to be supplanting them.

The only other arts characteristic of the village are the making of ceremonial masks and other paraphernalia and the manufacture of musical instruments used in the various ceremonial dances. There are individuals who make drums, gourd rattles, "Mexican" harps, flageolets or whistles, and violins. Guitars are used a great deal, but no one in the village manufactures them. An occasional mask, Mexican harp, or violin is made for sale to a curious outsider, but the manufacture is designed chiefly to meet only the needs of the village ceremonies.

HISTORY

The men and women of Pascua who are over forty move in an atmosphere of the recent past. When the young men get together informally in the evenings, they play guitars, drink muscatel and whiskey, and sing the Mexican songs they have learned from their phonograph records. When the older people get together, they do not sing—they talk. They may listen to the stories of the two remaining men who fought under the last great Yaqui war leader, Cajeme. They often tell one another of their travels after Cajeme's defeat by the Mexicans in 1887, how they secured work in various parts of Sonora, of the songs sung by the Southern Pacific Railroad gangs with whom they worked, or how they crossed the border into the United States. The story of how Francisco Valencia got across at El Paso as a member of a circus troupe is a favorite one. The lives of most of them are full of incidents of violence, flight, and escape. Their presence in Pascua Village is a result of the series of events which stirred Sonora from 1875 to 1912, beginning with Cajeme's first uprising and continuing until the Revolution put an end to Porfirio Díaz's campaign of Yaqui extermination. They are all refugees, and they do not forget it.

The Mexican background.—The Yaquis, when first encountered by Spanish explorers, occupied the lower portions of the river which is today called the Yaqui, in southern Sonora. They were one group of a people closely similar in culture and speaking languages which ethnologists have grouped together under the name "Cahita." The Yaquis were the northernmost of the Cahita-speaking peoples. Older sources give an amazing number of "tribes" classifiable as Cahita. Besides the Yaqui, some of these were the Mayo (who occupied the lower portions of the Mayo River Valley immediately to the south of the Yaqui territory), the Guasave (on the coast), the Oguera, the Ocoroni, the Ahome, the Tehueco, and many others.[1] Of these, the only surviving groups today are the Yaqui and Mayo. If the others ever indeed were distinct groups, marked off by anything except place of residence, they have disappeared. It is estimated that as early as 1620 the Cahita people numbered between 80,000 and 120,000.[2]

The first encounter between the Yaquis and whites was in 1533, when a portion of the Guzmán expedition reached the Yaqui River and was forced to retreat before an armed attack on the part of the Indians.[3] This set a keynote for Yaqui-white relations which has been dominant ever since. Yaqui "uprisings" have occurred in 1764, 1825, 1832, 1840, 1867, 1887, 1901, and 1926, to mention only the major ones.[4]

[1] Cyrus Thomas and John R. Swanton, *Indian Languages of Mexico and Central America* (Bureau of American Ethnology Bull. 44 [Washington: Government Printing Office, 1911]), pp. 11–17; Ralph L. Beals, "Historical Reconstruction of Cahita Culture" (manuscript).

[2] Carl Sauer, *Aboriginal Population of Northwestern Mexico* ("Ibero-Americana," No. 10 [Berkeley: University of California Press, 1935]), pp. 5 and 32; Ralph L. Beals, "Present-Day Yaqui-Mayo Culture" (manuscript).

[3] H. H. Bancroft, *History of the North Mexican States* (San Francisco: A. L. Bancroft & Co., 1884–89), I, 54.

[4] *Ibid., passim.*

It is the rise of José María Leyva ("Cajeme") in the 1870's which marks the historical horizon of the Yaquis of Pascua. They remember him by his full name and point out that his Yaqui nickname means "does not drink," for he disciplined himself by drinking water only once a day. He seems to have been war chief (*'wikoijaut*) of the important town of Torim and later to have become war chief of all the eight Yaqui towns after about 1880. Cajeme united all the Yaquis under him, made an alliance with two of the Mayo villages, and kept his army in an active state of revolt until the Mexican government under Díaz was able to put a large enough force in the field to defeat him. This happened in 1887, and Cajeme was executed in the same year. His army was dispersed, and many Yaquis were deported from the Yaqui country to work on the *haciendas* of Sonora. Others escaped into the Bacatete Mountains, which has remained until the present a breeding-ground of sporadic raids and insurrections.

Encroachment on Yaqui lands, which had been the basic source of Mexican-Yaqui hostilities, continued after the defeat of Cajeme. Another uprising occurred in 1895, and after this Díaz inaugurated his campaign of "Yaqui extermination." Yaquis were shot down as they worked in their fields, and thousands were rounded up and shipped to Yucatan to work in the henequen plantations.[5] It was during the height of this "slave trade" in the years immediately following 1900 that most of the present Pascuans entered the United States. Many fled the Yaqui country and at first took up residence in various places in Sonora, but even escape to such places did not bring security, and many

[5] Carleton Beals, *Mexican Maze* (Philadelphia: J. B. Lippincott Co., 1931), p. 185; H. Baerlein, *Mexico, the Land of Unrest* (Philadelphia: J. B. Lippincott Co., n.d.), p. 139; J. K. Turner, *Barbarous Mexico* (Chicago: C. H. Kerr & Co., 1911), *passim*.

consequently moved on across the border into the United States.

Yaquis in Arizona.—Prior to 1900 the Yaquis who had crossed the border came individually, without relatives or possessions. Later they came in small family groups. The majority of adults now in Pascua came in this way. Many of those who entered after 1900 had never been in the Yaqui country. They were children of parents who had left the river pueblos before or during the Cajeme revolts and had taken up residence elsewhere in Sonora. They had lived peacefully at Guaymas or Hermosillo or in other places among Mexicans, renouncing Yaqui customs because of their fear of deportation or execution.[6]

This later movement of Yaqui families into Arizona continued steadily from 1900 until about 1912. A small settlement was begun near Nogales, Arizona, just across the border, as early as 1901. Another settlement of this early period was Guadalupe, established near Phoenix about 1904. Most of the adults now in Pascua did not settle together at first. They took jobs on the railroads and allowed themselves to be moved about in Arizona, New Mexico, California, and even Oregon. This period of movement from place to place in southwestern United States continued until about 1910. By that time, however, several centers of Yaqui settlement, in addition to those at Nogales and Phoenix, had been established. With the development of irrigation in southern Arizona, the demand for farm laborers in the vicinity of Tucson, Phoenix, and Yuma increased, and Yaquis began to settle near these centers.

The history of Pascua.—The village of Pascua, as a defi-

[6] Aleš Hrdlička, "Notes on the Indians of Sonora, Mexico," *American Anthropologist*, VI (new ser.; 1904), 51–89, esp. 68 and 71.

nite territorial unit, has been in existence only since 1921, but Yaquis and a few Mayos were settled in the vicinity of Tucson as early as 1904 or 1905. A few were living at this time in the northern part of the city in "Barrio Anita," others were settled on a ranch north of the city called "Tierras Flojas," and still others were living just south of Tucson in a place called Mezquitál. In 1909 Yaquis from these three areas joined together for the first time to hold an Easter *fiesta*, their fears of revealing themselves as Yaquis having at last abated. The Easter ceremonies have continued annually since that time, but in 1915 the North Tucson Yaquis separated from those of Mezquitál, and each group has maintained its own separate Easter *fiesta* down to the present.

In 1918 an event occurred which resulted in knitting more closely all the Yaquis of North Tucson and ultimately bringing about the establishment of the village of Pascua. Many Arizona Yaquis had maintained an active interest in events in Sonora after their arrival in the United States. In 1917 a group of Tucson Yaquis organized an armed expedition into Sonora in the belief that the fighting then going on was an uprising of Yaquis against the Mexican government. This little band started from Tucson for the border, but they were stopped by a detachment of federal cavalry, a Negro unit from Fort Huachuca, just before they crossed.[7] They were brought back to Tucson and held before the federal court there on a charge of "violating the neutrality of the United States" by attempting to transport arms into Mexico. In the period before the trial, while the prisoners were being held in jail, the Yaquis of Tucson were greatly stirred and one man in particular, Juan Muñoz, called "Pistola," made efforts to secure the

[7] *Arizona Daily Star* (Tuscon, Ariz.), January 11, 1918.

release of the prisoners. He brought the families of the Tucson men before the court, pleaded for them, and tried to explain to whites in Tucson why the men had made the attempt to enter Mexico. It was believed by the Yaquis that it was as a result of Pistola's efforts that the men were ultimately released.

The Tucson papers had their own version:

> The Yaqui "army of liberation," eight men and one child, disbanded yesterday in the federal court and gave its promise that if the court deemed it desirable to deal with it leniently, it would return to the fields and ranches from which it had gathered and think no more of Mexico and the outrages it heard that the Mexican government was inflicting upon its tribesmen. . . . . It developed . . . . that the Yaquis had told the truth from the time they were arrested at the border by the army patrol. There was all sorts of evidence that they were bound for Mexico to aid their relatives fight the Sonora government, which they heard had been massacreing their tribe, driving the Yaquis off the land that they had fought for nearly two centuries to keep, and was capturing and dumping them in the sea off the west coast of Mexico. . . . . Because of their truthfulness there was really no defense that could be set up against the charge of attempting to violate the neutrality of the United States. Therefore, it was decided yesterday to enter a plea of guilty which was accordingly entered in the morning for the army. The court cross-examined the Yaquis briefly. They could see that they had broken no law, had intended to break none at any event, they said. Perhaps it was wrong to go to the defense of their fellow-tribesmen but in their view it was cowardly to do otherwise. They had always been hard-working men, interfered with the rights of no one, and knew little of the law. However, if the court said it was wrong, it must be wrong. They were not wise like the court. If the court wished them to stay in the United States, turn a deaf ear to the tales of outrages coming to them from Mexico, to the appeals of relatives for help even, they would do as the court said. Solemnly they promised. Thereupon the court said he would consider for a few days what should be done.[8]

Whatever Pistola's real part in the liberation of the "*prisioneros*," as the Yaquis still refer to them, he immediately became prominent among both whites and Yaquis of

[8] *Ibid.*, February 17, 1918.

Tucson. It was due to his activities and those of whites associated with him that Pascua was founded a few years later.

Juan Pistola was a Mayo Indian whose early history was much like that of the other Arizona immigrants. Fleeing the Yaqui-Mayo country in his early youth, he worked in placer mines in Sonora and eventually drifted, after many hardships, across the border, settling in Tucson. He was totally undistinguished among Tucson Yaquis until the trial of the "*prisioneros*." He was known only as a hard drinker and for an extensive police-court record. What seems to have distinguished him from other Yaquis was that he knew many of the officials in the city hall and county courthouse. One of these was Kirke Moore, a lawyer. Pistola constantly sought advice from Moore during the years from 1918 to 1922, when he was establishing his place as leader of Tucson Yaquis. Much of his power evidently derived from his association with Moore and with other white men in Tucson, who were able to assist him and his followers in many ways.

The position which Pistola assumed very soon after the release of the "*prisioneros*" is indicated in the following newspaper account:

> In a proclamation issued by their committee and with the sanction of Captain Juan Pistola, who holds the titles of captain, general commander, representative and adviser in general to La Colonia de la tribu Yaqui who are residents of Tucson and Pima County, the authorities, city, county, state, and federal, are advised that newcomers of their tribe should be reported to Pistola, who will see that they are kept under peace, law and order while they are in this country.
>
> A copy of this strange proclamation, by an authority that is absolute among Yaquis in Arizona, was sent to the Star with the request that it be published. The English version is as follows: "The colony of the Yaqui tribe, residents of the city of Tucson in Pima County, Arizona, hereby give notice to the authorities, civil and military, local and

federal, and to whomever it may concern, that Juan Pistola is their captain, general commander, representative and adviser in general, and whatever transaction affecting one, either or all of their colony of alien friendly Yaqui tribe now residing throughout Arizona or who may come into this country in future from the state of Sonora, Mexico, so that authorities may advise their said general and captain of any newcomers and thus enabling their said captain and general commander to keep them under peace, law, and order while in this country.

Given in Tucson this 8th day of October, 1918
By their committee and consent of their said captain and general commander, Juan Pistola, whose address is North of Barrio Anita, Tucson, Arizona

[*Signed*] JOSE MATUS, LUCAS CHAVES, MARTIN VALENCIA — *Committee*

JUAN PISTOLA, *Captain General Commander-in-chief*[9]

This proclamation was also painted on oilcloth and spread on a placard about three feet square. The placard was then taken to all Yaqui houses in Tucson, and at each Pistola and the committee stood while Lucas Chavez, the only literate member of the group signing the document, carefully read the words to the householders. This reading of the proclamation was evidently regarded as the equivalent of an election, for from that time forth Pistola, until his death in 1922, assumed the title of *comandante-general* of all the Yaquis in Arizona and in Tucson assumed the role as well as the title.

By no means all the Yaquis of Tucson took kindly to Pistola's assumption of leadership. There had already been a split over the Easter ceremonies between the Barrio Anita and Mezquitál groups, and this was intensified as a result of Pistola's new activities. He attempted to maintain a police force for the purpose of keeping order at

[9] *Ibid.*, October 9, 1918; also document in possession of Lucas Chavez.

fiestas in both North and South Tucson. At one of these in South Tucson a young man was killed in a brawl, and Pistola was blamed by the man's father for the death. Pistola was acquitted of the murder charge, but friends of the boy turned against Pistola, and a definite anti-Pistola faction grew up in South Tucson. Pistola's lack of popularity there was further increased by his announcement that he would not support the activities of a secret society with headquarters in Tucson which had as its aim the shipment of arms to Sonora Yaquis. Although Pistola had once been active in this work, the influence of his white friends was now strong enough to make him give it up in order to maintain the power and leadership which he had won.

In the spring of 1921 Pistola, Kirke Moore, a banker named John Metz, and a real estate man named Franklin conceived the idea of a Yaqui village, which was to be the center of a "Yaqui Nation" in Arizona, with Pistola at its head. Franklin offered to provide a plot of land of forty acres at the northwest corner of Tucson. This was to be sold in small lots to all families who were supporters of Pistola, and a portion of it was to be set aside as common property to be used as a plaza for ceremonies where "the Yaquis would not be molested by Mexicans or any others who were not of their religion."[10] The land was surveyed, and the followers of Pistola began to build houses on the lots. Some were already settled as squatters on the land. The village was called Pascua because, it is said, the idea for it was conceived on Easter Sunday, 1921. It became the nucleus of the present Pascua Village.

The foundation of Pascua made the breach between North and South Tucson Yaquis more definite and by no means operated, as the whites had hoped, to bring all the

[10] Statement by Lucas Chavez in personal interview.

Yaquis into line behind Pistola. There were now two distinct factions—the Pascua group headed by Pistola and the Mezquitál group headed by Nestor Muñoz. The latter, however, never had the definitely organized government which Pistola worked out for his group. The details of Pistola's political organization will be discussed at another point. Suffice it to say here that, in addition to his policing activities, Pistola was active in many other ways. He kept in touch with Tucson whites and secured work for his followers, obtained charity relief and medical aid, and just before his death was planning the organization of a village court to deal with disputes of various kinds. He died, however, in 1922, before his organization was fully worked out.

At the time of Pistola's death the population of Pascua seems to have been about 200, and more Yaquis were moving in. Pistola's most active assistant at his death was Francisco Matus, a resident of South Tucson. Pistola asked that Matus take his place, and an election was held at which he was given the title which Pistola had assumed. Matus, however, failed to gain the support of Pistola's followers. Among other things, he antagonized Pascuans by bringing Papagos from South Tucson to police a *fiesta*. While Pistola had evidently devoted himself honestly to obtaining all possible aid for his followers from the whites of Tucson, Matus carried on none of this work. It is said by Pascuans today, for example, by Pistola's secretary, that Matus secured a good job for himself and then proceeded to forget the needs of his followers. Consequently, by the time of his death in 1928, he was no longer recognized by any but Tucson whites as the Yaqui leader.

SUMMARY

It is possible now to point out some of the historical factors which have a bearing on the present organization of the village and on the attitudes of the individuals who compose it. In the first place, Pascua is composed of persons who have come from different places in Sonora. They have had varied early experiences both in Mexico and in the United States, but there is a pattern nevertheless to which these early experiences conform in greater or lesser degree. They have come to the United States not with economic gain in view but rather for the purpose of escape from an oppressive political regime; they are refugees, not seekers of more comfortable living. We can distinguish three phases in the lives of most of them. First, the formative periods of many of the adults coincided with a period of intense feeling on the part of Yaquis against Mexicans, culminating in war and a well-developed spirit of nationalism under Cajeme. Second, there was a period following defeat which was characterized by a loss of Yaqui customs and close association with Mexicans, first in Sonora, then in the United States. Third, there was a separation from Mexicans in the United States and a regrouping of Yaquis in their own villages, with a subsequent revival of Yaqui customs. This revival was followed by an organized attempt on the part of some Yaquis to establish formal channels of relationship between white and Yaqui culture—an attempt which was short lived but which resulted at least in establishing a geographical unity for Pascua.

CHAPTER II

ECONOMICS

NO PASCUAN ever lives directly on the natural environment for more than a few days at a time. In the summer or autumn there are prickly pears, mesquite beans, chickweed, and certain grasses which can be used for food. Most families have had, at one time or another, to resort to picking and cooking chickweed and grass, but the needs of a family of five exhausts the supply within walking distance of the village in a few weeks. Hence there can be little reliance on the natural environment. Existence is wholly dependent on the establishment of relationships with individuals outside the village. If for any reason the economic relations of a Pascuan with outside persons are broken off for an extended period, it becomes necessary to depend on other Pascuans who have maintained such relations.

There is, further, no important addition to the food supply through agriculture carried out by Pascuans on their own land. The village is situated beside an irrigation ditch, and there are some thirty wells from which drinking water is obtained. But the abundance of water cannot change the character of the land. Over the greater part of the village there is no covering of soil that goes deeper than two or three inches. A half-dozen families have scraped together enough soil for garden plots which they water by hand from their wells or from the irrigation ditch. The largest garden plot, however, is not more than fifteen feet square. A few rows of beans and a few hills of corn are the most that they can maintain, perhaps sufficient food for two weeks for a family of five. The small importance of such garden plots is indicated by the fact that only six households have bothered to make them and that three of these are used only for the growing of flowers and for a native tobacco which is valued as a medicinal plant.

Thus the economic life of Pascua is closely interlocked with that of the surrounding people. To exist, Pascuans must enter into the economic system of the Americans. This they have done, but that does not mean that their economic life is identical with that of Americans. It is not. Not only are their attitudes toward economic labor different but also there are economic institutions in the village which differ from those outside.

THE MEANS OF SUBSISTENCE

An outstanding feature of the economic life is its season al variation. The kind of work engaged in varies, for the great majority of individuals, with the season of the year. Moreover, the division of labor varies with the season, and the whole of the village life is affected by these seasonal differences. In some measure, the community life is suspended from the early part of September until January. This is the cotton-picking season, and most of the families leave the village to take up residence on cotton ranches. They return at certain times for ceremonies, such as All Souls' Day in November, and a few families drift back before the cotton-picking is finished because they are tired of it or because of illness, but during this period of three or four months the village has the air of being deserted. A few ceremonial officials remain in the village and carry on the regular round of ceremony, but attendance is scant and irregular.

During the rest of the year, from January until September, most of the houses are occupied continuously. The men and a few women go out to work by the day and return each night. The community life is resumed. Some families occasionally move out for a few weeks or months to some ranch, but the majority stay in the village until cotton-picking begins again.

In the cotton fields men, women, and children work in family units; during the rest of the year remunerative labor is engaged in almost exclusively by men, the women occupying themselves only with house work.

The work of males.—Nearly all the males above the age of fifteen work for wages outside the village. There are only two who do not. These two make a kind of basket which they peddle on the streets of Tucson. The wage-workers engage mainly in three types of occupation: ranch work (chiefly irrigation and irrigation-ditch cleaning), the making of adobes for housebuilding, and labor in railroad section gangs. These are the major occupations, eighty-two of the men in Pascua being so engaged when they are not picking cotton. The majority of these are ranch workers. There are only three men whose work can be classed as skilled labor: a truck-driver and two cement workers. The others have no settled occupations but work in any class of unskilled labor which they can secure. Ten of the latter were employed during 1936–37 on federal W.P.A. projects. Table 1 indicates the classes of work engaged in by Pascua males of different ages.

In the occupations which have become the traditional Yaqui ones there are only slight differences in pay. The adobe-makers (who always do piece work) make as much as $15 a week, but $11 or $12 is more usual. A job rarely lasts for more than a month at a time. Some adobe-makers go to the place where they are working and set up a camp in which they stay during the job, coming home only for week ends. The majority remain in the village and go to the job daily. Adobe-making is the only job which results in co-operation between individual Pascuans. An adobe crew consists of three persons who divide between them-

TABLE 1

Occupations of Pascua Males

Class of Work	Age Group							Total
	15–19	20–29	30–39	40–49	50–59	60–69	Over 69	
Ranch hands	9	10	17	7	9	6	0	58
Adobe-makers	3	2	3	2	2	0	1	13
Railroad labor	2	3	2	2	2	0	0	11
Odd jobs	4	3	3	0	0	0	0	10
W.P.A.	0	3	4	2	1	0	0	10
Basket-makers	1	0	0	0	1	0	0	2
Cement workers	0	0	1	1	0	0	0	2
Truck-driver	0	0	0	1	0	0	0	1
Total	19	21	30	15	15	6	1	107

selves the $12–$15 per thousand adobes, which is the usual rate of pay.

Railroad labor pays about $13 a week. Most Pascuans who engage in railroad work remain in the village, going back and forth to the Tucson yards. Periodically, however, some family will go to a section house and remain there for a few weeks or months at a time. Life in the section houses is not, in general, regarded as desirable because of crowding, although it is admitted that the houses are warmer in winter than Pascua houses and that there are more conveniences.

The wage for ranch work varies according to place. In the vicinity of Tucson the weekly pay is from $7.50 to $12.00. Outside of cotton-picking season most Pascuans who do ranch work stay in the village and go out to the near-by farms daily. However, at Marana, twenty miles north of Pascua, the pay is slightly higher, ranging from $9.00 to $13.50 weekly. A few families are drawn by this higher wage, but those who have gone say that it costs more to live in Marana than it does in Tucson and that hence there is little advantage. The population of Marana is largely recruited from Pascua and the South Tucson Yaqui district.

Cotton-picking stands apart from the other occupations not only in its seasonal character but also in wages and the conditions of labor. It has been said that the whole family engages in the work. A family of six makes from $15 to $30 weekly, depending on the condition of the cotton and on the regularity with which they work. It is thus the most remunerative of all the occupations. While the other occupations are characterized by individual contacts in the relations between employers and Yaquis, in cotton-picking the whole family enters into the relationship. The ranchers send trucks to Pascua and carry whole families and groups of families away with them. Sometimes a single family lives during the whole season in a small house or tent beside the ranch house, doing almost all the picking themselves and during the time becoming intimately associated with the rancher's family. More frequently a group of two or three families from Pascua occupy adjoining tents or houses on the ranch some distance from the ranch house. Often they are associated on the ranches with Yaquis from other villages or with Mexicans or Americans. Not all Pascua families go out to pick cotton away from the village. In 1936 nineteen remained in Pascua during the season, the heads of ten of which were employed by W.P.A.

In summarizing the wages and working conditions, we may say that in the most usual occupations wages range from $7.50 to $15.00 a week. In the lowest paid of these, ranch work, there are more Yaquis than in any of the others. The wages which Yaquis receive in their three traditional trades are at the bottom of the general wage scale in southern Arizona. Pay is higher in cotton-picking, but only because the whole family works, not because the rate is higher.

The securing of work is largely an individual matter. That is, each man gets a job either through his own efforts or as a result of having previously established a contact with some employer. Sometimes a person secures a job through the contacts of his relatives or his *compadres*, but there is no real organization of work contacts. There is no recognized individual who acts as representative of the village, as Juan Pistola formerly did, through whom an employer can recruit workers. Employers often find it necessary to make house-to-house canvasses to fill their needs.

During 1936–37 Pascuans spent very little time looking for work. Labor was not abundant in the Tucson region, and employers were constantly seeking workers. Yaquis have a reputation for being "good workers." Employers, with hardly an exception, say that "Yaquis work better than Mexicans." There is a saying that a Yaqui is worth three Papagos and two Mexicans. Employers say that they cannot expect a Yaqui to work regularly six days a week, but they agree that, while they are working, they work hard and usually rapidly. It is their speed and enterprise which causes them to be ranked above Mexicans and also above other Indians. As a consequence of this reputation and of the scarcity of labor in recent years, Yaquis have been in an advantageous situation in the labor market. Their attitudes toward work in 1936–37 were very probably influenced by the situation. Many worked and stopped work when they pleased, in the knowledge that they could get jobs whenever they wished to.

The work of women.—With four exceptions, the women of Pascua spend their time in household tasks during the season of residence in the village. There are four women, all under thirty, who work for wages as housemaids and laundresses in Tucson. They make from $7.00 to $12.00 a week, or, in other words, only slightly less than the men.

There are two women, both over fifty, who are professional midwives and herb doctors. Their practice is carried on exclusively in the village, and they charge for their services. They are, however, unable to compete with the county doctor, who gives his services free, and they are therefore not frequently used by Pascuans.

Summary.—The people of Pascua are entering American economic life at the lowest income level. For the most part it is the men who secure jobs and participate in the production aspect of economic life, but women also participate. In some ways economic activities tend to break up the community life. During cotton-picking season the village is nearly deserted, and families are scattered under varying conditions throughout the Santa Cruz and Gila valleys. During this time, however, the family units remain together and are even more closely associated than when they are in the village, for men, women, and children work together in the fields as well as eat together and occupy the same household.

THE LEVEL OF SUBSISTENCE

The average weekly wage in Pascua has been calculated from a study of the incomes of a sample of fourteen male adults.[1] Over the three-month period studied the weekly wage averaged about $6.14 and ranged from (omitting persons with no income) $0.26 to $11.72. An adult male in Pascua, outside the cotton-picking season, supports four persons on the average besides himself. Thus the average income per person per week amounts to slightly less than $1.23.

The County Welfare Board estimates that $1.96 per person per week is minimum allowance for an individual in the Yaqui village. It is an interesting fact that the estimates of Pascuans themselves fall considerably below this level. Seven estimates by individuals in the village give a range of from $0.71 to $2.00 per person per week, with an average of $1.28. This estimate is very close to the calculated average income per person. It should be noted that no estimate by a Pascuan includes clothing. All are inclusive of food only, while the Board's estimate includes clothing as well as food. None of the estimates include rent. Persons who live in Pascua proper do not pay any rent, although those who have moved to Barrio Belén and have not yet paid for their lots pay a dollar a week to the real estate collector.

Those Pascuans who will make an effort to estimate how much it costs them to live invariably fail to include the cost of clothing or anything other than food. They say that they buy clothes when the income is for a time unusually large, as during the cotton-picking season, or when a surplus of food happens to be on hand at payday. Food

[1] See below, p. 50.

alone seems to be regarded as a constant necessity. The expenditures of a household consisting of nine persons was obtained for a week in April, 1937. Only food was bought during this week when the total income for the household was $15. The expenditures are as follows:

Flour	$ 3.14	Potatoes	$ 1.59
Lard	4.00	Onions	0.30
Dry beans	1.50	Meat (beef)	2.75
Coffee	1.00		
Sugar	0.48	Total	$14.86
Salt	0.10		

This budget, with its average expenditure of about $1.65 per person for food, might stand as more or less typical for the village. But it is not intended to give the impression that money is spent in any such regular fashion. The food budget is often cut to buy gasoline to run an automobile, to give money to a relative in need, to defray the expenses of a *fiesta*, or for any of a number of reasons. Moreover, in general, the income is not steady; it may lapse entirely for a week or two or it may be considerably more than the figure given above. A characteristic of Pascua life is that income and expenditure are extremely irregular.

THE USE OF MONEY

Subsistence being derived almost exclusively through wages, the use of money is general throughout the village. Every person handles it and lives by means of it. Relations with whites are mainly of the sort which involves, first, the exchange of labor for money and, second, the exchange of money for food and other means of existence. The relations which a man has with his employer are confined almost entirely to matters involving the exchange of labor for money. There is rarely any bargaining in such matters. The employer states his wage, and the Yaqui accepts or rejects it. Occasionally an adobe-maker, particularly the older and more experienced ones, bargain with an employer. But usually bargaining is not a verbal process. It consists in the acceptance of a job at a given wage, followed by quitting, if the Yaqui is dissatisfied, and return to the village. The employer may come for him again and raise the wage, and the Yaqui may go back, but there is little of even this sort of bargaining.

In the exchange of money for food and other necessities, it is usually the women who are involved. Hucksters and butchers, who may be Chinese, American, or Mexican, make daily visits to the village, driving their trucks from house to house. Purchases are made with reference to the needs of the moment. The hucksters are frequently called in a bantering fashion "robbers" (*coyotes*), and there is a certain amount of bargaining and haggling. Not all the food is bought from the traveling traders. The stores of Tucson, chiefly those which are Chinese owned and which cater to the lowest-income groups in the city, are patronized, and at least one member of a household, usually a woman, will make one trip a week to buy at these stores. One of the Chinese-owned stores often extends credit to a Yaqui for as much as several weeks when he is not working. The Chinese owner says that every debt owed him by a Yaqui has always been cleared from the books not later than the cotton-picking season following the contraction of the debt.

Within the village the chief use of money between Yaqui and Yaqui is in the form of gifts and credit. Relatives living in different households are constantly helping one another with small money gifts, particularly in connection with defraying the expenses of ceremonies. Not only the claims of relatives but also those of *compadres* and "godparents" are met regularly with the payment of small sums. Every person is expected to assist a *compadre* in paying the expenses of a *fiesta* which the latter is faced with giving. In addition, *compadres* and godparents have the right to ask for small loans. Interest is never charged in such transactions.

There is little exchange of money in the village except in the instances mentioned. Occasionally, a Yaqui rents his automobile to another, but other tools are lent without compensation. A few Yaquis cut and haul wood and sell it to others in the village. A Yaqui never hires another to work for him for wages, although the *maestros* (leaders of ritual services) receive sums of money for saying prayers for the dead on certain occasions.

Pascuans make no use of banks in Tucson or elsewhere. There is a saying: "A Yaqui never saves a cent." It is true that no systematic saving goes on, and no family was found which would admit to any extensive surplus. However, families frequently find themselves unable to spend all that they make during the cotton-picking season and bring the money back with them in old purses and stockings to Pascua. They then live on this surplus through the Easter ceremonial season or for as long as it lasts.

In short, relations with persons outside the village who are not Yaqui are almost entirely through the channels of money exchange. Relations between Yaquis within the village also take the form of money exchange very often, but they are of a different character.

Kinship and other types of social obligations are fulfilled by the payment of money, at least in part, but the exchange of goods or services for money between Yaquis is rare. Money is extensively used and so is credit; but, although the principle of interest is known, no one seems to make use of it in his credit dealings with Yaquis, and none is aware of it in his dealings with outsiders. Surpluses are small or nonexistent, and there is no cumulative surplus of any kind, in the form of money, being built up by any individual.

PROPERTY

The forty acres which were set aside as the original village area no longer holds all those individuals who act as members of the Pascua community. During the last nine or ten years there has been some movement of families who originally held lots in Pascua into the adjoining *barrio*. This has not been due to overcrowding on the Pascua acres. More than half the Pascua lots are now unoccupied, and about one-third of the area has never been occupied since the foundation of the village. The movement is directly traceable to the persuasion of a real estate development company which has offered lots in the adjoining subdivision. They have not been offered at a price cheaper than those in Pascua, but the agent of the company has spoken individually to Pascuans and has in some obscure way influenced them. Some Pascuans believe that the Catholic church of Tucson has been concerned in the matter—that the real estate company and the church have been working together to draw Pascuans away from the Yaqui church by having them settle in closer proximity to the newly erected Church of Santa Rosa in Barrio Belén. Those who have taken up residence in Belén give various reasons for moving. One man moved, he says, because his wife died in his Pascua house and he no longer wished to live there. Others recognize an economic disadvantage in that they now have to pay rent and seem unable to assign a definite reason for moving.

The community is still continuous territorially, but the boundaries of the original Pascua Village are well recognized. Those who live in Belén are spoken of as living in a different *barrio*. They are not permitted to use the adobe dirt from the unoccupied portions of Pascua. It is held that this is the common property of those holding Pascua lots and is reserved for their use only. It is also said that the plaza and the church are the common property of Pascuans and not of those who now live in Belén. Nevertheless, there is no exclusion of the Yaquis of Belén from the Pascua church or plaza. They participate equally with Pascuans. No one in Pascua at present assumes responsibility for administration of the waste land (i.e., the unoccupied area from which adobe dirt is taken for building or other purposes), but the residents of Barrio Belén admit their lack of right to it and do not make use of it. The management of the plaza is in the hands of the ceremonial societies, as is the upkeep of the church and other public buildings. As members of ceremonial societies, Yaquis of Belén assume equal responsibility in these matters with Pascuans.

Only three persons in Pascua have paid for their lots and have deeds to them. For nearly ten years after the foundation of the village, a collector came regularly in an effort to collect the instalments which buyers of lots had promised to pay. Few Yaquis, however, paid regularly, and for the last six or seven years collections have been made only occasionally. Pascuans act as if the land were theirs, but many have a sense of insecurity and a feeling that the land might be taken away from them at any time.

There is no clear-cut sense of individual ownership of

either house or lot. Individuals have their specific possessions, such as clothing and tools, but the management of houses and household goods is a joint affair, involving all who live in a household. The oldest individuals, whether male or female, seem to have the strongest voice in management. Decisions such as, for example, the remodeling of a house after the death of one of its inhabitants are made in conferences participated in by all the adults of the household. There is rarely any definite assignment of property after the death of an adult member of a household. The person dies and the management of the property goes on as before—in the hands of the whole group. No disputes arose in such connections in Pascua during 1936–37, and none was reported as having taken place in the past. In one instance, a man told a member of a household before his death that the house was to be regarded as the property of his oldest son and that the latter was to have the disposition of his automobile and the household goods. It happened, however, that the land contract had been in his wife's name. After the man's death, the wife planned and worked out the remodeling of the house, the son continued the registration of the automobile in the dead man's name, and the wife took the responsibility for the lending of some ceremonial paraphernalia which had belonged to the dead man. In other words, the son did not assume responsibility for the property but left it in the hands of his mother, the oldest woman of the household, despite the deposition of the dead man.

In the matter of inheritance little need arises for the specific allocation of property after a death. The household goes on as before, and the needs of the group determine the use of the goods. The absence of agricultural land no doubt simplifies the property situation. Older persons say that on the Yaqui River there was a definite procedure in the disposal of agricultural land after the death of a person. The pueblo '*kovanau* (*gobernador*) always took charge. He allotted the land which the dead man had been working to either his eldest or his youngest son, depending on which was the more industrious and better able to manage it. There were no fixed rules of inheritance for the house, the land on which the latter was built, or its furnishings. Often the youngest son was still living with his parents, it is said, when the latter died, and hence he continued in possession of the house and household plot. In other words, the system which some of the older people remember seems to be much the same as that now obtaining. The deciding factor in the disposal of agricultural land was the recognition, on the part of the person receiving it, of obligation to work the land; and the disposal of other goods depended on the needs of persons who had formerly had some interest in them. Ownership was and is less a matter of rights over things than of obligations to and needs for the things.

There is much of this same character in the ownership of ceremonial articles. A *matachín* dancer owns his dancing paraphernalia, people say, not because he makes and pays for it himself but because it is the insignia of service in the dance society and must be buried with him at death to show in the other world that he has rendered that service. It is part of his social personality and could have no meaning in the hands of anyone else. It is also said that he "owns" the paraphernalia because he must use it in his dance on stated occasions. Another type of ownership of ceremonial goods illustrates the same principle. Several families in the village have possession of images. One family, for example, "owns" the image called "Santa Cruz."

The image is kept in their house, and they originally paid for it. The family, however, as a result of this ownership has certain obligations to the whole village. It is their duty to hold a ceremony on May 3 each year—a ceremony which is public and which involves the co-operation of all the ceremonial societies. The expenses of the ceremony, as well as certain definite ceremonial duties, must be assumed by the family owning the image. If a person who has such an image has not sufficient money to hold the ceremony at the proper time, he is ashamed and may lose prestige in the village. He may avoid the latter if he holds at least a private ceremony and burns a few candles before the image. Thus the ownership of an image involves not only the right to keep it in one's house but also an obligation to do certain things by which benefits are brought to the village as a whole.

Concepts of property are inextricably bound up with the two ideas of obligations to things and the needs of persons for the benefits derivable from things. Rights over things are not to be dissociated from the other two aspects of ownership. The tradition that inheritance of land should be dependent on ability to work the land is indicative of the general attitude toward ownership of property in Pascua today. It is regarded as natural that a person, even a stranger, coming to Pascua should make use of a vacant house without payment to its owner. Julio Olivas is "ashamed" to ask rent for his house when he returns to the village and finds that a Mexican family has occupied it. He cannot even suggest that they leave, because they tell him that they have no place to go. Accordingly, he takes up residence in his father's house until they have found another place. A deed gives title to land to a certain person mentioned by name, but the ownership and management of that land may be in the hands of a family council headed by his eldest brother or sister. Property does not descend from one specific person to another; it is used first by one group of persons and then by another, and the use is determined by needs rather than by fixed rules.

ECONOMIC ASPECTS OF THE "FIESTA"

Except for the occasional organization of an adobe-making crew of three or four men, Pascuans do not co-operate with one another in the production aspects of economic life. They co-operate only in the distribution of economic goods. We have already mentioned the use of money in the fulfilment of obligations to one another of blood relatives and of *compadres* or godparents. The fundamental social unit, the household, usually consisting of one or more elementary families related by blood, invariably shares whatever money is brought in by any of its members. It is not infrequent for one man with a job to support for several months a household consisting of several elementary families, although there may be one or two other able-bodied men living in the household. The kinship relation enjoins the sharing of whatever one has with one's relatives. This holds good whether the relatives are occupying the same household or not. The *compadre* relationship also requires a certain amount of mutual economic assistance, but the aid which *compadres* render one another is more usual in connection with the sudden and unexpected necessity of holding a *fiesta* than with the demands of ordinary daily life. The *fiesta* is a frequently recurring phenomenon which makes demands on the economic resources of a household to such an extent that they can rarely be met without outside assistance of some kind.

The *fiesta*, it may be briefly stated here, is a ceremony

usually connected with a crisis in the life of an individual, such as death, marriage, baptism, or sickness. When a person dies, three ceremonies are necessary: one at the time of death, one within nine days after the death, and one a year later. Marriage and baptism each require an elaborate ceremony, and a serious illness often results in a family's contracting to give one or more ceremonies in payment to a god for assistance in curing. The ceremonies are expensive affairs. They cannot be held without the co-operation of one or more ceremonial societies, and it is always expected that a large number of nonparticipants will attend. The ceremonial performers and the general public must all be fed during the course of the ceremony. In addition, the household must be decorated in certain prescribed ways, and, if the ceremony takes place in winter, large quantities of wood must be supplied to provide heat for those attending. All this requires money.

The least expensive type of *fiesta*, a baptism, may be carried out for six or seven dollars because only the families of the baptized child and his godparents and one member of a ceremonial society (a *maestro*) are expected to attend. But at *fiestas* of the other types provision must be made for considerable crowds. At a funeral, for example, there may be a dozen members of the *matachín* dance society, several *maestros* and the female chanters who accompany them, as well as thirty to a hundred nonparticipants. The cheapest funeral recorded in 1936–37 cost $9.00. It was an extremely simple affair, being organized for a man who had no relatives in the village and consequently no one to take great interest in the ceremony. Other *fiestas* cost from $14.00 to $80.00, a usual cost being about $25.00.

A *fiesta* is almost invariably an emergency, an economic as well as a personal crisis. A wedding may be planned in advance and frequently a baptism is postponed and prepared for, but the first two death ceremonies cannot be predicted. It was *fiestas* connected with death which were most common during 1936–37. Preparations have to be made hurriedly and appeals have to be made to all relatives and *compadres* for financial assistance. It is in this connection that the great importance of such relationships may be seen. Surpluses of money being rare, the crisis of the *fiesta* can rarely be met without the economic co-operation of kin and *compadres*.

These are not, however, the only channels of economic co-operation. There is co-operation on a wider basis which functions through the ceremonial societies. The economic functions of the societies will be dwelt on in detail below. Here we shall merely indicate briefly their more important duties in connection with the economic aspects of the *fiesta*. The members of the male dance societies, in their respective seasons, have the obligation to perform certain labor in connection with the preparation of a household for a *fiesta*. They must prepare the ground surrounding a house for the necessary dances and other ritual activities and set up the ceremonial paraphernalia; in addition, they have the duty of cutting and hauling wood for the fires necessary in cooking and heating. All this labor is performed without remuneration from the household giving the *fiesta*, except for meals during the course of the work.

Besides this the dance societies are required to enlist the aid of the whole village in behalf of the persons giving the *fiesta*. They do this through an institution called the *limosna*. The *limosna* is conducted by the dance societies just prior to the ceremony. They go from house to house throughout the village and, in the name of the patron of their society, either the Virgin Mary or Jesus, ask for food or money as contributions. The details of this important economic institution will be discussed more fully below. It is sufficient here to say that it is a frequently recurring feature of life in Pascua. One was conducted at least every two weeks during 1936–37.

The *fiesta*, it is evident, is an institution which is closely linked with other institutions by means of which economic co-operation may be effected in the village. The institutions of group labor and the *limosna* are the only channels through which the village ever acts as a unit in economic matters. It should be noted that they operate in connection with ceremonial occasions only. There is an exception to this rule, however; the *limosna* may be used for other purposes which will be described below. Under whatever circumstances it is used, it is always under the control of one or the other of the ceremonial societies.

ECONOMIC ATTITUDES

The idea of economic advantage operates in the village in an apparently erratic fashion. Calixtro Estrella, a man of thirty, has within the last three years turned from ranch work to adobe-making and laying. His reasons for the shift are quite definitely those of an "economic man." He has recognized the difference in pay—the two or three dollars more a week which the adobe trades yield. He, moreover, recognizes the fact that he works fewer hours for this higher pay, and this he counts as a great advantage. His own summary of the matter is that formerly when he worked on the ranches he never had more at the end of a week than enough for food for his wife and children; but now, he says, he has enough for a little beer and he has time to drink that beer. The fact remains that Estrella actually makes less money now than he did formerly, for, having made the change, he now refuses to take a ranch job under any circumstances, even when there are no adobe jobs in Tucson. Another man, Julio Olivas, also recognizes the differences in pay between adobe and ranch work. He has a large family to support. Nevertheless, he refuses adobe-making jobs when he has the chance to choose between them and ranch work. He is familiar with the techniques of the former, but he says that he has always been a ranch hand and he likes that better. The few extra dollars do not matter much, he thinks. Olivas' attitude toward labor is the one which seems to characterize the majority of Pascuans. We have seen that most of them remain in the lowest paid of the three traditional Yaqui occupations—ranch work. That this is forced on them by the general economic situation seems doubtful. Almost all have had a hand at railroad work, and many have been successful in it to the point of becoming foremen or assistant foremen. But they have not liked railroad work and have drifted back to the village to make their livings from the ranches.

The point is that any individual, in making a decision as to the kind of work he shall do, considers many factors besides the wage. Some of these may be simply summed up as "working conditions." Railroad labor is unattractive to most Pascuans because it is "hard." Cotton-picking is attractive because the freedom that goes with piece work accompanies it; one can work when he pleases and take a day off when he pleases. But there are other kinds of factors. Holding a railroad job involves being sent about from section house to section house and consequently remaining away from the village for extended periods or altogether. Pascuans say with considerable unanimity that they do not like section houses. Cotton-picking also involves staying away from the village, but the houses in which one lives are often like the houses in Pascua and usually there are other familiar families as neighbors. The factors which complicate the operation of the principle of economic advantage are bound up with noneconomic activities in the village. It is necessary, therefore, to examine the latter in order to arrive at an understanding of the economic life.

Activities of Pascua males.—A record was kept of the daily activities of what was considered a representative sample of male adults in the spring of 1937. An analysis of these activities is shown in Table 2 (p. 50). A few points in connection with this table need explanation. The column headed "Days Worked" refers to days during which the individual was occupied outside the village working for wages. The column headed "Days Loafed" refers to time spent in various ways but not in remunerative labor or in ceremonial labor in the village; most men spent such days either in sitting or in sleeping at home, doing small jobs about the house or lot such as cultivating a garden plot or repairing a house roof, visiting in the various houses in the village, or walking to town and wandering around the streets. "Days at Home Working" refers to time spent in some systematic work about the home, such as constructing a new house or *ramada*. The column headed "Days Engaged in Ceremony" refers to activities in connection with *fiestas* or other types of ceremony in the village. "Days Combining Ceremony and Work" were days on which individuals participated both in work for wages outside the village and in some ceremonial activity in the village. The words in parentheses following the names of the individuals indicate the ceremonial offices held by them. The nature of these offices will be discussed fully below. It should be noted that four of the persons held no ceremonial offices. This proportion, four out of fourteen, is representa-

TABLE 2

ACTIVITIES OF PASCUA MALES (APRIL 5–JUNE 24, 1937)

Person	Age	Occupation	Average Weekly Income	Days Worked	Days Loafed	Days at Home Working	Days Engaged in Ceremony	Days Drunk	Days Looking for Work	Days Combining Ceremony and Work	Days Sick	No Record	Total
C. Matus (*maestro*)	50	Ranch hand	$11.72	41	3	....	10	....	1	27	0	0	81
T. García (*matachín 'kovanau*)	50	Ranch hand, adobe-maker	1.42	10	29	....	32	5	1	1	....	3	81
I. Valenzuela	36	Odd jobs	4.65	36	16	5	....	6	9	....	....	9	81
M. Valencia (*maestro*)	66	Odd jobs	0.26	2	49	....	15	....	....	....	15	....	81
T. Olivas (*maestro*)	44	Ranch hand	0.00	....	35	....	16	....	....	....	23	7	81
S. Silva	55	W.P.A.	11.00	59	19	....	....	1	....	....	....	1	80
R. Alvarez (*moro*)	75	Adobe-maker	5.81	45	11	2	2	9	....	....	....	12	81
J. M. García (*maestro*)	85	Not working	0.00	....	24	15	38	....	....	....	....	4	81
J. Cervantes (*matachini*)	88	Odd jobs	0.00	....	36	15	20	....	....	....	....	10	81
M. García (*matachini*)	40	Gardener	7.24	51	7	....	12	5	....	4	....	1	80
D. Lucero (*matachini*)	18	Railroad worker	8.07	42	19	....	14	....	4	....	....	2	81
L. Vasquez (*pascola*)	60	Ranch hand	0.51	4	4	47	17	7	....	1	....	1	81
P. Flores	30	Ranch hand	5.17	40	32	4	....	4	....	....	....	1	80
B. Valenzuela	45	Ranch hand	11.72	68	11	1	....	....	....	....	....	....	80
Total	....	....	....	398	295	89	176	37	15	33	38	....	....

tive of the proportion of men over ten years of age in the village who are without ceremonial duties of any kind.

The totals of days spent in the various kinds of activities have significance only as a general indication of the relative importance of the types of activities. It will be noted that work for wages consumes more time than any other single activity, that "loafing" ranks next, and that ceremonial duties are third. But this order of importance holds good only for the group as a whole, not for each individual studied. For an understanding of the place of these various activities in the village life, it is necessary to consider the individual variations.

Perhaps the most striking fact indicated by the table is the scarcity of "steady" jobs. Only two men, the first and last ones listed, worked the full quota of working days set by the American calendar for the period; each of these men worked 68 days. There were, however, two other men who had "steady" jobs: S. Silva worked for W.P.A., and his number of working days is low only because the W.P.A. working calendar excludes Saturdays, and M. García had regular employment extending throughout the period, but he was somewhat irregular in working at it. None of the others had single jobs which carried them through the whole period. A number had three or four different jobs; others had a single job which lasted only for a portion of the three months. The full notes on the work records indicate that the general work pattern consists in taking a job for a week or two, stopping work for a week or more, taking another job, etc.—alternating periods of work with periods of loafing. The "steady" job is an exception; the periodic layoff the rule.

Undoubtedly Yaquis, in following this work pattern, are following a pattern which obtains in unskilled labor for

Arizona Mexicans and Americans generally. An adobe-making job rarely lasts for more than a month, and, when one is over, it is necessary more often than not to spend some time getting in touch with new employers. Ranch work also to some extent consists in periods of intensive labor with periodic layoffs. But it will be noted that the two men who worked most regularly during the period were ranch hands who worked during the whole time for the same employers. A thorough study of working conditions in southern Arizona would be necessary before it could be determined to what extent Yaqui work habits are imposed on Yaquis by the general economic system. There is a good deal of evidence indicating that these habits are strongly influenced by the social and ceremonial system obtaining in the village.

A second important fact indicated in the activity records is that ceremonial duties occupy a large amount of time. Only four individuals—those without village offices of any kind—spent no time in ceremonial labor. The period studied was by no means the richest in ceremonial activity during the year. The three months preceding—the Easter ceremonial season—is the period during which most time is devoted to ceremony. April, May, and June in 1937 were characterized by an unusual number of child funerals resulting from an epidemic of measles, but in other respects the amount of time devoted to ceremony was not unusual. It might be taken as typical for the year.

It will be noted that one of the individuals who held a steady job, C. Matus, also participated in the maximum number of ceremonies. Of the four who had steady jobs, two also had ceremonial offices and two did not. These facts, together with the indications of Table 2 as a whole, show that there is no definite correlation between steadiness of work habits and absence of ceremonial duties.

Nevertheless, the Pascua ceremonial system does influence the economic activities of Pascuans in certain ways, and an effort will now be made to show in what manner this takes place.

Attitudes toward work and ceremonial labor.—The activity which is the main feature of participation in either wage labor or the ceremonial societies is called, in Yaqui, *'tekipanoa.* A man who goes out to work on a ranch or the railroad for pay is carrying on *'tekipanoa.* So is a member of a ceremonial society who dances or chants at a ceremony. Both kinds of activity go by a single name, but the attitudes toward them are very different.

Work for wages receives no sort of public recognition in the village, while work for a society is publicly approved at least once a week throughout the year. A sermon delivered by a *maestro* or some other public official is a constant element in every ceremony. The characteristic feature of each sermon is the mention of the ceremonial societies which have participated, an expression of thanks to them on behalf of the village, and an enjoinder to appear and carry on their *'tekipanoa* at the next ceremony.

In ordinary family life one often hears a person appraised on a basis of his ability to provide for his family or, in other words, his steadiness as a worker. This sort of appraisal is rarely final, however. The discussion of a man's merits almost invariably leads to mention of his participation in ceremonies if he is a member of a society, or of his recognition of his obligations to hold ceremonies if he is not. A man is interesting or worth talking about if one can discuss his behavior in the ceremonial society to which he belongs. A man who has never participated in a ceremonial society is especially pointed out and is given a special name, which literally translated means "not chosen."

On the other hand, a man who has worked steadily year

after year, as a few have, seems to have no standing in the community for that reason. What social prestige there is in the village is closely bound up with ceremonial participation.

The best way to support these statements is to list a number of examples:

León Valencia is a young man of thirty. He has worked steadily for the last twelve years at a near-by dairy. His employer says that he has missed hardly a day during this time. In the employer's opinion, Valencia is the best Yaqui in the village, because "he works steady and doesn't even quit for Easter." Valencia was promised to the *matachín* society when he was young and danced for it as a boy. His obligation has been forgotten neither by himself nor by others in the village. He excuses himself for not dancing by saying that he has to work to support his family. Actually his activity in behalf of his family has gone far beyond that of any other Yaqui in the village. He has the best house of any, the only one with a floor and a real stucco front. Others in the village say that he is "*mal por Dios*" because he has stopped dancing. When one expresses admiration for his economic success, it is dismissed with the comment "Oh, he is like a Mexican." He is still considered a part of the community only in that a *limosna* party always includes his house.

The most universally respected man in the village, Eduardo Valenzuela, against whom the investigators heard no bad word during the year of study, is one who has worked regularly all his life and at the same time has fulfilled his somewhat unexacting duties as a member of the male altar society. It is not held against him that he has worked hard enough to pay for his lot, but he is not praised for that. The basis of the respect that people have for him is always given as follows: "He knows more than anybody else about what should be done at the Easter ceremonies."

Celso Matus, *maestro* and head of the *fariseo* society, is also a member of another society. His active participation in these societies is a frequent subject of comment in the village. However, in the last two years he has begun to work regularly day by day, except during the Easter ceremonial season. Public opinion in the village is now rather strong against him because he lets his interest in work interfere at times with his duties as a member of the ceremonial societies.

Teodoro García, the present leader of the *matachín* society, is, from an American point of view, the most shiftless man in the village. He has no family at present and has a record of working only a few weeks each year. He has no property and not even a house of his own. Yet he is a busy man; he fulfills regularly his exacting duties as leader of the *matachín* society. He is not a man who enjoys the universal respect of the village. But the criticism that is leveled against him takes the form of disapproval of his inadequate knowledge of his ceremonial duties rather than of his dislike for work. People rely on him for the organization of ceremonies, and there is no doubt that he is a figure of importance.

Thus it would seem possible to say that prestige in the village depends much more on ceremonial activity than it does on income or possession of property. In other words, the values of the village are much more strongly centered about the ceremonial institutions than they are about the institution of wage labor. The lack of importance in Pascua of the economic values which obtain in the surrounding community is further apparent in the absence of class groupings based on income or property possessed. There is, as we have seen, difference in income; there is not much in regard to the income available for those who work, but there is considerable variation in actual average income. There are persons who average as much as $11.00 weekly the year round and others whose average is less than $5.00. With such differences in income it would be expected that there are differences in amount of property possessed. This is the case. There are a few persons who own their lots and houses, while the great majority own no land and are even squatting in houses built by others to which they have no legal claim. The range in value of property possessed is from nothing at all to $350. There is little correlation between property possessed and village participation. What there is, is inverse; most of those whose property may be valued above $300 participate relatively little in the community life. The correlation is not, however, very precise. There are several families with that amount of possessions who are also regular participants, and there are others who own nothing whose participation is infrequent. Constant and regular participation does not seem to work against the possession of property in amounts which are the maximum for any in Pascua.

Since participation in the work of the ceremonial societies has no value outside the community, while steadiness of work habits not only is highly valued but also plays an important part in anyone's getting a job, we should expect that there would be conflicts involved in any individual's participation in the two cultures. We have hinted in the examples given at the nature of the conflicts. The leader of the *fariseo* society was pointed out as losing prestige because he was regarded as paying more attention to his work on the ranches than to his work as a member of a ceremonial society. The man himself recognizes that there is a conflict, and his manner is one of almost constant apology for failure to perform his ceremonial duties while he holds down his job. He says that he works as hard as he does because his daughters have been sick and he has to get the right kind of food for them. He evidently wants to be re-elected head of the *fariseos* next year but has given up hope of this because he is conscious of the widespread disapproval in the village. But in 1937, and also the year before, Matus quit his job for one month during the Easter season expressly for the purpose of having time to fulfil his duties as *fariseo* leader. He kept his family going meanwhile on money he had saved for the purpose during the cotton-picking season. This conflict has not been settled yet, except through an admittedly unsatisfactory compromise between the two patterns effected by Matus himself.

Seven years ago José Robles was elected head of the *matachín* society. He fulfilled his duties for less than a year. Then, without telling anyone why at the time, he began to neglect them. He let them go more and more until eventually they were taken over by the present leader, Teodoro García. Robles says now that he dropped his duties because he could not carry them on and also keep a steady job. He regarded the steady job as more important than the prestige of leadership in the society. However, Robles has maintained his connection with the society and dances on important occasions as its leader. He does this only when it does not conflict too greatly with his work. He is a respected person in the village and is still spoken of frequently as a potential leader. He has worked out an adjustment between ceremonial activity and work which he can maintain only so long as he remains an ordinary member of the society. It is evident that leadership in the society and constant attention to a job are not compatible.

The sort of adjustment which Robles has made is the kind characteristic of nearly every other member of the *matachín* society. It is entirely possible to remain a member of the society in good standing without participating in every ceremony. Participation in all the ceremonies in which the society is concerned is necessary only for its leader. At any one ceremony only a small number of the members is necessary—eight or ten out of sixty-one. Consequently, periodic participation is the usual thing, each member dancing when, for one reason or another, he is out of work or when the activity does not conflict greatly with his job. Thus it is apparent that the conflict between the work pattern and the ceremonial pattern is resolved by most individuals in the partial acceptance of both. Leadership, however, requires an evaluation of the latter above the former, and it is in this connection that we see instances of acute and as yet unresolved conflict.

SUMMARY

Being entirely without economic resources in the form of agricultural land or products derivable from the natural environment, Pascuans have necessarily accepted roles in the economic system obtaining among Americans and Mexicans of southern Arizona. It cannot be said, however, that they have been assimilated into that economic life. They maintain property ideas and even certain economic institutions, such as the *limosna*, which are by no means identical with those in the surrounding culture. Moreover, they have not been assimilated in the sense that they wholly accept the values current in the surrounding economic life. Not only is their standard of living below that of the lowest-income Americans but Pascuans themselves do not, in general, entertain the idea that it could be higher. They estimate their needs at a lower figure than do the charity agencies in Tucson. Along with this acceptance of a low standard of living goes an irregular and only partial acceptance of the American job pattern. Steady work habits and regular participation in the surrounding economic life with the objective of increasing amounts of property held are not highly valued in the village. The social prestige that accompanies such activities among Americans is not associated with economic labor in Pascua. Prestige in the village depends on other kinds of activities associated with a system of ceremonial organization. An interest in the latter tends to retard economic assimilation. It now becomes necessary to examine in some detail these retarding factors if we are to explain the fact that Pascua has merely accommodated itself to, not been assimilated into, American economic life.

CHAPTER III

KINSHIP

WHEN the leader of a dance society starts out to organize a ceremony in the village, he begins by going from house to house and explaining at length the time, place, and occasion of the *fiesta*. He frequently says, as he sets out to do this, that he is going to tell *todos los parientes* (Yaqui: *'siʾime wa'waim*), "all the kin." He means by this "all the Yaquis in Pascua." It is customary not only for a dance leader but also for anyone else in the village to speak of all other Yaquis and particularly of those in Pascua as "relatives." Moreover, the common terms of address in greeting are Yaqui kinship terms. Men call one another "father" and "brother" and speak to women as "mother," whether or not there is blood relationship between them. This is a general custom. Kinship terms are loosely used and widely extended, but this does not mean that kinship relations are indefinite or that they are unimportant as an organizing factor in the social life. Everyone knows who his real kin are, and kinship remains an important principle in the social organization.

KINSHIP TERMS

The kinship terminology which is actually in use in the village is a composite of Yaqui and Spanish terms. No one makes use of or even knows a complete list of Yaqui kin terms. On the other hand, all know Spanish terms, and many can give extensive lists of them. Older people and a few of the younger women know many Yaqui terms which they never, or very rarely, use in ordinary speech. From some of these persons it was possible to obtain a partial kinship terminology in Yaqui. The terms were secured only with difficulty, and there was much disagreement in the lists, even between those of individuals who felt confident that they were familiar with the Yaqui terminology. Most persons disclaimed much knowledge of the Yaqui terms and gave what they did with doubts and hesitations. The Yaqui terms may be seen in Figures 3, 4, 5, and 6.

Evidently there is indication that the Yaqui system of terminology is of a "Yuman" type, with similarities to the fragmentary systems already published by Radin for other North Mexican tribes such as the Opata and Tepehuan[1] and by Bennett and Zingg for the Tarahumara.[2] It will be noted that there are disagreements with the fragmentary Yaqui system obtained by Kroeber.[3]

The characteristics of the system obtained in Pascua which suggest that it is Yuman are the following: (1) the prominence of differentiation of relatives according to the sex of the speaker; (2) the differentiation of parents from parents' siblings and of parents' siblings from one another; and (3) the importance of relative age distinctions. Two other important features of the Yuman type, namely, the complex cousin terminology based on relative ages as well as sex of generational links and the emphasis on male lineages, are not indicated in the Pascua data.

The differentiations according to sex of the speaker occur

[1] Paul Radin, *Mexican Kinship Terms* ("University of California Publications in American Archeology and Ethnology," Vol. XXXI, No. 1 [Berkeley: University of California Press, 1931]), pp. 3–4.

[2] Wendell C. Bennett and Robert M. Zingg, *The Tarahumara* (Chicago: University of Chicago Press, 1935), pp. 220–21.

[3] A. L. Kroeber, *Uto-Aztecan Languages of Mexico* ("Ibero-Americana," No. 8 [Berkeley: University of California Press, 1934]), p. 23.

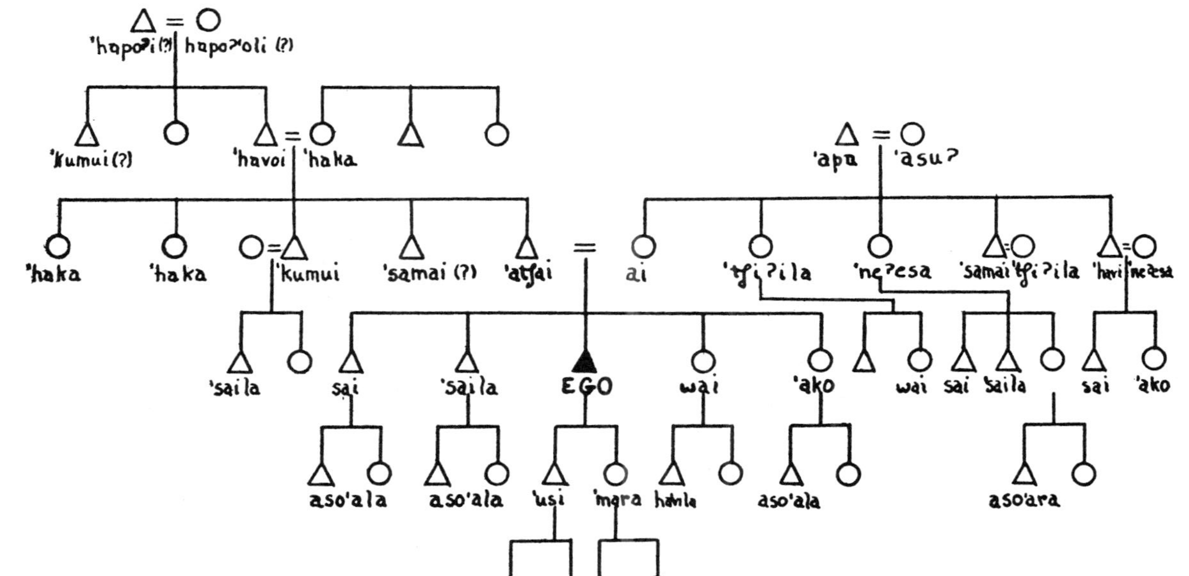

FIG. 3.—Yaqui kinship terminology: Pascua (male speaking)

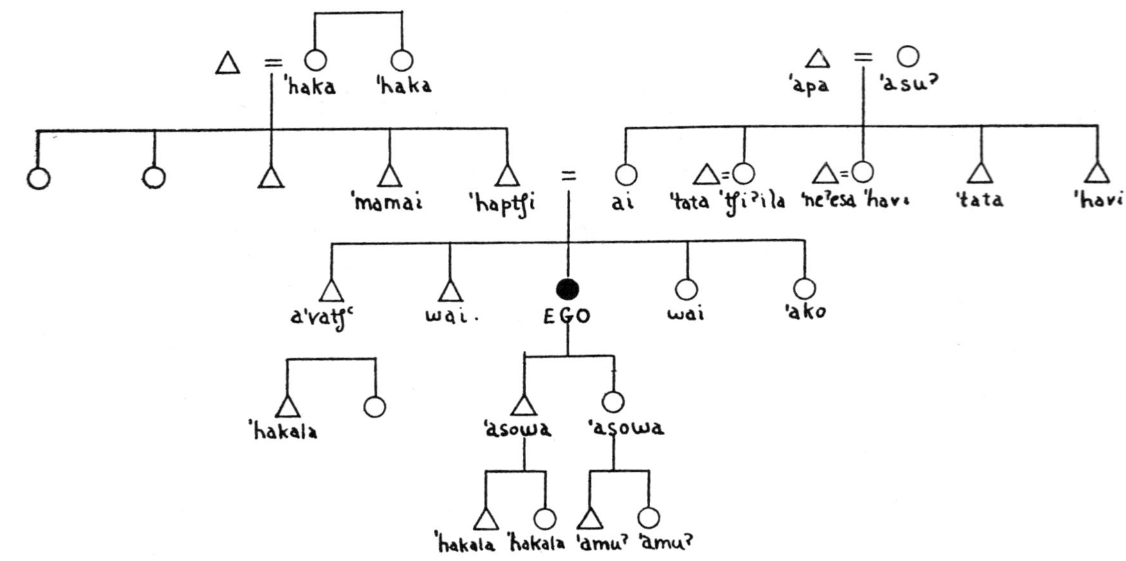

FIG. 4.—Yaqui kinship terminology: Pascua (female speaking)

in the first ascending, first and second descending, and also in ego's generation. A man and a woman refer to the mother by the same term but use different terms for the father. A man differentiates all siblings according to rela-

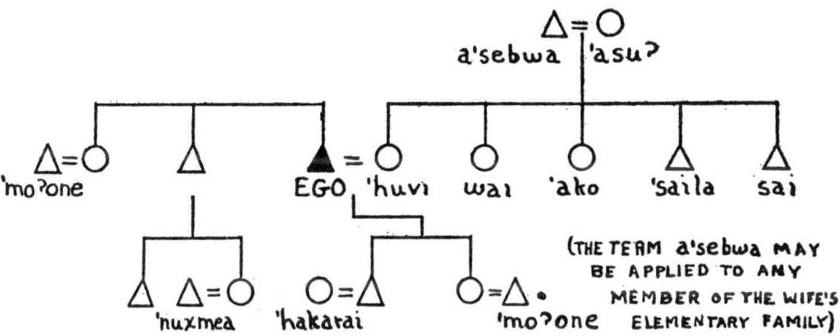

FIG. 5.—Yaqui affinal terminology (male speaking)

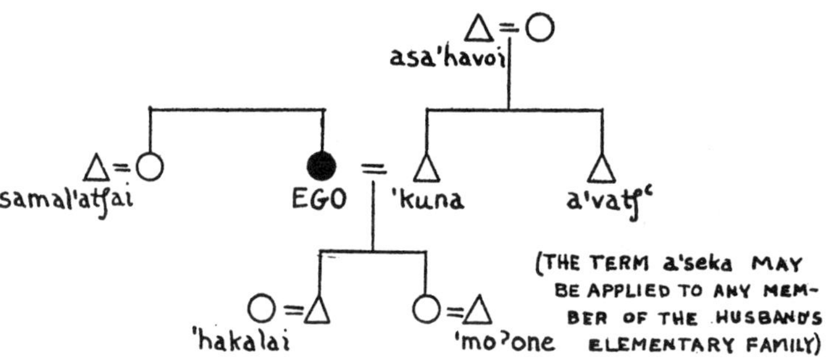

FIG. 6.—Yaqui affinal terminology (female speaking)

tive age as well as sex, while a woman differentiates her older siblings by sex, but not the younger ones. A man differentiates his children according to sex; a woman uses different terms from those of her husband for children and does not differentiate between them according to sex. Men and women use different terms for grandchildren.

In a Yuman type system the distinctions between persons in the first ascending generation are important for the classification of cousins. In Pascua the cousin terms are not remembered, but the distinctions in terminology for the members of the first ascending generation are retained, although they are infrequently used.

The relative age distinctions are apparent in ego's and in the first ascending generation. They are alike recognized by males and females. Generations are kept distinct except in the case of females on the father's side, who are merged in the first and second ascending generations.

In the discussion which is to follow it will be well to remember these characteristics of the "older" or Yaqui terminological system. It will be seen that some of these features are now obliterated, while some are in active existence. The system of terminology which follows (Fig. 7) is the one which a majority of families in Pascua use. The terms are familiar to everyone. The Spanish terms which appear in it are not used as vocatives, with the exception of *mamá* and *papá*. All the Yaqui terms, on the other hand, are in regular use as vocatives. The terms given for siblings, for parents, and for children are in constant use as vocatives, as are also those given for grandparents, with the exception of *papá grande* and *mamá grande* and *abuelo* and *abuela*. The latter, like all the other Spanish terms, are used only in indirect reference to the designated relative. Uncles, aunts, nephews, etc., are addressed usually by their personal names.

The borrowed Spanish terminology has evidently taken the place of all the terms for the more distant relatives. Cousins, uncles, aunts, nephews and nieces, grandchildren, and even grandparents are referred to in Spanish terminology. The Yaqui terms that remain are almost entirely

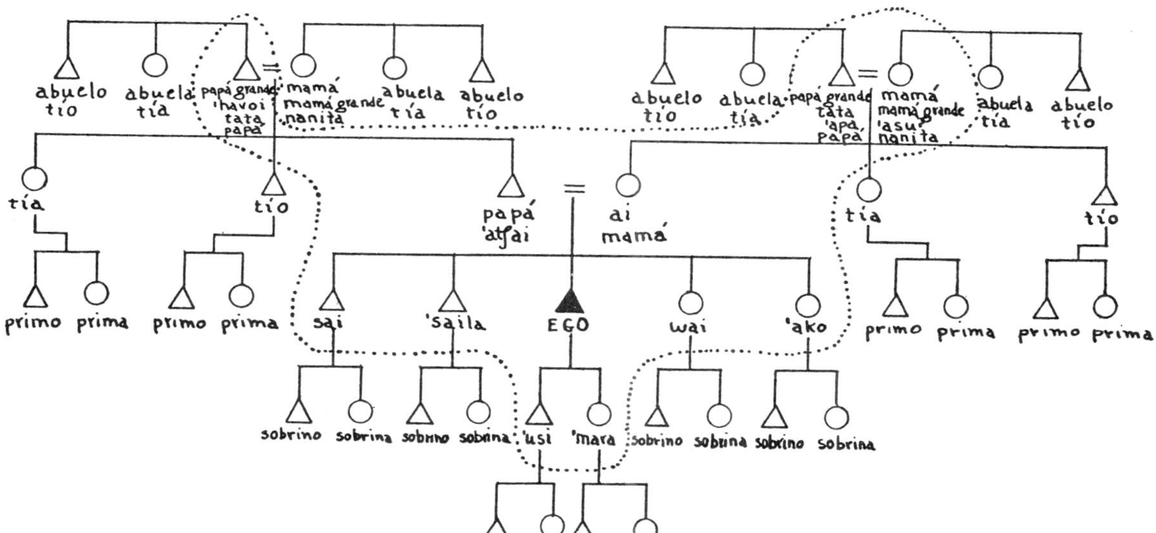

Fig. 7.—Yaqui-Spanish kinship terminology: Pascua (male speaking). The chart is a composite from the terms in use by thirteen individuals. Where more than one term is given for a relative, disagreement in the individual lists is indicated. In such cases the term occurring most frequently in the lists appears at the top, those occurring less frequently, below.

confined to members of one's elementary family, although the grandparent terms are still in use to some extent. The Spanish terminology has obliterated the remembered distinctions between relatives in the first ascending generation. Even father's siblings are not distinguished from mother's siblings. In the second ascending generation there is a further tendency to obliteration of distinctions based on maternal or paternal connection, as a consequence of the encroachment of the Spanish grandparent terms on the Yaqui ones.

The characteristics of the present system may be summarized as follows: (1) the mergence or equivalence of maternal and paternal lines; (2) the differentiation of sexes according to the sex not of the speaker but only of the relatives referred to; and (3) the recognition of relative age distinctions within a generation (but this is apparent now only in the persisting Yaqui terms for ego's siblings and is definitely not a feature of the overlaid Spanish system). In other words, two of the important features of the "older" Yaqui system have been entirely obliterated and a third persists only in part where some of the Yaqui terms have been retained.

It was mentioned at the beginning of the chapter that there is a loose use of kinship terms. The kinship chart (Fig. 7) gives some indication of what was meant by this statement. In most households where a grandfather is present, for example, he is spoken to as *papá* or sometimes as *'atʃai* by his grandchildren as well as by his children. *'Atʃai* 'joʔ*owe* ("older father") or *papá grande* are recognized as proper in such instances, but these terms are rarely used in practice. The same sort of usage applies to grandmothers, who are ordinarily addressed as *mamá*, *'mala*, or *ai*. The implications of this situation will be discussed more at length below. There is a similar tendency toward a loose usage of *tío*, *tía*, *primo*, and *prima*. Almost any relative, not a parent or grandparent, who is older than the speaker may be referred to at various times as *tío* or *tía*, if it is not important at the time to make the exact nature of the relationship clear. Similarly, *primo* and *prima* are used to refer to persons related to the speaker if they are of about the same age or younger. Although such loose usage is customary, an individual is usually found to know quite definitely the real relationship to himself of persons so designated.

The use of kinship terms in greeting has also been briefly mentioned. The terms which are used in this way are all Yaqui ones and are those used in designating members of one's elementary family. There is a tradition in the village that all Yaquis should regard one another as related: *'itom wa'waim jo'emem* ("We Yaquis are kin"). In accordance with this idea, the kinship terms are used whenever one Yaqui greets another. A man older than one's self is greeted as *'atʃai;* one of about the same age is called *sai* or *'saila.* Women are addressed as *'mala* by men and by one another. These terms are much used in ordinary greeting and in conversation in the village and may even be extended to non-Yaquis who gain the respect of the villagers.

KINSHIP BEHAVIOR

The most inclusive statement which can be made about kinship obligations in Pascua is that they are somewhat generalized. There is interest in the specific type of blood relationship which persons bear to one another, but kinship behavior outside the elementary family is not characterized by numerous varying patterns. In general, a maternal uncle is treated about the same as a paternal uncle and either of these much the same as a cousin or a great-uncle. The important thing in the eyes of a Pascuan is not so much the specific kind of kinship tie but merely the general fact of any kind of blood relationship. It is probably relevant to recall in this connection that many Pascuans had been separated from relatives for years before entering the United States. Those who did come in the company of relatives rarely came with more than three or four. Moreover, there has been much moving from place to placc since arrival in the United States, with consequent separation of children from parents, brothers from one another, etc. In other words, conditions have not been favorable for the development of large, stable kin groups. The kin groups in Pascua are small and, moreover, miscellaneous; that is, the kinds of relatives which an individual has near enough at hand to play a part in his life are, outside the elementary family, extremely varied. For example, there are three men in Pascua at present who have no blood relatives whatever. One man has only his married daughter. A woman, besides her own elementary family, has only the family of her married sister. Another man has only his wife and children and his wife's parents.

The specific types of kinship behavior are to be observed in the relations of elementary families, but the patterns here, like the kinship terms, may also be extended. A grandfather may act as a father toward his grandchildren, or a grandmother as mother, and this is to be observed regardless of whether the former is connected through maternal or paternal lines. Relative age within a household often seems to be as important in determining behavior as specific types of blood relationship. Nevertheless, there are types of behavior which are recognized as pertaining to specific kinship relations. These can best be discussed as elementary family patterns first, with subsequent mention of the ways in which they are extended.

Parent-child.—The chief differences apparent in the behavior of father and mother toward children result from the economic division of labor. The father provides food and other necessities, while the greater part of the physical care of the children falls to the mother. But the training of the child is carried on by both parents jointly. Girls learn domestic work from the mother, but training in social etiquette and in the elements of ritual behavior is carried out by either mother or father, whoever is most interested or best equipped. A father concerns himself as much with his daughter's training as with his son's. He or the mother, or both, may teach them to cross themselves, to kneel, and to recite a short prayer, such as the Ave Maria.

Parents have the obligation to secure ceremonial sponsors, "godparents," for their children, until the time of their marriage. The nature of these sponsors will be discussed below. They are extremely important in any individual's life, and the obligation to provide children with them is strongly recognized in the village. Either father or mother may take the initiative in obtaining sponsors, and the decision as to whom to get is ordinarily jointly made. Another responsibility which is accepted jointly is that of making the decision to promise a child, when seriously ill, to ritual service in a ceremonial society. This obligation is taken at least as seriously in the village as the one to secure godparents, although opportunity to exercise it may never arise.

The obligations of children to parents may be summed up as "respect" relations. Obedience is expected from children and likewise by parents from grown sons and daughters. In addition, it is a strong and generally recognized obligation of children when grown to initiate the three necessary ceremonies at the death of a parent and to take an active part in assisting ceremonial sponsors and others in the ceremonies. They must also observe certain rules of mourning in connection with the first and third of the ceremonies. The care of parents when old is also regarded as the proper duty of all children, regardless of age.

Sibling-sibling.—The oldest male and the oldest female sibling in a family are expected to share jointly in the care and training of their younger siblings. The oldest child of a family, whether male or female, is considered responsible for the conduct of his brothers and sisters and usually takes his responsibility seriously. Younger siblings often show a strong attitude of respect toward an oldest sibling, and it is evident that this persists throughout life. Brothers and sisters are expected to be co-operative and friendly, particularly after they have grown up and married. It is cause for censure if they are not.

Extension of kinship behavior.—None of the relations described for parents in regard to children is confined exclusively to parents. In households which consist of a single elementary family the parents fulfil these functions; but in households consisting of more than a single elementary family these parental functions may be more or less jointly shared with other men and women of the household. A mother's or father's parents usually take an active part in the training of grandchildren, share jointly in the selection of ceremonial sponsors, and assist when able in their economic support. Similarly, the respect relations of children to parents, apparent in a single elementary family household, are extended to grandparents in households where the latter are present. There is ordinarily a stronger degree of respect on the part of children toward such grandparents than toward parents, but otherwise the relation does not differ from that between the latter and their children.

In these extensions the guiding principle is that of relative age, and the relations involved may be summarized as ones of respect and authority. Authority characterizes the behavior of parents, parents's parents, and older siblings. Respect characterizes the behavior of children and younger siblings.

Joking relationships.—In one household in the village a well-developed joking relationship exists between brothers-in-law and sisters-in-law. In a few other families there are traces of such a relationship, but in the majority there is not even knowledge of it. In the household in which the joking relationship exists there happen to be two sisters married to two unrelated men. Between each of the men and his sister-in-law there is maintained a consistently disrespectful attitude, characterized by deliberate misinterpretation of words, refusal to consider seriously anything said by the other, and constant bantering. The people in the household regard the relationship as a traditional form of behavior. In some other households where the relationship does not obtain, there is embarrassment and sometimes laughter when the Yaqui word *'moʾone*, in the sense of brother-in-law, is mentioned. No such attitude seems to be associated with the Spanish word *cuñado*.

Several old people in the village have some knowledge of the joking relationship between brothers-in-law and sisters-in-law, although it is not practiced in their households. They say that they can remember when it was in use in their families in Sonora. In general, their attitude toward it might be summed up as a feeling that it is not respectable. One woman of eighty remembers that her first husband disliked the joking behavior, and as a result she did not encourage it in her household. Another man of sixty-five is convinced that "good families" among the Yaqui never practiced it.

General kinship behavior.—Other than those which have been mentioned there are no specific patterns of kinship behavior in the village. There are, however, ties of a general sort between kin. Any individual seeks assistance when he needs it from any persons who he knows are related to him by blood or through marriage. When he is faced with giving a ceremony for any reason, he seeks out his relatives and asks them for money or food or other necessary contributions. Cousins, nephews, brothers-in-law, and uncles, as well as nearer kin, are asked for such assistance. It is generally felt in the village that a relative is obligated to help as much as he can in such instances. The same sort of obligation is felt and acted on also when the occasion is not a ceremony but merely lack of a job or sickness in the family. There is, in other words, voluntary mutual assistance between relatives, regardless of type of relationship.

Other general obligations of kin which are recognized in the village are certain ritual ones connected with death. When a person dies, it is considered proper for all his relatives to appear at the three death ceremonies and to take an active part in the ritual connected with them. These activities are obligatory for all persons related by blood who occupy the same household as the dead person and also for all members of the two elementary families to which the latter belonged. They are voluntary for other persons who are related by blood. The parts played by the relatives in the death ritual are allocated not according to specific relationship but rather according to the relative ages of the whole kin group participating. The leadership of the ritual processions at the funeral and the death *novena*, for instance, falls to the oldest male of the group present and not necessarily to a son or a father or other designated kind of relative.

The general kin group also plays a part in other ceremonies, in fact, at any the scene of which is the household. In such ceremonies again, the leadership of ritual processions is taken by the oldest male of the household, sometimes by the oldest male of all the relatives present, or possibly by the oldest female if all the males are youthful. In all ceremonies, whether they are connected with marriage, baptism, death, sickness, or of a kind not connected with personal crisis, an effort is made to gather as large a group of relatives as possible, in which the most distant as well as the closest kin are included.

The place of in-laws in such ceremonial kin groups is not altogether clear. There seems, however, to be as much concern to gather in-laws as to gather blood relatives; a brother-in-law, moreover, if he has seniority, may assume the ceremonial leadership during a ceremony as readily as a blood relative.

MARRIAGE

The way in which groups of people related by blood enter into relationships with one another may best be seen by observing the marriage ceremony. There is, in fact, no other way in which kin groups, as such, co-operate with one another in Pascua.

There have been changes within the lifetimes of persons in Pascua in the methods by which marriage is effected. An older way of marriage arrangement exists side by side with a newer way. This applies to the marriage preliminaries only; the essentials of the consummating ceremony have not changed in recent times.

The older method of arranging a marriage required that the parents of the boy and girl concerned make all the preliminaries, usually with the latter playing no part whatever in the proceedings. Within the last five years marriages have been arranged in this manner in Pascua. One was so arranged in 1936–37. But two others in the same year were arranged in another way. In these the boy and girl concerned made the first overtures themselves, bringing their families into the arrangements only after they had made their own decision to marry. Whether or not the couple themselves make the first arrangements, the parents and other relatives still play an important part in the final ceremony. The three marriages which took place in the village in the first seven months of 1937, involving couples of about the age of twenty, were all carried out with the old-style Yaqui wedding. There are records of only three weddings in the village which did not follow the old Yaqui pattern for the ceremony.

Formerly, the parents of a boy took the initiative in arranging for a marriage. After they had decided on a girl, they went to the house of her parents and arranged with them for the marriage. Now it is not regarded as necessary for the boy's family to begin negotiations; they may be begun from either side. The only rule involved in the mating of persons is that they not be known to be related by blood.

At the wedding itself the couple is not much in evidence during the full day of ceremony. The parents and the marriage sponsor (unrelated by blood) of the couple make all the arrangements and try to secure as many as possible of their relatives. The sponsors of the boy and girl take them in to the Catholic church in Tucson in the early morning, have them married there in orthodox fashion, and then escort them back to the village to their respective houses for the eight or ten hours of Yaqui ceremony.

A group composed of relatives and *compadres* of the boy prepares a feast at the house of his parents. The relatives and *compadres* of the girl do the same at her house. The ceremony is consummated with processions, first, of the man's group of relatives to the bride's house, where they are feasted, and, second, of the girl's group of relatives, now in company with the groom's, to the latter's house, where all are feasted again. The exchange of feasts between the two groups is regarded as an equal ceremonial exchange and is accompanied by another exchange. The girl's kin group brings a basket of *tamales* to the groom's house during the course of the day and sets it down by the *patio* cross outside the house. It is taken in by the women of the groom's kin group, who later return the empty basket with money or something else which they regard as the equivalent of the *tamales* which the basket originally contained. Both exchanges are regarded as equal.

During the ceremony the boy's relatives accompany him in a body whenever he is required to appear in public. They escort him to the girl's house when the exchange of feasts begins, and they escort him back to his own house. Similarly, the girl is accompanied by the whole group of her relatives, until the point is reached in the ceremony where she is taken from her escorting group by the boy's relatives and ceremonial sponsor, in a sort of capture, and rushed into the house of the boy's parents. When the ceremony is over, the couple remains temporarily at the boy's parents' house. This does not, however, imply patrilocal residence at present, whatever may have been the past situation. Now a couple may live in the household of either the boy or the girl, or they may set up their own establishment immediately.

The marriage ceremony is gone through with only once during a person's life, even though there may be a subsequent change of mate. It is regarded as altering a person's social status in certain important ways. The nature of the changes will be discussed more fully below.

THE KINSHIP GROUPS

The fundamental rights and duties which are the expression of the relationships between individuals who are connected by blood have been discussed. We have made some mention also of temporary associations of relatives at various ceremonies. The personnel of such groups is not fixed by custom but may vary, and usually does, for even the same household on different occasions. There are, of course, more formalized kinship groups which are relatively permanent in their personnel and which constitute the basic social units of the village. These are the families and groups of families composing households. It is from the observation of such groups in their daily life in Pascua that the above discussion of the principles of the kinship structure has been built up.

The family.—Of the ninety-five elementary families in Pascua, twelve include couples who are not married to each other. Only two sets of these couples have never gone through any marriage ceremony of any kind. All the others have been married at some time in their lives, but not to the partners with whom they are now living. Death is responsible for the change of spouse in some instances, but there is also a number of persons whose former spouses are still living—with other persons.

There is a general ideal in the village that the marriage ceremony is a binding obligation and that two persons who are married to each other should remain together throughout life. This ideal is no more strongly expressed by older persons than by younger. They say that it was formerly the custom to bury alive persons who insisted on separating from each other and taking other spouses. It was not wrong, however, for a woman to leave a man who was drunken and failed to provide for her and her children. It was proper for her to do this and to come back to the house of her parents. It was also proper for a man to leave a woman who had sex relations with other men after her marriage. He need not, further, recognize any obligation to support her in such case. But it was not considered proper for the parties to such separations to take other spouses. Only if the first partner died was it proper to take another spouse. This ideal of behavior is clearly not lived up to at present.

Separations have taken place in recent years for the causes indicated above, but they have also taken place because of mere mutual incompatibility, and most of the persons so separated have proceeded to find other partners and to live with them. The second *maestro* and leader of the *fariseo* society, a prominent man in the village, is, for example, living with a woman to whom he is not married. His former wife lives in another place not many miles away with another man. The children of the former union live with the father and his new spouse. The new arrangement is not pointed out as wrong and does not seem to operate against the prestige of the man in the village. It is, in fact, the accepted way of adjusting to situations of husband-wife separation. Nearly all the most prominent persons in village life are living under similar conditions. The head *maestro*, a leader of a female ceremonial society, the oldest and most respected *pascola* dancer, two other *maestros*, as well as some of the less prominent persons, are not married to their present spouses.

Obviously, then, change of spouse with no new marriage ceremony is an accepted method of adjustment. The Yaqui and the Catholic ideals of no divorce are expressed in having only a single marriage ceremony for any individual—in other words, only ceremonially.

Separation for whatever cause is not usually accompanied by a complete breaking-off of relations between parents and children. Either or both of the parents may continue to be regarded as such by the children, despite living in different households. The complicated case of Pablo Ochoa illustrates what often happens. Ochoa was married to a woman who had had children, a son and a daughter, by another man who had died. The children continued to live with their mother and her new partner. The children grew up, for a few years, under Ochoa's care and called him "father." Then he and their mother separated. Ochoa began to live with another woman. Ochoa's former partner also took another spouse, going to live in Libre with this man. The children of the woman divided their time between Ochoa's house in Pascua and their mother's in Libre. Ochoa began to have children by his new partner, but he continued to contribute to the support of the other children. The latter regard Ochoa as their father and his first wife as their mother. At the deaths of both in 1937 they acted in the ritual capacity as son and daughter of each. The son, moreover, acts at present as older brother of the children whom Ochoa had by the second woman with whom he lived. It may be calculated that this son has no biological relationship with these "brothers" and "sisters" of his. This situation is unusually complex, but it illustrates a typical attitude. The parent-child relationships seem surprisingly strong, and they remain despite husband-wife separations unless there are complicating circumstances, such as extreme enmity between husband and wife which results in preventing any continuing association between a child and a parent.

The family is, therefore, in one sense an unstable institution in Pascua. There is frequent change of spouse and no effective public sentiment against such change. It seems to be rare for an individual to go through life with a single spouse. It is the older persons in the community, the prominent members of it, who are most frequently found to be living with persons to whom they are not married. Despite the readiness with which spouses may be changed, there is a strong tendency for the standard parent-child relationships to be maintained, although there is no definite pattern which these relationships may take and no community machinery for maintaining them.

The household.—The kinship relations which we have described develop in the household, which may be regarded, rather than the elementary family, as the fundamental social grouping in Pascua. By "household" is meant a group which eats in common, shares the means of subsistence, and occupies a house or possibly more than one house jointly. There are sixty such groups in Pascua, the majority of these being composed of more than one elementary family.

The groups classed as households are composed of from one to twenty-four members, the majority having between seven and fourteen individuals. The number of elementary families in a household ranges from one to five, the majority consisting of two. Twenty-seven (less than half) of the households are composed of a single elementary family.

Those households which are composed of more than one elementary family do not conform to a single pattern. There is indication of a tendency in the village to develop a type of extended family, consisting of parents and their married children, but such a form is by no means universal at present. There are at present only twelve such extended families. In these households there is no accepted pattern as regards sons or daughters remaining with the parents after marriage. In some there are only married daughters, in some there are only married sons, and in others there are both married sons and married daughters. There are also households occupied by persons with their married nephews, nieces, and granddaughters. There are, besides, four households in which the families living together are unrelated by blood.

It is evident, therefore, that the household pattern in Pascua is not a fixed one. Moreover, any given household will vary in composition during the course of a year. In Yaqui a household is called *ho'aʾkame* and the people of a household are called the "children of the house": *'siʾime nau 'wepul ho'aʾpo jo'emiarim*, which means literally "all together children in one house." This terminology seems well to fit the situation in the village. The house, or group of houses, remains the one constant feature of the household. The families who occupy it come and go. There are households of more than one family in which the persons occupy a single house and *ramada*, but there are only one or two of these. The usual household has two or three houses all occupied jointly by the household group, whenever they are in Pascua together. In many households the unit families seem to have regular sleeping quarters—for instance, a room which is reserved for each family; but almost as frequently persons sleep where they can, on floor or bed in any room. The cooking is done by any or all of the women, all of whom know the techniques. The men may work at different times or all may be holding jobs at the same time. Earnings are shared by the whole household group. A man who is working steadily may support for weeks not only his "own" family but also the two or three or more other families who live in the household.

The shifting nature of the personnel of a household may be indicated by citing the example of the Rosario Flores house group. The three houses and two *ramadas*, with a well and garden plot, are occupied by Rosario Flores, a widower of about seventy-five, the family of his son Julio Olivas, his unmarried daughter María, his married daughter Nicolasa and her husband and children, the family of a godchild named José Valenzuela, an unmarried son Juan, and the family of an unrelated woman named Jesusa Alvarez. These persons never occupy the household all at once, except for three or four weeks at Easter. In the summer months, for example, only old Rosario, the unmarried girl María, and the family of the son Julio Olivas are there. During the cotton-picking season from September until January everyone leaves except the old man. He remains in one of the houses, closes up the others, and often takes his meals at a neighbor's. But on All Souls' Day in November everyone comes back to the household, except the family of Nicolasa, which remains on a ranch more than a hundred miles down the valley. They are soon off again, however, to the cotton fields, leaving old Rosario alone until the middle of January. Then slowly the houses fill up. Three weeks before Holy Week everyone who belongs to the household is there, with the exception of the unmarried son, Juan. Juan will return only for Holy Week itself, and immediately on Easter Sunday night he will be off again to his ranch job near Casa Grande. The others stay on through the spring after Easter, the men working occasionally, but gradually jobs take them away, until by July only the old man and the family of his son Julio are left again.

This is more or less typical of the Pascua household. Not all households have such a shifting personnel, but most do. The coming and going of families is a prominent feature of Pascua life. The nucleus of the household group is usually a blood-related family, but it will have been noted that blood relationship is not always present. "God-children" or "godparents" may join a group or even persons who have not this relationship, and they may become permanent members of a household. The household in Pascua might be thought of as a loose confederation of elementary families, not necessarily related by blood and by no means fixed as to composition in accordance with a traditional pattern.

Nevertheless, the household, at any given time, has a definite organization. Some middle-aged men in Pascua say that a man is always the "head" of a household. Many middle-aged and older men do not say this, and it seems fairly clear that sex is not the determining factor in establishing the seat of authority in a household. Although personal qualities are important, the determining factor is ordinarily age.

In two of the households of the village the oldest members are males, one of these living with the families of his two married daughters, the other with his own wife and children and a married sister. These two men are the oldest males in the village, nearly eighty, and both are senile and inclined to have little interest in the practical affairs of the household. A great deal of respect is paid to both; their statements are listened to with gravity, however irrelevant they may be, and the children show considerable circumspection and some awe. A decision, however, such as, for instance, whether a daughter may become godmother of a neighbor's child or at what time the family will take to the cotton fields for the annual picking, lies in the hands of the oldest women in both houses. It is recognized that no real decision can be made by the old men, and the women readily accept the responsibility and direct the affairs of the family.

In other households where women are the oldest persons and still in possession of their faculties it is frankly admitted by males and females alike that they refer their problems to the old women. In other houses, for instance that of Rosario Flores, the oldest man is the dominating figure. It is impossible to point out a household where the oldest person is disregarded, except for the two special instances mentioned above, and it is impossible to generalize by saying that either males or females are the dominant authorities. In general, all adults share in decisions in a household and in general it is the oldest person to whom all defer when disputes or disharmonies arise.

The inheritance of the house or houses which constitute the basis of every household group has been sufficiently discussed under "Property" in the previous chapter.

A household also has members who are not in the world of the living. The dead members of the elementary families who make up a household are considered to be members of the latter. Each elementary family keeps a small book, usually a ten-cent-store notebook, and each time a relative of any member of the family dies the name of that person is entered in the book. The books are called by Pascuans by the same name that is applied to the soul of a dead person, *animam*, a slightly Yaqui-ized form of the Spanish word for "spirit." In the following pages these important little lists of ancestors will be referred to as Books of the Dead. No household is without one or more of them. One frequently contains more than two hundred names of adult dead and nearly as many names of children. The dead are divided always into three groups in the book: adult males, adult females, and children (among whom sex is not distinguished except by the name). Only the Christian name of each individual is listed, but it is always followed by any ceremonial title which the person may have had in this life. The books are not secret and are not kept hidden. They are open for the inspection of anyone who wishes to look at them and are objects of pride in a family. The duties which persons have in connection with the Books of the Dead will be dwelt on below.

The wider kin group.—It has been mentioned that there is a saying current in Pascua that all Yaquis are kin and that elementary family kinship terms are extended throughout the village and beyond. We have emphasized the fact that this does not involve any confusion as to who are one's real relatives. The extended terms are definitely recognized as "respect" terms only.

The general term for blood relatives, *wa'waim*, and its Spanish translation, *parientes*, are used by everyone in referring to other Yaquis. We have noted that a dance society leader often uses the expression in this way when he is giving public notice of a ceremony. He applies the term to the Yaquis of other villages almost as readily as he does to the Yaquis of Pascua.

This usage does not have a basis in any belief that all Yaquis actually are related by blood. At least no one in

Pascua today believes such a thing. There is no myth current in the village, other than that of Adam and Eve in the Garden of Eden, which indicates that Yaquis trace their descent to a single ancestor. The only thing which might be connected with the usage is the common reference to images of the Virgin Mary and certain other representations of her as *'itom ai*, "our mother." No one, however, says that he believes that all Yaquis are descended from the Virgin Mary or from any aboriginal equivalent of her.

However, certain forms of kinship behavior seem to be associated with the extension of the general kinship term to all Yaquis. When a ceremonial society official announces that he is going to tell all the "kin" about a *fiesta*, he means that he is going to go from house to house and make a formal announcement and at the same time conduct a *limosna*. That is, he goes to the households of the village for assistance just as a man goes to the houses of his blood relatives and asks them for help whenever he is faced with giving a *fiesta*. Just as the reference to Yaquis outside the village may be as "relatives," so also the *limosna* method of obtaining aid for a *fiesta* may be extended outside Pascua to other Yaqui villages.

The use of Books of the Dead by families has just been mentioned. There is a similar interest in the dead of the village as a whole. This interest is expressed by the head *maestro* on many occasions but particularly in those ceremonies which are held each evening during the month of October. At these the *maestro* recites a list of names of dead persons which follows no particular family line. The dead persons named are the more famous Yaqui leaders, such as Cajeme, various "generals" prominent in Yaqui uprisings, and, finally, dead village leaders, such as Juan Pistola, Francisco Salvador, and others. These village dead are referred to as *pueblo 'animam* in the same way that the names in the Books of the Dead are referred to as *familia 'animam*.

There is more emphasis on blood relationship in certain sermons which the *maestro* gives at the end of every service. In these he ordinarily introduces what he has to say with a long list of kinship terms, such as *'itom aim*, *'itom 'atʃaim*, *'itom 'apam*, *'itom 'asum*, etc. These expressions mean "our mothers," "our fathers," "our grandfathers on our mother's side," "our grandmothers on our mother's side," etc. He usually mentions the fact that "our mothers" nursed us and took care of us and that respect is due them and all other relatives of the first, second, and third ascending generations. He goes on to explain what they expect of the villagers and how the ceremony just completed was in part for these dead ancestors. The *maestro* is thus a spokesman who constantly emphasizes in his sermons a unity of the village expressed as being based on a relationship to dead ancestors.

It is clear from what has been said that kinship terms are used commonly in a way which expresses not only a unity within groups actually related by blood but also a unity of the larger group comprising all Yaquis whoever they may be. This idea of a kinship unity, including all Yaquis and particularly the village of Pascua, is not accompanied, however, by a belief in actual blood relationship. No such belief exists. The usage may be compared with the Christian saying that all men are brothers, but it plays a considerably more vital part in the lives of the people and receives much more frequent overt expression.

RECENT CHANGES IN KINSHIP BEHAVIOR

There is a widespread belief among persons over forty in the village that younger persons lack respect for older.

This idea is usually put in the following form: "Nowadays the boys and girls don't care what the older people say; they don't do as we used to do when we were young." Then examples are cited of how young people used to behave, and these are compared with the behavior of young people now in the village.

It is maintained consistently by persons in their sixties and seventies that when they were young all marriages were arranged by parents or a village official sometimes called *'piskanjaut* (Spanish, *fiscal*) and that the couple concerned had nothing to do with it. They are also consistent in saying that their parents required them, as children, to stand before the *patio* cross in the house yard each day, in the morning and evening, and either recite a Catholic prayer, say the Rosary, or give some Yaqui ritual salutation to the parents. One seventy-year-old man maintains that children had to get down on their knees frequently before their grandparents (both maternal and paternal) and that no child could address his grandfather without first being spoken to. This is not confirmed by any other statements. There are also several other unconfirmed statements in regard to kinship customs. One man says that he was forced to assume ceremonial duties in the Yaqui River pueblo of Belén because his mother was born there, although he no longer lived there and his father had come from Rajum; he says that he was regarded as *belonging* to his mother's pueblo. Another old man says that children were required to paint the eyebrows of their parents in the funeral ceremony, a custom which would be in great contrast with the present avoidance of the body by relatives.

Of these practices, we have seen that the custom of parents' arranging for children's marriages is still carried on in

Pascua, although it is not the exclusive method. The custom of children going through daily ritual under the direction of parents before the *patio* cross is no longer carried on, although there is good evidence that such a custom was in vogue in one family after it had arrived in the United States about thirty years ago. There is no indication of survivals of the other customs mentioned. Before these data can be taken as evidence of changes in kinship behavior, they will have to be checked further.

It is clear that, despite the widespread belief that children do not have respect for their elders, there is still a definite social hierarchy based on relative age. If what the elders believe is true, then an extreme degree of respect for older persons must have prevailed in earlier Yaqui society. To an American viewing Yaqui society now in Pascua, there is a much better-developed sense of respect for older persons than in his own society.

An obvious recent change is the dying-out of the use of Yaqui kinship terms. Several old persons are quite convinced that they know the old terminology and will proceed to give it to an investigator. They soon find that they know less than they thought, and it is obvious that their lists do not check very far with other lists. Nevertheless, the oldest people do *know* more kinship terms than they actually use. Those which they do not use, such as those for members of the second ascending generation and for all but parents in the first ascending generation, are, of course, not being taught to the younger persons, who seldom or never hear them. They are therefore dying out, and, when necessity for expressing such relationships arises, as it frequently is doing with the development of kinship groups in the United States, Spanish terms are resorted to.

SUMMARY

The basic principles of organization indicated as being of importance in the older Yaqui kinship terminology are, with one exception, no longer of importance. Sex differentiation does not seem to be expressed in the actual kinship organization, although it appears as a survival in the kinship terminology of the elementary family. We shall see later that sex distinction is expressed rather extensively in the ritual. The maternal-paternal lineage distinctions are also not apparent in the present organization. (Children do not even take consistently the names of either father or mother.) But one of the older important principles is still very strong—that of relative age. It is relative age rather than generation which has remained important in that part of the social organization determined by kinship.

We have seen that there is not a wide systematization of kinship behavior. Kinship relations are more or less generalized. Although the relations cannot be said to be highly organized, yet kinship is the basis of formation of certain groups. All these—the general group which forms at a ceremony, the elementary family, and the household—are rather loose in organization and varying in personnel. Nevertheless, they exist and play a part in the social life. Particularly important is the household, in which the organization of the family tends to be merged. Whatever strength the kinship principle has depends on the behavior established in the household and perhaps also on the objectification of the household kin group in the ritual which is carried out at the time of a household *fiesta* and at the time of a marriage, when kin groups function ritually as such.

In addition, there is an extension of kinship terms, and

to some extent usage, to the wider group of the village and even to all Yaquis of whatever village or region.

The present kinship system is a fusion of Yaqui and Spanish elements, certainly in terminology and probably in behavior pattern. It is evident (Fig. 7) that certain aspects of the old Yaqui terminology are more resistant than others to the encroachment of Spanish. The elementary family terms remain Yaqui, while those for more distant kin have become, or are becoming, Spanish. The significantly operating factor in this different acceptance of terms would seem to be the character of the social groups in which the terminology is involved. That is to say, the intimate primary group of the elementary family preserves Yaqui tradition more effectively than the less intimate, wider kin group. The role of these groups in the preservation of kinship tradition may be indicated by reference to the conditions in Sonora toward the end of the nineteenth century which resulted in the atomizing of Yaqui society. Elementary families as well as the larger kin groups were broken up, but the former were quickly re-established while the latter have only slowly begun to develop, as stable Yaqui settlements have appeared in the United States. The parent-child and sibling terms have remained Yaqui, it may be suggested, because the elementary family has had continuous existence throughout the recent period of social change and, consequently, persons have had more occasion to use these terms. Spanish terms have been substituted for the Yaqui ones for more remote kin, because the groups in which they were used went out of existence and consequently the Yaqui terms were lost. With the redevelopment of such groups, need for designating the persons in them has arisen, and Spanish terms have been borrowed to fill the need.

CHAPTER IV

CEREMONIAL SPONSORSHIP

THERE are persons in Pascua who have not a single relative, by blood or by marriage, but there is none who lacks a *compadre*. One of the older men, who entered the United States alone and has now survived the wife of a childless marriage, lives by himself without knowledge of where any of his wife's relatives live. He says, nevertheless, that he feels quite secure. Does he not have a *compadre* of long standing in the house next door? And does he not have a godchild in another house near by? These people, together with his many other *compadres* and godchildren, will help him if he gets sick and take care of his body and possessions when he dies. He shrank from the idea of going to the hospital when he had pneumonia and consistently refused to be taken there. He was dangerously ill for more than a month, and during this time a man of about eighty, one of his *compadres*, made daily visits, bringing food and medicine. When the old man recovered, he said, "I did not go to the hospital because I would have been alone. Here I had my *compadre* to take care of me."

The relationship which exists between this man and his *compadre* is one of a kind which links all the persons of Pascua with well-recognized and binding ties. It often has the elements of what in Western society is called "friendship," but there is a great deal more than that in it. Friendship in our sense may be entirely absent, yet certain definite mutual obligations continue to be recognized and the bond still holds. The *compadre* and godparent-godchild

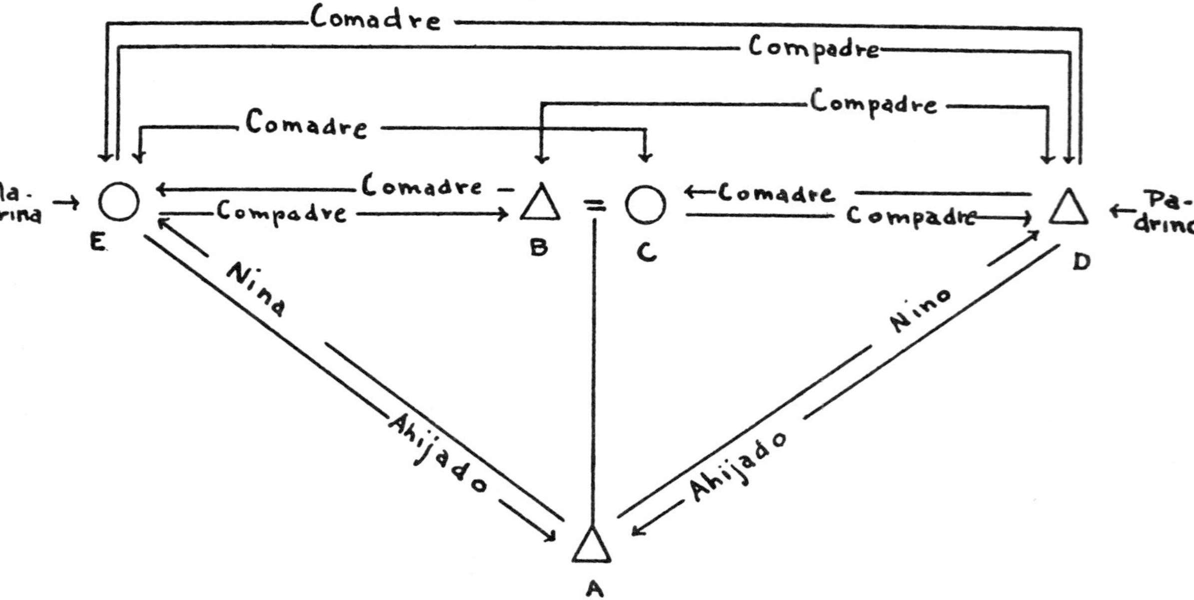

Fig. 8.—*Padrino-compadre* terminology

(*padrino-ahijado*) relationships are formalized into an institution which is at least as important an element in the social structure as kinship. The behavior which the institution enjoins is possibly more precisely formulated than is kinship behavior.

TERMINOLOGY

A *padrino* is, briefly, a ceremonial sponsor, one who sees another person, the *ahijado*, through a ceremony of the personal-crisis kind. There is a definite set of terms which applies to persons who stand in this relationship to each other and to certain of the relatives of both the sponsor and the person sponsored. In Pascua both Spanish and Yaqui terms are used to express these relationships. The use of the Spanish terms may be made clear by Figure 8.

In the diagram, A is a male whose ceremonial sponsors are the male D and the female E. The parents of A are B and C. The arrows point in the direction of the person to whom the term included in the arrow is applied by the person at the base of the arrow. For example, A calls his male ceremonial sponsor *nino* and is in turn referred to by D as *ahijado*. Similarly, D and B are *compadres*, and D and E are *compadre* and *comadre* to each other. The arrows pointing to D and E from no designated person indicate that the male and female sponsors of A are referred to as *padrino* and *madrina*, respectively, by anyone either outside or inside the relationship. The terms *comadre*, *compadre*, *nino*, and *nina* are the only ones used as vocatives.

The Spanish terms given, with the exception of *compadre* and *comadre*, have Yaqui equivalents. They are as follows:

padrino, nino....*'vato 'atʃai* (male speaking); *'vato 'haptʃi* (female speaking).. (*Va* is the Yaqui word for "water" and refers here to baptism.)

madrina, nina....*'vato ai* (male or female speaking)

ahijado.........*'vato 'usi* (male speaking); *'vato 'asowa* (female speaking)
ahijada.........*'vato 'mara* (male speaking); *'vato 'asowa* (female speaking)

All the Yaqui terms are used as vocatives as well as referents. In Yaqui speech *compadre* is always *'kompai* and *comadre* is *'komai.*

The terms, either the Spanish or the Yaqui, are in constant use in the village. They are heard somewhat more frequently than are kinship terms. There is no one above the age of ten who is not familiar with, or does not make use of, all of them.

Figure 8, however, is not quite complete. To be so, it would have to show also the spouses of the *padrino* and *madrina* and the grandparents of the *ahijado.* The *compadre* and *comadre* terms are extended to these persons. Thus (referring to Fig. 8), B and C would address the wife of D as *comadre*, and she would reciprocate by calling them, respectively, *compadre* and *comadre.* The husband of E would, similarly, be called *compadre* by B and C. Further, if the parents of B or C or of both are living in the household of the latter, it is likely that they, too, would be addressed as *compadre* and *comadre* by D and E, and they would use the same terms for the latter. Accompanying the use of the terms in these extensions there would be the appropriate reciprocal behavior.

The terms are extended even farther. An individual does not have only a single set of ceremonial sponsors. Theoretically at least, he may have any number. All the sponsors of any given individual, no matter of what type they may be, also use the reciprocal *compadre* and *comadre* terms to each other as well as to the parents and grandparents of the person sponsored. Thus the simple act of ceremonial sponsoring brings persons from a number of different families into a system of defined relationships in connection with which there is a specified set of terms.

THE NATURE OF CEREMONIAL SPONSORSHIP

A ceremonial sponsor is one who assumes certain duties on behalf of another person during certain ceremonies. These ceremonies may be described as personal crisis rites. In Pascua ceremonial sponsors appear in the following: baptism, confirmation in the Catholic church, confirmation by rosary in the Yaqui church, the ceremony of the *hábito*, confirmation in any of the ceremonial societies, and marriage. Status as ceremonial sponsor is established only in these ceremonies. In fulfilment of the obligations established on these occasions, sponsors appear and perform certain ritual acts in the ceremonies connected with the death of the person sponsored. The sponsorship obligations end with the death of the sponsored person, but those between *compadres* and *comadres*, established through the *ahijado*, continue after the death of the latter.

Selection of a ceremonial sponsor.—The selection of a ceremonial sponsor usually falls to the parents of the person to be sponsored. In the great majority of cases the latter is unmarried, a young boy or girl, although it may happen, in confirmation in the *fariseo* society or in the ceremony of the *hábito*, that the person is already married and not living with his parents. In such cases the sponsor is selected by the person himself.

It is not required that a sponsor be outside the circle of blood relatives of the person to be sponsored. A man may select a sister to be the *madrina* of his child, or a brother or other relative to be a *padrino*. Ordinarily, however, an unrelated person is selected. Neighbors are frequently chosen as sponsors, and usually there are ties of friendship or at least cordial familiarity existing between the parents and the persons chosen before the selection is made. The *compadre* relationship, therefore, is often merely a formalizing of an already existing bond. Sometimes in Pascua sponsors are sought outside the village in Libre or Marana, or even among the Mexican population of Tucson.

When the parents make the selection, they go to the house of the person chosen and informally ask him or her, frequently offering a small gift at the same time, such as a pot of flowers or some food. The child accompanies the parents and is told, as soon as the agreement is made, to call the person *nino* or *nina*. This form of address continues from that time on. No return gift is made by the sponsor, but he incurs certain expenses either at the time of the ceremony or later.

Baptism.—The ceremony of baptism is carried out at the Catholic church in Tucson. As soon as possible, after the birth of a child, the parents select a male and a female sponsor. The sponsors take the child into the church in Tucson, pay the fee to the priest, answer the necessary questions which the priest asks, and bring the child home again. The parents may or may not accompany the sponsors to the church. Meanwhile a feast has been arranged at the home of the child by its parents. When the sponsors return, they, and as many of their relatives as care to come, eat with the parents and their relatives at a common table. The sponsors are expected to furnish whiskey or wine to drink and also soda pop for the women and children. A *maestro* is present and also eats at the table. When the feast is finished, the family of the child, the sponsors, and the *maestro* go to the *patio* cross in the yard, where a brief ceremony is performed. The essential features are a sermon by the *maestro* in which he tells in detail the mutual obligations established between sponsors and family, formal presentation by the sponsors of their Christian names for use by the child, and a formal expression of gratitude by the child's parents to the sponsors for their activities, present and future, on behalf of the child.

Confirmation in the Catholic church.—Confirmation in the Catholic church is accompanied by a less elaborate ceremony. Every Yaqui in Pascua is baptized, but probably not half have been confirmed in the Catholic church. Only one sponsor is necessary for the ceremony, a male sponsor if the child is male or a female sponsor if the child is female. The sponsor takes the child to the church, unaccompanied by the parents, pays the necessary fee, and sees that the child does what is required during the service. When the child is brought home, there is no feast or other formal ceremony establishing the relationship.

Confirmation by rosary.—Confirmation by rosary is regarded as the equivalent of confirmation in the Catholic church and is called by the same name. It is, however, a very different ceremony and always takes place in the Yaqui church in Pascua. Every adult Yaqui has been confirmed one or more times by rosary. Two sponsors are necessary, a *padrino* and a *madrina*. They accompany the child and his parents to the Yaqui church, take the child to the altar, and go through a ceremony there with him. They show him how to kneel before the altar, how to cross himself, and how to kiss the images on the altar and cross himself before each one. Then each places a wooden Yaqui rosary about his neck, making the sign of the cross before his face with it as they hold it between the child's finger and thumb. They bring the child back to the front of the church, where they present him to the parents. Then each sponsor makes a short speech, formally presenting his Christian name to the parents for use by the child. The *maestro* describes the obligations established, as in the case of baptism, and there is a brief ceremony in which the new sponsors touch the hands of the parents and their relatives and those of the other sponsors of the child, each in turn. There is no feast or other ceremony following the one in the church.

Ceremony of the "hábito."—When a child or older person is sick and all the usual remedies have failed, the assistance of the gods may be sought. The person may be promised to a ceremonial society on condition that the selected god make him well, or his parents or other relatives may contract for him to do a penance of some kind. The most frequent penance among the Pascua Yaquis is the wearing of the *hábito*. The *hábito* is a simple dresslike garment of cambric, its color depending on the saint of whom aid has been sought. Most of the *hábitos* seen in Pascua were brown, the color proper to St. Francis Xavier. The resort to the *hábito* penance is frequent in Pascua for both males and females of all ages.

The penance cannot be accomplished without the assistance of ceremonial sponsors. Sometimes the ceremony of putting the *hábito* on is combined with confirmation by rosary. The ceremony is often carried out at the Papago mission dedicated to St. Francis Xavier. Two sponsors are necessary, a male and a female. The sponsors and the parents, if the person is a child, take the child into the church and place the *hábito* on him before the altar, where he is made to cross himself. If the ceremony takes place at the Mission of San Xavier, the child, with his *hábito* on, may then be taken to a near-by shrine by his sponsors. There is no further ceremony or feast, and the formal hand-touching ceremony between parents and sponsors is not carried out. The child must wear the *hábito* until it wears out.

Confirmation in a ceremonial society.—In order to be accepted into any of the male or female ceremonial societies, a person must be sponsored. The ceremony which accompanies admission to a society is called "confirmation." The candidate has to have both a male and a female sponsor. The ceremony is carried out in the Yaqui church, where the sponsors perform certain rituals. There is no feast or other ceremony following the initiation.[1]

Annual confirmation of a "fariseo."—There is a peculiar form of sponsored ceremony each year in connection with members of the *fariseo* society, which goes by the name of confirmation. At the conclusion of the *fariseos'* part in the annual Easter ceremonies, each member of the society is taken into the church by a previously selected male and female sponsor. The sponsors take care of his paraphernalia and perform certain ritual activities, which will be described below. These sponsors are classed by Yaquis as *padrinos* and *madrinas*, along with the others mentioned, and they have obligations common to those of the other types. They differ in that their ceremonial duties are undertaken three times, in three successive years, after which new sponsors are selected by the *fariseos* for the next three-year period. The status as ceremonial sponsor continues after the three years of service are over.

Marriage.—In the marriage ceremony a groom has to have a male sponsor and a bride a female sponsor. These sponsors take the couple in to the Catholic church in Tucson in the early morning of the day of the wedding, pay the fee to the priest, attend the service, and bring the couple out to the village again for the day of Yaqui cere-

[1] See below, p. 132, for description of ceremony.

mony. The *madrina* takes the girl to her family's house and the *padrino* takes the boy to his family's house. Prior to the day of the wedding, both the *padrino* and the *madrina* have been involved in making the arrangements for the ceremony, together with the relatives of the couple. The *padrino* has secured *pascola* dancers and a quantity of whiskey ready for the part of the ceremony which takes place at the boy's house. The *madrina* has also hired *pascolas* and has joined in the making of *tamales* to be used in the wedding ceremony. During the wedding the *padrino* must accompany the boy in procession to and from the bride's house, escort him into the latter, and finally must take a leading part in the ceremonial "capture" of the bride. The *madrina* in her turn is constantly with the bride until after her "capture" by the *padrino* and the groom. The *padrino* and *madrina* pour out the drinks at the end of the ceremony at the groom's house. There is no special feast for the ceremonial sponsors, but they sit at the feast tables with the two groups of relatives.

The number of ceremonial sponsors.—If an individual goes through with one of each of the ceremonies described, he will have established relations with ten ceremonial sponsors: two for baptism, one for confirmation in the Catholic church, two for confirmation by rosary, two for the ceremony of the *hábito*, two for confirmation in a ceremonial society, and one for marriage. There are many adults who have such a set of ceremonial sponsors. But there are many who have never been confirmed in the Catholic church, and there are a number of men and an even larger number of women who are not members of ceremonial societies. Thus there are many persons who do not have ten ceremonial sponsors. It is rare, however, to encounter an adult who has not been baptized, confirmed by rosary, presented with the *hábito*, and married. In other words, almost everyone in Pascua, male or female, has from five to seven ceremonial sponsors.

On the other hand, it is common for a person to go through with the ceremony of confirmation by rosary more than once. A number of men belong to more than one ceremonial society, and it will be remembered that a member of the *fariseo* society has a new set of sponsors for every three years of service in the organization. Thus there are many individuals in the village, particularly men, who have more than five ceremonial sponsors. Some men have as many as fourteen or fifteen during the course of their lives.

THE NATURE OF THE OBLIGATIONS

The ceremonies described above mark the establishment of a set of mutual obligations between sponsors and person sponsored, between sponsors and certain relatives of the person sponsored, between the latter and certain relatives of the sponsors, and, finally, between sponsors and other sponsors. These mutual obligations are accompanied by certain well-recognized behavior patterns. The obligations and the behavior patterns are operative from the time of the ceremony in which the relationship was established until the death of the persons concerned.

"*Ahijado*"-"*padrino*."—The *ahijado* is expected to treat his *padrino* "like a father." People in Pascua are very clear on this point. They say that an *ahijado* must have "much respect" for his *padrino*. This takes the form of polite and formal greetings whenever they meet and involves the use of respectful terms of address, of which *nino* is one. An *ahijado* feels that he may go to his *padrino* for advice whenever he is in trouble or is confronted with a problem. He also expects his *padrino* to help him in case of need with money or food or other necessities. This sort of relationship applies also to *ahijado* and *madrina.*

The *padrino* is regarded as having a permanent interest in the welfare of the *ahijado*, particularly in connection with his health. The *padrino* is consulted by the parents of the *ahijado* when the latter is ill. The decision to call a white doctor is sometimes placed in the hands of the *padrino*. If a child is dangerously ill, he is usually taken to the *padrino's* house. If an *ahijado* is an adult, not living with his parents, and becomes ill, a *padrino* is often given the responsibility not only of deciding as to the kind of treatment but also of actually caring for the sick *ahijado*.

The *padrino* is further expected to maintain an interest in the training of his *ahijado*, particularly in seeing that the latter learns the rudiments of personal ritual, such as making the sign of the cross and learning a simple prayer like the Ave Maria.

Just as the *ahijado* relies on the *padrino* for economic assistance in times of need, so the *padrino* relies on the former. There is a well-developed sense of mutual responsibility which involves assistance at times when one is out of work, ill, or faced with the sudden necessity for giving an expensive ceremony. The assistance of *ahijados* is sought as frequently as that of blood relatives at such times.

"Compadre"-"Compadre."—Compadres and *comadres* always address each other by the reciprocal terms, *'kompai* and *'komai*, and it is rare for a person who stands in the *compadre* relationship to another not to refer to the latter as his *compadre* when mentioning him. The relationship is regarded as equally important as the *padrino-ahijado* relationship. It is characterized by a mutual "respect" behavior. This means, specifically, that feelings of friendship

are to be maintained between *compadres* and that the hospitality of one's house is never denied to a *compadre*. These relations apply between all persons who call each other *compadre*. They are accompanied by mutual economic assistance in times of need.

There is a special relationship existing between *padrinos* of baptism and the parents of the child baptized. It will be remembered that, immediately after the baptismal ceremony, the parents of the child gave a feast to the sponsors. This feast is definitely regarded as establishing an obligation of the sponsors. They must, if their *ahijado* dies unmarried, give the funeral *fiesta*, which involves, among other things, giving a feast to the parents of the child. This feast at the death of the *ahijado* is regarded as a return payment for the feast given the sponsors when the child was baptized. It is thought of as the essential feature in the whole relationship between baptismal sponsors and their *ahijado*'s parents. It is possible for other kinds of sponsors to give the feast if the original baptismal sponsors are dead or absent, but they are thought of in such cases as substitutes for the baptismal sponsors.

The funeral feast is given by the baptismal sponsors at the house of one or the other of them, not at the house of their *compadres*. The obligation to give the feast in this way, or to give a feast at all, exists only until the marriage of the *ahijado*. If the latter dies unmarried, the feast is given in the manner described above. If the *ahijado* dies after marriage, then the baptismal sponsors render assistance in the funeral feast, but it is not held at their house and it is the relatives, not the sponsors, who have the responsibility for making the arrangements.

Ritual obligations of "padrinos."—Every *padrino* of a person, no matter of what kind, has a definite set of ritual obligations at the death of the latter. It is these ritual obligations at funerals and death *novenas* which are regarded as the consummation of the relationships between *padrinos* and *ahijados*. The obligations are reciprocal. The ritual duties at death are the same for *ahijados* in relation to *padrinos* as they are for the latter in relation to the former.

Every person, married or unmarried, must have three *padrinos* and three *madrinas* to prepare him, when he dies, for the grave and the next world. Relatives of a dead person are collectively called the *dolientes* or mourners. It is not proper for them to prepare the body in burial clothes or to see the body lowered into the grave. The preparations, which involve intimate and extended contact with the dead body, fall to the group of three *padrinos* and three *madrinas*. It is said that the relatives would feel their sorrow too deeply if they did these necessary things.

The essential duties which the *padrinos* have to carry out for any dead *ahijado* are not the same for an unmarried as for a married person. If the dead person is unmarried, the *padrinos* carry the body to the house of one of the baptismal sponsors, and the whole funeral ceremony takes place there. If the dead person is married, the funeral takes place at his family's house, and the *padrinos* perform their ritual duties there. In the former case all the funeral preparations are carried out by the *padrinos;* in the latter case the *padrinos* merely assist the relatives, who take the initiative. Otherwise the duties of the *padrinos* are the same for married and for unmarried persons.

The important ritual duties of the *padrinos* are the preparation of the body for the next world. The *madrinas*, three or more, remove the everyday clothes from the body and replace them with a simple blue dress, covered by a white one, which they have made of voile. The dress is the same for male or female. If the dead person is unmarried, many-colored paper flowers are also affixed to the dress, a crown of paper flowers is placed on the head, and wings at the shoulders. Then the sponsors go up to the body in pairs, a *padrino* and a *madrina*, and each one places a Yaqui rosary about the neck of the dead person and two *wikosam*, or "breechclout strings," about the waist. When they have finished, the body is thus equipped with six rosaries and twelve *wikosam*. The rosaries indicate in the other world that he was a Yaqui-Catholic here, and the *wikosam* are used by the angel-guardians to lead the person out of this world into the other.

The other ritual obligations of the *padrinos* consist in the carrying of the body to the cemetery and placing it in the grave. The activities at the grave are ones which no relatives can with propriety perform; they must remain hidden, out of sight, until the body is safely in the grave.

THE "PADRINO" GROUP

The group of ceremonial sponsors which performs ritual duties at a funeral is called a *compañía;* there is no Yaqui term for this group. Its personnel is by no means fixed, but there is an accepted ideal as to its composition. It should be headed by the sponsors of baptism and should normally have, besides, a *padrino* and *madrina* of the rosary. Any other sponsors or godchildren of the dead person may join it.

The group normally takes form in the following fashion. As soon as a person dies, his baptismal sponsors (if they are not already aware of the death) are informed by relatives. It then becomes the duty of these sponsors to hunt up all other sponsors of the dead person and bring them together to assist in making the preparations for the funeral. There are many variations from this ideal organization of the group.

If the dead person is an adult, it commonly happens that his baptismal sponsors are dead. In that case the organization of the group falls to a sponsor of the rosary ceremony or perhaps to any sponsor who can be reached most quickly. If the dead person is very old, it is usually the case that all his *padrinos* and *madrinas* are dead. It then falls to any of his godchildren to organize the sponsor group. In the absence of any *padrinos* or *madrinas*, a group may be composed only of godchildren, *compadres*, and *comadres*. A number of funerals in Pascua in 1936–37 were carried out by groups with such composition. *Compadres* were readily substituted for sponsors or *ahijados*. One *compañía* was organized by a *comadre* who had been the *fariseo madrina* of the dead man's son the previous year. In this case, some of the *padrino* group were not even *compadres* of the dead man. They were simply villagers who could be got together on short notice and had had no formal relationship with the man prior to the ceremony. After the ceremony, however, these persons were regarded as *compadres* of the dead man's wife, and one of them insisted that the dead man's children should maintain the respect relationship of *ahijado-padrino* with him in the future.

The ritual associated with "padrino" groups.—The only times at which the sponsors of a person function together as an organized group is at a death ceremony or at a ceremony in which the person is acquiring new sponsors, such as confirmation by rosary in the Yaqui church. On all such occasions there is a standard ritual in which the *padrino* group participates with the family of the person sponsored.

This ritual is the same in pattern as that which is carried out after a baptism subsequent to the formal presentation of names by the baptismal sponsors. It is essentially a public expression of thanks on the part of the family in behalf of the *ahijado*. It is an important and indispensable part of every funeral, death *novena*, confirmation by rosary, marriage, baptism, and confirmation in a ceremonial society. It is, moreover, the final ritual at the end of the Holy Week ceremonies, when it is carried out by the whole group of *fariseo padrinos* and *madrinas* and the persons who have taken part in the Easter ceremonies.

At a funeral, immediately after the dead body has been outfitted by the *padrino* group with rosaries and *wikosam*, the relatives of the dead person line up at the *patio* cross. The group of *padrinos* comes out and lines up facing them. A formal speech of thanks is made by the eldest of the relative group; this may or may not be followed by a short speech of acknowledgment by one of the *padrinos* or *madrinas*. When the speeches are over, the *padrino* group files past the relative group, each *padrino* and *madrina* with his right hand touching the shoulder and hand of each member of the relative group. The standard Yaqui greetings are murmured each time by each person, the *padrinos* taking the initiative with "'Dios em *tʃ*a'niam, 'kompai," and the relatives each replying "'Dios em *tʃ*i'okwe, 'kompai." The circuit of the relatives by the *padrinos* in this manner is made three times, each time with a repetition of the hand-touching and exchange of greetings.

This little ceremony, or some variation of it, is a constant element in all *fiestas* in which groups of *padrinos* take part. In some kinds of ceremonies the lineup of groups is different. For instance, in the ceremony of confirmation by rosary, the previously established sponsors of the *ahijado* line up with the relative group, and the newly made sponsors touch their hands and greet them as though they were relatives of the godchild. In other words, it appears as if the baptismal sponsors are identified with the relatives and are accepting the new sponsors as an addition to a larger co-operating group of relatives and sponsors.

There are other forms of ritual characteristic of *padrino* groups. At funerals when the parents of the dead person are given the feast in return for the baptismal feast, the *padrino* group does not eat at the table with them but stands around the table in a circle, each one holding a candle for the feasting relatives.

It is the *padrinos* and *madrinas* who furnish drinks, whether whiskey or soda pop, at ceremonies where drinking is an essential part of the ritual. The baptismal *padrino*, for instance, provides whiskey at a baptism, pours the drinks and passes them around, and often makes a short speech urging the persons present to drink and enjoy themselves. Precisely the same thing is done by the groom's *padrino* at a wedding. It is the *padrinos* and *madrinas* of the *fariseos* also who provide the whiskey and soda pop for the necessary drinking at the close of the Easter ceremonies.

THE IDEAS UNDERLYING CEREMONIAL SPONSORSHIP

The sponsoring system may be regarded as a sort of extension of the kinship system. In this view the *padrinos* and *madrinas* are auxiliary mothers and fathers. We have seen that the terms used in Yaqui to express the relationships between godparents and godchildren are in every case modified kinship terms which are in use in the elementary family. It is, moreover, common for a Yaqui in Pascua to refer to a *madrina* as his "other mother." There are cases of young men calling the sons of their *madrinas* "brother" (*sai*) and one instance of a man regarding the son of his godchild as his grandson and calling the latter by the ordinary kinship term for that relative. Aside from these verbal extensions, there is evidence for the above view also in the characteristic behavior. That of godchildren and godparents has many of the same elements as kinship behavior between parents and children, such as respect, mutual economic assistance, and the father-like regard of the *padrino* for the *ahijado*. The constant bringing of *padrinos* into problems connected with child care and training further bears out such an interpretation.

The *compadre* relationship, however, defies interpretation in kinship terms. It is more and less than a sibling relationship. It must be classed in a distinct category from any of the kinship relationships. It seems to be an outgrowth of and development from those relations which are fundamental in the *padrino* system, namely, the godparent-godchild relations which are so obviously modeled on kinship lines. The latter are accompanied by the *compadre*, or, as we might say, co-parent, relations which constitute a different order of relationship, effecting a wider grouping of individuals within the village than does kinship and serving to form into co-operative units many different groups already organized on a kinship basis.

There are certain aspects of life with which the *padrino-compadre* system is especially concerned. These are, as we have indicated, personal crises and sickness. The personal crises have mainly, in Yaqui thought, to do with preparation of an individual for life after death, although they are also connected with status in society in this world. Baptism, for example, is regarded as having significance for the status of the child after death, and the relationship established with the sponsor is frankly regarded as an insurance that the child will be properly prepared for life after death when it dies. This preparation can be carried out only by someone outside the child's elementary family. On the other hand, initiation into ceremonial societies also requires the assistance of persons who are classified in the same category with *padrinos* of baptism. The sponsor of an initiation ceremony assists in the change of status of a person in society in this world, and the same is true in marriage.

One of the most important functions of certain ceremonial sponsors is in connection with illness. The ceremony of the *hábito* is purely and simply a ceremony to ward off illness. The ceremony of confirmation by rosary is also often regarded in this light. The Yaqui rosary is worn constantly around the neck by many Yaquis. Like certain charms against witchcraft, it is considered to ward off evil, particularly the evil of sickness. It is sometimes worn as a charm against witchcraft. An already established *padrino* may place a rosary around the neck of an *ahijado* when the latter is ill, in an effort to cure him. We have mentioned that sponsors of all kinds are frequently consulted as to what to do when their *ahijados* are sick. Before a man who was dying of tuberculosis, for example, could receive treatment of any kind, it was necessary for a fellow ceremonial society member to go to the neighboring village and consult the man's *padrino* of baptism. It was only when the latter's consent was obtained that a doctor was permitted to see the sick man. *Padrinos* are thus especially concerned in the physical health as well as in the social status and spiritual welfare of the persons whom they sponsor.

The idea of ceremonial sponsoring is not considered as being confined to human beings. Churches and images may also be sponsored. For instance, the cross called Santa Cruz, which is the essential image in a *fiesta* celebrated on

May 3 (the Finding of the Holy Cross), always has two attendants, a man and a woman, who are called the *padrino* and *madrina* of the image. They are required to give the *fiesta* in honor of Santa Cruz and also to perform certain rituals in connection with it during a ceremony on the eve of the feast day. Yaquis in Pascua classify these sponsors as being of the same kind as the ceremonial sponsors of humans.

The importance with which Yaquis regard ceremonial sponsorship is indicated in the content of sermons given by the *maestros*. Whether or not a ceremony is directly concerned with ceremonial sponsorship, it is customary for a *maestro* to incorporate in the sermon with which he ends the ceremony a series of statements detailing the obligations which *padrinos* have toward *ahijados* and the mutual obligations of *compadres*. A *maestro* does not invariably include such remarks in the sermon, but he frequently does. The failure of the present head *maestro* to do this sufficiently often has brought censure on him recently from the second *maestro*.

In sermons at funerals and at other ceremonies where *padrino* groups are participating, the presence of the sponsors is always mentioned, and they are officially thanked by the *maestro* for their parts in the ceremony, along with the participating ceremonial societies. The head of a ceremonial society also, when he is making his rounds on a *limosna*, addresses the people of a household as *kom'palem* and *ko'malem*, which are plural for the Yaqui-ized Spanish *kompai* and *komai*. Thus the *compadre* and *padrino* relationships are recognized in formal statements by the official spokesmen of the village, and their importance is emphasized in many ceremonies of various kinds.

HOW THE SYSTEM WORKS

By the time a child is nine or ten he usually has two or three *padrinos* and the same number of *madrinas.* He knows who they are and where they live and has been trained to address them as *nino* and *nina.* He is often not so sure as to which kinds of *padrinos* they are, that is, which ones are baptismal, which are *del rosario*, or which are *del hábito.* In his mind they are all just *ninos* or *ninas.* After the age of about ten, however, he begins to make the distinctions between them and can tell which are which. They are as clearly distinguished from the rest of the adults in the world as are his relatives and the members of his household. The horizon of his personal relationships with adults thus goes beyond his own household, extending into several others in the village. It is not unusual for a boy in his teens to describe his *ninas* as his "other mothers" or to feel as much at home in their houses as in his own.

By the time a person is married, however, he has begun to move out of the world of the *padrino* relationships. Some of his *padrinos* have died. In many instances in Pascua *padrinos* have moved away from the village by the time their *ahijados* have grown up, or *padrinos* who were acquired in other villages when the *ahijado*'s parents lived elsewhere are no longer associated with the family.

But with the coming of the first children after marriage, a man or woman begins to acquire *compadres* and *comadres.* Whether the children live or not, the *compadre* relationships entered into through them remain. Persons find their childhood friendships made permanent in the *compadre* relationships which they enter into when they ask old friends to sponsor their children. In addition, they are asked to sponsor children and begin to acquire *ahijados* in many households in the village. There is no adult in Pascua without *ahijados* and *compadres*.

The definiteness of the early *padrino-ahijado* circles disappears. The child who could name and place in households all his *padrinos* and *madrinas* finds, as an adult, that it is very difficult for him to name all his *compadres* and *comadres*. He knows without question who the *padrinos* and *madrinas* of his children are and hence can name these persons as his *compadres* and *comadres*, but he does not keep constantly in mind those persons to whom he is also *compadre* as a result of being *padrino* himself of some child whom they also have sponsored. Adults in their early twenties say seriously that they cannot count all their *compadres* and *comadres*. This is not strictly true, but it is, nevertheless, the case that a person would have to consult many people before he could make a complete list of his *compadre* relationships.

The result of this situation is that a circle of people in the relation of *compadre* to one another never functions completely as such. That is, there is a certain selection by any person of the *compadre* relationships which he keeps constantly in mind. He remembers and maintains those with his children's *padrinos* and does the same for those entered into with parents and relatives of children of whom he has become *padrino*. But he usually forgets many of the other *compadre* relationships which have been established. Some of these he may remember and maintain because the persons are neighbors or because he likes and associates frequently with them. But the others lapse, unless someone in need remembers them and comes to him for assistance. He would not think of denying them in such cases.

It is commonly said in the village that all Yaquis are

compadres and *comadres* to one another. It is not uncommon for a person to call another *compadre*, although he cannot definitely point to a ceremony in which such a relationship was established. It may not be actually true that all the adults of Pascua stand in the relationship of *compadres* to one another, but the feeling is general that they should all act so. If *compadre* circles in the village were to be traced out in detail, it is conceivable that many of them would be found to be almost village wide.

The looseness with which the *compadre* terms are sometimes used is not a reflection of indefiniteness in those *compadre* relationships which have been selected for emphasis by the various individuals. People are constantly aware of the latter and take them seriously. A man does not begrudge having to devote the proceeds of two days' work of wood-hauling to a *fiesta* for a *compadre* whose child has died and of whom he is the *padrino* of rosary. Another man does not hesitate to go into debt to assist a *compadre* in making a *fiesta*, even though he is *compadre* only by virtue of extension of the term from the *fiestero*'s son.

We may view the *compadre* aspect of the *padrino* system as an all-pervasive network of relationships which takes into its web every person in the village. Certain parts of the network, here and there about the village, are composed of strong and well-knit fibers. Here the relationships between *compadres* are functioning constantly and effectively. Elsewhere there are weaker threads representing relationships which have never been strengthened by daily recognition of reciprocal obligations. These threads nevertheless exist and may from time to time be the channels of temporarily re-established *compadre* relationships.

The network is a reality, and it is an organized system. Individual patterns of behavior within it may vary somewhat, but they all have something in common, and the unity of Pascua would not be so great if it were not for the common body of understandings which it defines.

SUMMARY

The *padrino*, or ceremonial sponsor, system in Pascua is as definite a system of relationships as is that based on kinship. We may speak of a social structure based on ceremonial sponsorship as readily as we may speak of a structure based on blood relationship. A *padrino* group is as clearly an organized structure as is an elementary family, and the persons involved in one of the former are linked by relationships of the same general kind as those involved in a kinship structure, both economic and ritual. The emphasis, however, is on ritual relations in the *padrino* structures, while in the families the emphasis is on economic obligations.

The *padrino* structure is much more complex than is the kinship structure. A person may be a unit in an unlimited number of *padrino* structures. It is possible that he could be an active member of every *compañía* in the village and thus be in the position of maintaining relationships of a formal sort with every individual there. We do not know whether such a condition exists, but it is entirely possible. Thus while a person during the course of his life is a member of only two elementary families, he is a member ordinarily of many more than two *padrino* structures.

If we think of an elementary family as a structure composed of a person, his parents, and siblings, we may think of a *padrino* structure as composed of a person, his parents, and his ceremonial sponsors. The ceremonial sponsors of a person will ordinarily be members of the generation next above him, that is, of the same generation as his parents.

He is thus linked quite definitely by a system of social obligations to a number of different individuals outside his own elementary family and in the generation above.

On the other hand, we have seen that, just as a man acquires children and becomes a member of a second elementary family during the course of his life, so every man acquires *ahijados* and thus enters into *padrino* relationships which link him to the generation next below as securely as he is linked to the generation next above. Also in the course of his downward linkage he necessarily finds himself extending his *compadre* relationships in his own generation, because he acquires *ahijados* only as a result of accepting such relationships with the parents and other sponsors of the *ahijado*. Thus the *padrino* structures carry social links through three generations in much the same way that the elementary family structures do.

The greater complexity of the *padrino* over the kinship structure is apparent in the working-out of the *compadre* relationships. Through them obligations are established between an individual and many other individuals of the same generation. These relationships are further extended to certain relatives of the latter. This results in the social linkage of many families into co-operating groups. The general custom of seeking *compadres* outside the circle of blood relations widens the sphere of any individual's social relationship beyond those of blood and family. The *padrino* system is thus a formal social institution based on ritual obligations which formalizes the relationships between groups already organized on a basis of blood.

CHAPTER V

THE CEREMONIAL SOCIETIES

WRITTEN after the name in a family Book of the Dead is the village office which each ancestor held. One may have been a *matachín* dancer, and accordingly *matachini* will appear after his name in the book. If a man has been a *fariseo* or a *maestro* or if a woman has been a *cantora*, it is recorded in the book. A *maestro* who has been asked by a family to hold a service in honor of their ancestors reads the title as well as the name of each. In some of the books titles like "captain," "general," and "war chief" appear, all reminiscent of the warlike days of a generation or more ago. At present the only titles being written into the books are those designating persons as members of ceremonial societies or as *pascola* dancers. In Pascua there are now five societies for men and two for women.

THE MEN'S SOCIETIES

One hundred and nine of the males in the village, or about one-fourth of the total population, had membership in ceremonial organizations during 1936–37. The five societies to which they belonged were as follows: the male altar group, the *matachinis*, the *fariseos*, the *caballeros*, and the Coyotes.

The male altar group.—Members of this group are called either by the title *maestro* or *'temasti*. A *maestro* is a man who knows how to lead any religious service. The term is sometimes translated as "lay priest" or "lay reader," a translation emphasizing the fact that the *maestro* is not ordained by the Catholic church but that his activities correspond to some extent with those of a priest. In Pascua the *maestro* not only is not ordained by the church but is not at all recognized as a part of the Catholic organization. He is not considered, as *maestros* apparently were on the Yaqui River, to be a lay assistant who ministers to a group of Catholic believers between visits of an ordained priest; he is considered unnecessary because of the proximity to the village of an established church and hence is regarded as being entirely outside the Catholic hierarchy of ministrants. There is no co-operation whatever between the *maestros* of Pascua and the Catholic church of Tucson.

There are four *maestros* resident in Pascua. Besides these, there are a fifth, now living elsewhere but originally confirmed in the village, who appears only for the Easter ceremonies, and a sixth who is an itinerant but who appears at Pascua ceremonies more frequently than at those in any other village. The oldest of these is called the *maestro mayor* (Yaqui: *'maito 'joˀowe*). He is the leader of the *maestro* group and, in theory, is regarded as the chief organizer of all ceremony. It is his duty to see that the head of a dance society is informed of an impending ceremony and that he organize his group to take part in it. He must inform the heads of other societies and see that they prepare the church and the images in proper time. During the ceremony he has the responsibility for leading it and co-ordinating its different parts. Actually the present *maestro mayor* (1936–37) is extremely old—too old to carry out the duties which are assigned to him. Theoretically, in such a case his duties should fall to the next oldest (*maestro segundo*). As it is, however, they are divided between the latter and other officials, a situation which will be discussed at length below. It is our purpose here merely to point out that the *maestros* are ideally regarded as a group organized on a basis of age, with authority in the hands of the eldest.

Subordinate to the *maestros* are certain assistants called *'temastim*. Their duties are always supplementary to those of the *maestros*, but they are regarded as being a part of the *maestro* organization. The term *'temasti* (of Nahuatl origin) is frequently translated as "sacristan." There are two sacristans in Pascua at present.

Aside from the duties mentioned above, which might be classed as administrative, all *maestros* have the same ritual functions. Any number of them may be present at a ceremony, and there may be some division of labor between them in that case; but the knowledge of ritual that each has is basically the same, and anyone confirmed as a *maestro* is expected to be able to do all that is required in the leadership of any ceremony. The necessary duties are, briefly, the recitation, without reference to books, of the following prayers: the Ave Maria, the Credo, the Pater Noster, the Sign of the Cross, the Litany of the Blessed Virgin, the Salve, and Confiteor; these may be recited in either Spanish or Yaqui. The *maestro* must know the Catholic Mass for the Dead in Latin and the various *responsos* for the dead (also in Latin). He must know the standard form of the five Yaqui prayers for the closing of a service. He must be able to chant in the Gregorian style various chants in Latin or in Spanish. He must know Spanish sufficiently well to read certain ritual from a book, for example, the *oraciones* at the Stations of the Cross. In addition, he must be sufficiently ready of tongue to give a sermon in Yaqui at the end of a ceremony, which is improvised but which contains certain conventional ideas.

All this must be accompanied by a knowledge of the regular order of ritual at death ceremonies, at saints' days, and at other celebrations of the fixed calendar. With these tools a *maestro* can conduct any of the ceremonies in Pascua.

The sacristans have to know the Catholic prayers listed above and the proper responses to certain of them. In addition, they have a duty which does not fall to the *maestros*. They are charged with taking care of the crucifixes used in ceremonies and with the preparation of certain special ritual articles, such as the Box of the Sacred Heart used in procession during Holy Week. It also falls to the sacristan to prepare the temporary altar at a household for any ceremony the scene of which is a private house. In general, the principal duties of sacristans might be described as the care and arrangement of all altar paraphernalia which is not cared for by women.

The "matachinis."—A *matachini* is a costumed dancer. There is no purely Yaqui word for this type of performer. The *matachinis* dance at funerals, on Sundays during the spring and summer, and at various other ceremonies. Included in the *matachín* society are musicians, violinists and guitarists, who play for the *matachín* dances.

There are sixty-one *matachinis* in Pascua, including the musicians. Their ages range from eight to eighty, with the greater proportion between the ages of ten and thirty. Not all the members participate at the same time in a ceremony, the largest participation in 1936–37 being thirty-six. All but one of the sixty-one members, however, participated at one time or another.

Unlike the *maestros* and sacristans, the *matachinis* have a characteristic costume, or at least distinctive paraphernalia which they invariably use in their dances. The leader of the group, called the *matachín 'kovanau*, wears no costume at any time but carries a stick about three feet long made of *carrizo*, or native "bamboo." The musicians are not distinguished by their dress. The *matachinis* proper wear the usual blue cotton pants and ordinary shirt and shoes, but, in addition, each wears a headdress. The head is first bound with a bright-colored handkerchief and over this is worn the headdress. It consists of a framework of *carrizo* about twelve inches high, rounded at the top. The frame is wrapped with colored crepe paper, usually red. To each of the uprights of the framework are affixed bright-colored cardboard disks. The essential feature is a mass of bright-colored paper streamers affixed to the top of the frame, called *'sewa* or "flower." This headdress is worn invariably when a *matachini* is dancing. In the right hand a gourd rattle about six inches in diameter is carried; the rattles are shaken in unison during the dance. In the left hand is carried an instrument called a *palma* or *pluma*. It consists of a trident-shaped frame of *carrizo*, to the three points of which, and halfway down each branch, are fastened chicken feathers, often dyed some bright color. Every *matachini* carries these three items of paraphernalia. There is, however, another kind of dancer who is more fully costumed. These are called *malinches*. In addition to carrying the three articles mentioned—the headdress, *palma*, and rattle—the *malinches* wear a long white dress over their pants and shirts. Over the dress diagonally across the breast are worn red ribbons, and many strings of gaudy beads are worn about the neck. The *malinche* wears shoes like the other *matachinis*, and his pants often protrude below the skirt of his dress.

There are a number of different ideas current in Pascua as to the proper organization of the *matachín* society. It is held by one or two that the oldest member, excluding the musicians, is automatically the head of the society. Others say that whomever of their number the *matachinis* choose to elect may serve as head. In practice neither of these principles is carried out. The present head of the organization was not elected by the members of the society nor is he the oldest member of the group. In point of service in the society he is one of the newest. He assumed the leadership when a duly elected *'kovanau* defaulted as head because of conflicts with his work to support his family. The duties of the *'kovanau* are numerous. It is he whom the *maestro mayor* informs when the *matachinis* are required at a ceremony. It is then his duty to inform the various *matachinis* in the village—a duty which he performs by visiting the houses of the individuals and also by hanging up the *matachín* headdresses on the front of the church as a sort of public advertisement that the *matachinis* are to dance. It may also be his duty to gather a few *matachinis* before a *fiesta* and go from house to house in the village, giving notice and at the same time collecting food and money to assist whoever is giving the *fiesta*. The *'kovanau* must also be present at the church or household where the ceremony is held some time before it begins in order to see that things are in readiness for the dances and to set up the special *matachín* "altar" (if it is at a private house). During the ceremony the *'kovanau* co-ordinates the activities of the *matachinis* with those of the *maestros* and other ceremonial groups and, while the *matachinis* are dancing, has the responsibility of seeing that the dance is correctly executed, which involves constant vigilance on his part.

Beneath the *'kovanau*, the *matachín* society is commonly thought of as being organized on a military basis. Its older members are called *mo'nahas* (Spanish: *monarca*). Any policy affecting the group as a whole is always talked over between the *'kovanau* and the *mo'nahas*. A *mo'naha* may serve as *'kovanau* in the absence of the latter. The *mo'nahas*, at different times, act as the dance leaders. The *'kovanau* rarely dances, but the *mo'nahas* are primarily dancers. To them falls the responsibility of working out the dance patterns properly and of co-ordinating all the movements of the dancers. The *mo'naha*, when he is acting as dance leader, dances at the head of the center of the three lines of dancers.

At the head of each of the other two lines dance *matachinis* who are called *segundos*. They have the responsibility of co-ordinating the movements of their lines with that of the *mo'naha*. Next behind the *segundos* dance the *terceros*, who have no special duties. The others in the two lines headed by the *segundos* are collectively called the *soldados* and have no special duties.

The youngest members of the organization usually but not always are *malinches*. They automatically cease to have *malinche* status after marriage. They dance in the center line behind the *mo'naha* and have simply to follow his movements. It also falls to them, as initiates, to stand guard over the *matachín* paraphernalia whenever, during a ceremony, it is not in use. They also are frequently required to carry water and otherwise serve the members of the society while a *fiesta* is in progress.

The ritual activity of the *matachinis* consists solely in dancing. Their dances are a standardized set of patterns with some resemblance to European folk dances and the Virginia reel. The sometimes complicated movements are executed to the music of violins and guitars. Each dancer, at the same time that he is carrying out the movement necessary in the group patterns, shakes his rattle in time to the music, moves the *palma* in his left hand in certain rhythmic flourishes, and repeats constantly certain dance steps. The *matachinis* may dance in groups of from six to thirty, a usual number being eleven. They dance for an hour at a time at intervals during a ceremony and frequently take part in various kinds of processions.

The "fariseos."—The *fariseos* are frequently referred to collectively by Yaquis as *tʃapa'jekam*. In Yaqui *tʃapa'jeka* means "slender nose" and, in this connection, derives from the long, slender noses which are an essential feature of the masks worn by some members of the *fariseo* society; *tʃapa'jeka* is more frequently used to refer to this masked group within the society than to the members of the society as a whole. There is no Yaqui equivalent for *fariseo*.

The *fariseo* society includes, besides the masked *tʃapa'jekam*, a number of other kinds of ceremonial functionaries. In a sense they may all be considered dancers, since they all at certain times execute certain rhythmic steps in unison to the music of drum and native whistle. But, unlike the *matachinis*, the *fariseos* have a great many other ritual functions besides dancing. Their dances are always supplementary to their other activities.

The *fariseos* appear only during what we may call the Easter ceremonial season, that is, from Ash Wednesday until the Day of the Finding of the Holy Cross on May 3. During this time they take over all the economic and social functions of the *matachinis* as well as the ritual functions. They are present at every *fiesta* and at nearly every ceremony of whatever kind, just as the *matachinis* are during the rest of the year. But their ritual duties are by no means identical with those of the *matachinis*, and their social and economic functions are much more extensive.

The *fariseos* may be conveniently discussed as two subgroups within the society as a whole: the masked and the unmasked. The masked *fariseos* are the ones to whom the term *tʃapa'jeka* especially applies. (When that term is used hereafter, it will be applied only to this group.) The *tʃapa'jekam* are primarily clowns. They appear at various times during the Easter season wearing elaborate masks, a blanket or overcoat over the shoulders, and carrying long sword-shaped sticks painted red, black, and white in their right hands, and small dagger-shaped sticks in their left hands. They have important duties in their capacities as clowns during the Friday processions of Lent and throughout Holy Week preceding Easter Sunday. There were seventeen *tʃapa'jekam* in Pascua during Easter, 1937, all of whom were men between twenty-five and fifty.

The unmasked group of *fariseos* are sometimes referred to in Pascua as the "soldiers of Rome," a title which refers to the part they play in the ceremonies during Holy Week as persecutors of Christ. They wear the ordinary clothes of everyday life, except for the native Yaqui *guaraches*, or sandals. But each carries a painted stick in the form of a lance or a sword. They are in so sense clowns. They join with the *tʃapa'jekam* in their march-dance at various times during ceremonies, and two of their number, a flutist and a drummer, provide the music on such occasions.

The "soldiers of Rome" are organized in a military fashion. At their head is a man called "Pilato" (referring to his role in the Easter ceremonies as Pontius Pilate). There are three Pilatos in Pascua, the oldest of whom is regarded as having the leadership of the *fariseo* society. The leadership of the Pilato is, however, delegated in practice to the "captain" and his "soldiers." The responsibility for the organization of all the *fiestas* during the Easter ceremony falls to this captain. Authority rests ultimately with the Pilato, but the captain has the actual work of organization. He gathers together the *fariseos* for *limosna* parties, organizes them into work groups, and as well marches with them in all their ceremonial activities. He is responsible for the co-ordination of the work of the *fariseos* with that of the other ceremonial groups at all *fiestas* and ceremonies—a responsibility which requires a detailed knowledge of the elaborate ritual involved in the Easter ceremonies. In addition, the captain is regarded as political head of the village during this season. He overshadows in importance any other official during this time of year.

The captain is assisted by a sergeant (*sargento*) and by a group of the recent initiates into the society, the "corporals" or *cabos*. The work of carrying messages, rounding up *fariseos* from their homes, and doing various menial tasks during ceremonies for the participants is carried out by the *cabos*. Their activities are directed by the captain, but they are immediately supervised by the *cabo mayor*, an older member of the *fariseo* society.

In addition, there are among the unmasked members of the *fariseo* society a drummer, a flutist, and two flagbearers. The latter carry the official red banners of the *fariseo* society, making extensive use of the flags during ceremonies.

There were sixteen "soldiers of Rome" in Pascua who participated in the activities of the society in 1936–37.

The "caballeros."—The *caballeros* (Yaqui: *ka'bajum*) are an organization which, like the *fariseos*, appear only during the Easter ceremonial season. In recent years it almost died out, but it is apparently being revived. There were only four active members of the society in 1936–37, three of these being youths under twenty. But two more were dedicated to the society during the year. Their patroness is the Virgin of Guadalupe.

In the Yaqui River pueblos the *caballeros* are reputed to have been an important society, with police duties throughout the year as well as special ceremonial duties at Easter season. In Pascua only the latter functions remain. The *caballeros* are interpreted as being "good soldiers" as opposed to the "soldiers of Rome." They are "for Christ," while the latter are "against Christ." They wear no costumes but carry wooden swords and lances, and one of their number carries the blue flag which is the emblem of the society. The leader of the group is dedicated as such, not being either the eldest or elected by the others.

The duties of the *caballeros* are few. They march beside the two lines of the *fariseos* in all ceremonies and join the latter in saying rosaries at the altar during the night of a ceremony. Two of the *caballeros'* spears are always crossed in front of an altar when the *maestros'* portion of a ceremony is not going on before it. They take an important part in the final ceremony before the church on Holy Saturday in the last symbolic battle with the *fariseos*.

The Coyotes.—The Coyote dance society is practically extinct in Pascua. There were three members in the village in 1936–37, but they took no part in any ceremonies and fulfilled no other kinds of functions. It is reported that they have not participated in ceremonies for the last five years, possibly longer.[1] They formerly danced in Pascua only at the end of Holy Week each year. Each wore a headband to which was attached a foxskin and four tufts of feathers. They carried bows which were beaten with carrizo sticks as they danced.

[1] The Coyotes danced again during Holy Week in 1939, according to information supplied by Dr. Bronislaw Malinowski.

THE WOMEN'S SOCIETIES

Only fifteen women had membership during 1936–37 in the female ceremonial organizations. Many others, however, served in the capacity of *te'nantʃim* (bearers of the Virgins), without official obligation to any society.

The "ki'ostim."—The *ki'ostim* may be described as the female altar society. The women who belong to it have the following duties. They keep in repair all the images of the Virgin and all the altar cloths. They are not permitted to handle crucifixes. When a ceremony includes processions, they secure female bearers for the Virgins, carry out the ritual preparations of the bearers, and themselves march in the procession as attendants to the Virgins, scattering confetti or flowers over the images at the proper times. The preparation of the altar in the church is their special duty, but, unlike the *'temastim*, they are not responsible for the preparation of altars at household ceremonies.

The *ki'ostim* are assisted in their work by unmarried women called *'alpesim* (Spanish: *alférez*). These girls aid in the care of the images but also have other duties. They are flag-bearers. In certain ceremonies they wear a white cloth *rebozo* over which is fitted a red-and-green paper crown. They carry a red flag with a green cross in the center and perform certain rituals with the flag. When an *'alpes* marries, she automatically ceases to be an *'alpes* and may become either a *ki'osti* or a *cantora*.

There were three *ki'ostim* and four *'alpesim* in Pascua in 1936–37. The eldest *ki'osti* is regarded as the head of the group, but her duties do not differ from those of the other *ki'ostim*.

The "ko'pariam."—Female chanters are called *ko'pariam* (Spanish: *cantoras*). There are eight in Pascua. Their duties consist in accompanying the *maestro* group in the chanting of prayers and *alabanzas*.

MEMBERSHIP IN A CEREMONIAL SOCIETY

There is one universal way in which an individual, male or female, becomes a member of a ceremonial society in Pascua. The person is "promised" by his parents to serve in the society. Not all members of societies have become members in this way, although the great majority have. There are several other ways of acquiring membership.

The method next most frequent to that of the promise when ill is the apprenticeship method. One may become a *maestro*, a *cantora*, a *ki'osti*, or a *matachini* in this way. Three of the *maestros* and a half-dozen of the *matachinis* are now serving as a result of such voluntary entrance to the societies. An individual who adopts this procedure in the case of the *maestro* society simply attends services, sitting close to the *maestros*, and gradually learns the necessary elements of the ritual. He may also go to the house of a *maestro* for special instruction and copy into a book the prayers and *alabanzas*. There is a man in Pascua at present who is learning in this way to be a *maestro*. If a man wishes to become a *matachini* voluntarily, he practices the dance steps by himself or with a member of the society, begins to appear regularly at ceremonies where the *matachinis* are dancing, and eventually is asked to dance. A woman may acquire the ability to be a *cantora* in much the same way.

When membership is acquired by the apprentice method, the person is not regarded, however, as having all the obligations of membership until he is officially confirmed in a special ceremony with all the members of the society present. He may go on participating with the group for several years before he is officially taken in. Whether or not he is confirmed depends on the steadiness and seriousness of his participation during his period of apprenticeship.

There are certain special ways in which a person may become a member of the *fariseo* society. One boy two years ago was discovered to be making *fariseo* masks and selling them to the whites. He was immediately reprimanded, and the captain of the *fariseos* informed his family that he would be required to serve henceforth in the society. The boy became a *cabo* and has served since. It is said also that a man may be forced to join the *fariseo* society if he is caught in some immoral act, particularly in sexual misconduct, such as adultery. No cases of this sort, however, have been authenticated for Pascua. The head of the *matachín* society says that it is customary to recruit members for either the *matachinis* or the *fariseos* by asking men or boys to eat at the table with the members of the society during a *fiesta*. If the individual joins the group at the table, he is from then on considered a member of the society and must recognize the obligations of membership. So far as is known, this method of recruiting members for either of the two societies mentioned is not carried out at present.

The *manda*, or promise when ill, is the most general way of acquiring membership in all societies. The promise is usually made when the individual concerned is very young, anywhere from a year to eight or nine years of age. It is usually made by the parents of the person or by other relatives, but it is entirely possible for an adult to promise himself or to be promised by wife or husband. Cases of both sorts are known in Pascua.

The *manda* is resorted to ordinarily only when the individual is seriously ill and expected to die. When all ordinary means of curing have failed, both native and white, then the parents decide that supernatural aid must be sought. The father or mother or both may make the promise themselves or they may ask a *maestro* to come and witness it. The form of the promise is simple and may be as follows: "It is proper now for me to make a promise (*manda*). You are sick. If you should get well, you will serve as a *cantora.* If God (*Dios*) permits you to, you will do this ceremonial work (*'tekipanoa*) with good will and willingly." In this case the promise as *cantora* dedicates the child to the service of Jesus, for *cantoras* are regarded as serving Jesus primarily. If the child were promised to the *matachín* society, he would be automatically dedicated to the service of the Virgin, for the *matachinis* are regarded as being devotees of her rather than of Jesus.

When the child recovers, he is regarded as, from that time on, being a member of the society to which he was dedicated, although his actual participation in the society may not begin for several years. The usual age at which participation begins in all societies is seven or eight. Sometimes it is held off until the child is ten or older. Confirmation in the society may not take place for several years after participation begins.

Membership in all societies is considered as being for life. But this does not seem to mean that any individual promised has to serve continuously on all occasions throughout his life. Illness, absence from the village, or even disinclination (if it is not habitual) are considered legitimate excuses for not serving on a given occasion. Further, it is recognized that, as men get married, they will curtail their activities in the *matachín* society. It is said that they cannot dance all night frequently and still provide a living for their families. It is possible also to take a "vacation" from service in the *fariseo* society. This can be done only through appeal to the captain of the *fariseos.*

The promise operates in the following way. It is considered that, when the promise is made, an appeal is being directed to the Virgin or to Jesus for aid in curing. When the individual gets well, it is believed that the appeal has been heard and that an obligation has been established, therefore, between the person and either Jesus or the Virgin. As long as the individual serves well in the society to which he has been promised, the illness will not return and he will not die. But if he falters in his obligation, for example, consistently refusing to dance when asked to by the '*kovanau*, then it is thought that he will die. Married men who gradually discontinue their dancing for the *matachinis* after marriage, however, do not die. It is said that they have danced sufficiently in their youth to satisfy the Virgin.

The obligation to the Virgin or Jesus is regarded as fully established as soon as the promise is made, but it is thought that an official confirmation by the society should be made some time before the person dies. A member of a society who has neglected to have his confirmation during his life may be brought to the church on his deathbed for the confirmation. The confirmation in such a case in 1937 was regarded as being a method of cure. It was hoped that after it the young man would get well, although, as a matter of fact, he did not.

The confirmation is an elaborate ceremony, requiring the presence of the individual's relatives, a *padrino* and a *madrina*, all the members of the society concerned, and at least one officiating *maestro*. It takes place in the church and may be attended by all the village. It is not secret. The essential features of the ceremony are a speech by the *padrino* or a relative explaining the circumstances of the person's *manda*, a sermon by the head of the society describing the duties and obligations of the new member, and a brief ritual in which an image of the Virgin or a crucifix (depending on the kind of society) is taken from the altar and held over the head of the initiate and then moved in the sign of the cross before his face by the *padrino* and the *madrina*. There is no feast connected with the ceremony.

THE OBLIGATIONS OF MEMBERS

The sort of activities in which members of societies engage is frequently referred to in sermons as *'tekipanoa*, which is the same term applied to ordinary work for the means of subsistence. *'Tekipanoa* is work. The *'tekipanoa* of members of ceremonial societies is both ritual and economic. *Maestros*, *ki'ostim*, and *cantoras* have only ritual work to do, but members of the other male societies, the *matachinis*, the *fariseos*, and the *caballeros*, have, in addition to their dancing and other ritual activities, a certain amount of labor which is not purely ritual. In groups, they cut and haul wood, sweep the plaza before a *fiesta*, or perform other jobs necessary in preparation for *fiestas*. This is ceremonial *'tekipanoa* just as much as the purely ritual activity. It is this as well as the ritual work which is referred to in sermons as ceremonial *'tekipanoa*.

Ceremonial "'tekipanoa."—We have already touched on the sort of ritual activity which members of ceremonial societies have to do. The work of the *maestros* may be summed up as the conducting of all ceremonies, the recitation of prayers, the chanting of *alabanzas*, the reading of services of various kinds, and the giving of sermons. The *'temastim* assist in the recitation of prayers and chanting of *alabanzas* and are charged with caring for the crucifixes and the preparation of altars. The *ki'ostim* share the responsibility for the preparation of certain altars and have charge of the Virgins and other images used in ceremony; they are assisted in this by the '*alpesim*, who also are required to manipulate banners in certain ceremonies in which they are essential. The *cantoras* assist the *maestros* in the chanting of *alabanzas* and prayers. The ritual activities of the *matachinis* are confined to dancing. The *fariseos* have a number of ritual functions, including dancing, acting as clowns and buffoons, and the performance of various rites in their capacity as "soldiers of Rome" and "Pharisees" during the annual Easter ceremonies. The *caballeros* march with the *fariseos* and assist them in their various activities.

The activities which are not purely ritual are confined to the last three groups mentioned. One of the primary functions of these groups is the conducting of *limosna* parties. During the Easter ceremonial season the *fariseos* conduct all *limosnas*, with the assistance of the *caballeros;* during the rest of the year the *limosnas* are conducted by the *matachinis*.

Limosna means, literally in Spanish, "alms." As used in Pascua it refers to the collection of money, food, or other things from villagers by a house-to-house canvass as well as to the actual goods collected. There is no Yaqui word in use for the operation. The idea of the *limosna* takes many different forms in Yaqui life in Arizona. A Yaqui in one of the villages who was formerly a '*temasti* now lives entirely by making occasional *limosnas* through his own village and also through Pascua. The *maestro mayor* of Pascua, who is too old to work, also frequently obtains food for his family by making a personal *limosna* in villages near Pascua. There is no one who makes personal *limosnas* of this sort who has not been at one time or is not at present an active member of a ceremonial society. The personal *limosna* is a rather unusual thing, but the group *limosna* conducted by the members of a ceremonial society is frequent. There was in 1936–37 an average of one every two weeks in Pascua.

A group *limosna* is organized by the *matachín 'kovanau* or by the captain of the *fariseos*, depending on the season. He gathers some members of the society together, and they go to each house in the village. They always carry the image of the patron saint of the society: the *fariseos* take their crucifix, the *matachinis* their own Virgin (or an image of Christ the Child). No *limosna* can be conducted without the image. In addition, the *fariseos* always carry their society insignia, the lances and swords or costumes of the members, and the *matachinis* always take one *malinche* with them who wears a *matachín* headdress and carries a rattle and *palma*.

There is a standard procedure in conducting the *limosna*. The leader of the society makes a speech of set form to the people of each household, mentioning the occasion of the *limosna* and stating that the collection is being made in behalf of the Virgin or Jesus, as the case may be. Whether or not any contribution is made, the leader also makes a speech of thanks just before leaving. The members of the society conducting a *limosna* carry sacks in which the food contributed is put and a bowl is carried by the one carrying the image, in which cash contributions are placed. The persons in the household visited go through a ritual with the image. Each one crosses himself before it and kisses it, usually placing it first on a table or chair in the house and kneeling before it. The image is then carried to the next household by one of the family. If it is the Virgin, a woman carries it. If it is a crucifix, a man carries it.

The *limosna* is regarded as having a twofold function. It is said that the most important of these is that of giving notice of the ceremony. Every house is visited, and the society leader describes in detail the nature of the ceremony which is to be given and why it is being held, mentioning carefully the place and the approximate time. It is said that his giving of notice of a ceremony will insure the attendance of all villagers, which is important because every ceremony is a public function. The other purpose of the *limosna* is the gathering of food and money to defray the expenses of the ceremony. This economic assistance is sought in the case of ceremonies sponsored by a private household, such as funerals, as well as for a general village affair, such as a saint's-day *fiesta*. Whatever the type of ceremony, it is always the ceremonial society which makes the *limosna*. It happens sometimes that a family may give nothing whatever in the way of food or money. This is accepted as natural, and no stigma is attached to the family which is unable to contribute. It may show its good will simply by going through the ritual with the image and listening to the society leader's description of the ceremony. An average *limosna* in Pascua results in the collection of about a dollar and a half and thirty or forty pounds of flour, together with lesser quantities of other food, usually beans, coffee, and sugar.

Besides joining in the *limosna* party, the members of the *matachín*, *fariseo*, and *caballero* societies are required to assist in the preparations for ceremonies. The kinds of ceremonies involved are funerals, death *novenas*, death anniversaries, household *fiestas de promesa*, saint's-day *fiestas*, and the ceremonies of Holy Week. All of these require considerable amounts of food, wood for cooking and heat, and the preparation of places for dancers to perform and processions to take place. A certain amount of this work is carried out by the members of the households at which the *fiesta* is given, but there is usually a portion of it which is done by the members of a society. A group of *fariseos* may be gathered together by the captain and sent out for a truckload of wood; a group of *matachinis* may do the same thing in their ceremonial season. Before a big *fiesta* in the plaza, groups of *fariseos* or *matachinis* form and spend a day or two sweeping the plaza with brush brooms. Similar groups join in clearing spaces for dances and processions at private houses before a death anniversary ceremony or a *fiesta de promesa*.

The *fariseo* and *caballero* societies are charged also with policing *fiestas* during their ceremonial season. This means that they keep drunken persons away and maintain order generally in the vicinity. The *matachinis* do not have this function, and to a certain extent it is not being carried out by the *fariseos*, who are relying increasingly on police protection from Tucson.

In all these classes of activities no money payments are made to individual members of societies for services rendered by the organizers of a ceremony. *Fariseos* who assist a private family may be, and usually are, given a meal or two during the period of their work. For instance, a group of *fariseos* who get a load of wood for a *fiesta de promesa* are always given a meal by the household on their return with the wood. But no other payment is ever made. The members of societies are always fed, however, during the progress of a ceremony in which they participate.

There is one exception to this rule of no individual payments. The *maestros* who give *responsos* for the dead on All Souls' Day are paid two or three dollars apiece, or else whatever the family is able to pay, in return for giving the prayers. Except for this, all the ceremonial *'tekipanoa* in which members of societies engage is considered to be part of their obligation as members of the society and no special payments are made to them. The work is regarded as being done not for the individual concerned in the ceremonies but for the patrons of the societies, the Virgin or Jesus, and as such is payment to the latter in return for assistance in curing the members of the societies.

THE OBLIGATIONS OF SOCIETIES TO MEMBERS

In the sermon given by the head of the *matachín* society, when a new member is being confirmed, the *matachín 'kovanau* says that the *matachinis* are brothers (*sai* and *'saila*) to one another, that they should think of this fact often, and that it means that they must help one another in every way they can when any one of them becomes sick. The idea of brotherly assistance between members of a society is not merely an ideal. It is very strongly felt in the village and is, moreover, acted upon.

When a young man who was a member of both *matachín* and *fariseo* societies became ill in another village in 1937, it was learned that he had no relatives to care for him. A *padrino* brought him to Pascua, and immediately the *fariseo* society made a *limosna* to secure food. His brother lived in Pascua but was without the means to support more than his own family. The *fariseo* society accordingly took it on themselves to make frequent *limosnas* in the village to provide food for him. The *matachinis* also joined in this activity, and the man was supported through these efforts until he died.

There were two other incidents of a similar nature in Pascua in 1936–37. Each showed that the *fariseo* and *matachín* societies felt as much responsibility for the welfare of a member as do kin or *padrino* groups. Assistance was rendered principally through *limosnas* covering all the families in the village and organized by the societies, but also through appeals to individual members of the societies. Economic assistance is rendered not only to members but also to their families; and, when a member dies, societies make an effort to provide the widow with food and necessaries until she is able to find other means of support. The organization of such assistance by means of *limosnas* and individual appeals is the responsibility of the head of one of the male dance societies—the *matachín 'kovanau* or the captain of the *fariseos*. It does not matter what ceremonial season is in progress. The *fariseo* society must organize *limosnas* for a needy member whether or not the need arises during the *matachín* or the *fariseo* season.

It is not altogether clear to the investigators how needy members of the male and female altar societies, *maestros*, *ki'ostim*, and *cantoras*, are taken care of. No cases involving them came up during 1936–37. But it is said by the *matachín 'kovanau* that the *matachín* society would be obliged to make *limosna* in such cases, and appeals might be made to individual *matachinis* or *fariseos* as well as to *maestros* or *ki'ostim*. In other words, the *limosna* machinery of assistance is in the hands of the male dance groups, but its benefits may be shared in by all the other members of ceremonial societies. The dance groups are obligated to assist them just as they are obligated to assist their own members.

Besides these economic obligations, the ceremonial societies also have certain ritual obligations to members. These are in connection with death. If a *maestro*, *cantora*, or *ki'osti* is about to die, all the members of the society concerned gather at the deathbed and chant *alabanzas* or recite prayers. They are also obligated to attend the funeral in a body, although they seem to have no special ritual obligations at the funeral or *novena*. In the case of the *fariseos*, *caballeros*, and *matachinis*, the ritual obligations at death are more specific.

When a member of the *matachín* society dies, he is always buried in the full costume of a *malinche*. That is, he is clothed in a white dress with diagonal red ribbons across the breast, a headdress is placed on his head, a rattle in the right hand, and a *palma* in the left hand. He is placed in the grave with all this paraphernalia. A special ceremony is necessary during the funeral, in which the *matachín* '*kovanau* and a *malinche* place the outfit on the body. The *matachinis* also perform a special dance during both the funeral and the death *novena*. The belief is that the costume insures that the dead person will be recognized in the other world as a *matachini* and will receive the benefits of long service in behalf of the Virgin in this world.

Similarly a *fariseo* is buried in a *tʃapa'jeka* mask or other *fariseo* paraphernalia, and all the members of the society attend the funeral whether or not it takes place in the *fariseo* ceremonial season. A *caballero* is also said to be buried with his lance or sword, and all the *caballeros* attend the funeral.

THE COMPOSITION OF THE CEREMONIAL SOCIETIES

Men far outnumber women as active participants in the ceremonial life. Twice as many men as women during a year take active part in ceremonies. A census of members of ceremonial societies indicates that two-thirds of all the males over the age of ten have such membership, while less than one-third of the females are members. Women show more interest in passive attendance at ceremonies, but they do not have the opportunity for participation that men do. The ritual activities of women are strictly limited to the care of certain images and to assisting men in chanting some of the *alabanzas* and saying certain prayers. Men, on the other hand, not only chant and are charged with the care of images but also are the leaders of all services and have the important function of dancing as their monopoly.

At first glance it appears that the male ceremonial societies constitute a sort of age-grading system. We find that the membership of the *matachín* society averages much younger than that of any other group. The great majority of its members are between the ages of ten and thirty. The *fariseo* society, on the other hand, is composed of persons who are for the most part between the ages of thirty and fifty. All the resident *maestros* are over the age of forty, and it happens that the two '*temastim* are over sixty. In other words, there appears to be at least a rough correlation between the age of a man and his type of ceremonial participation. *Matachinis* tend to be young, *fariseos* tend to be middle-aged, and *maestros* and '*temastim* tend to be old.

There are, however, no restrictions in regard to age in any of the societies. One of the present *maestros* in Pascua was practicing at the age of thirteen, despite the considerable fund of knowledge necessary for the work. The youngest (nonresident) *maestro* is a man of twenty, and there is a '*temasti* of the same age in the neighboring village of Libre. *Matachinis* tend to be younger than members of other societies, but two of the present *mo'nahas* are nearly fifty and the '*kovanau* is past fifty. There are *cabos* in the *fariseo* society who are under fifteen and one Pilato is fourteen. There is evidently, therefore, no restriction on age in the societies. They are not organized formally as age-grading institutions.

Nevertheless, as we have seen, they do operate to some extent in that way, and this comes about in the following manner. Many individuals are members of more than one society. It developed, in the study of the composition of the societies, that a person claiming membership in the *fariseo* society, for example, would say that he had served formerly in the *matachín* society and still considered himself a member of the latter. He had been promised at different times to both organizations. Having a choice of serving in either, he devoted himself to the *matachinis* during his early years and then after marriage, under pressure of supporting a family, curtailed his activities in that respect and devoted himself to the *fariseos*, who are active only three months in the year and who therefore demand less of his time and energy. The custom of shifting activities from the *matachinis* to the *fariseos* in this manner seems to be widespread in the village, and it is also true that persons who are dedicated to the *matachinis* exclusively are expected in village opinion to dance less frequently as they grow older.

In point of numbers, as well as in number of ceremonies participated in during the year, the *matachinis* are the most important organization in the village. Their membership of sixty-one in 1936–37 included more than one-sixth of the total population of the village.

SUMMARY

The five male and two female ceremonial societies in Pascua are organizations which combine a number of different ritual with social and economic functions. The members of each society are recruited from all age groups in the village, but age is, nevertheless, to some extent correlated with type of ceremonial activity. The societies emphasize sex differences in their organization, and within any one of them relative age is an important principle in establishing authority and organizing the activities of the group. Change of status with marriage is a characteristic of two of them.

Members are linked through a set of mutual obligations which are characteristically expressed in economic assistance. The obligations link both living persons and deities, and the social personality of a member is regarded as continuing after death. The members of a society are obligated not only among themselves but also outside the societies in that they have to perform certain ritual and economic duties for other persons resident in the village. All these obligations are supported by a supernatural sanction operating in connection with a specific belief concerning disease and its cure.

The societies may be thought of as cross-cutting the other two important aspects of the social organization—kinship and ceremonial sponsorship. They are village wide in scope, including persons from every household in the village, as well as from every *padrino* group and *compadre* circle. The ceremonial life of the village is organized, led, and carried out almost exclusively by members of societies acting in their official capacities. They constitute groups organized independently of one another, which may function in certain ways without reference to one another, but they are also co-operating groups, whose joint activity is essential for the successful completion of nearly every type of village ceremonial.

Certain of the ceremonial societies, namely, the male and female altar groups, have features of present-day Catholic organization. Lay groups organized to care for altars on certain occasions are a part of church organization wherever Catholic churches exist. It is possible, therefore, that these Yaqui societies had no counterparts in the aboriginal culture, but the men's dance societies and possibly the women *cantoras* suggest North American Indian ceremonial societies. If the *maestros* had no aboriginal counterpart, it is, nevertheless, the case that Yaquis talk and think about them in the same way that they do about the *matachinis* and the *fariseos*. The *maestros* are treated as a definitely constituted group, not as a number of individual specialists with varying powers and abilities. Differences in knowledge and experience are, to be sure, recognized, but their powers to influence the supernatural world are regarded as equal, and they are dealt with as a co-operating priesthood rather than as individuals. It is possible that we have in the altar groups an application of Yaqui ideas of ceremonial organization to Catholic ritual functionaries. On the other hand, it is also possible to see them as another example of the result of compatibility between Catholic and Indian church organization which has produced a new institution neither one nor the other.

Whatever the historical origins of the ceremonial society system its significance for modern Pascuans lies in its role as maintainer of those values which chiefly differentiate Yaquis from the surrounding population. It is through the ceremonial societies that the group ceremonial life continues to function. It is, moreover, in connection with the activities which they demand that significant conflicts are produced in the lives of Yaqui men. It seems doubtful, in view of these conflicts, that the societies would continue to exist if their functions remained entirely ritual. As we shall see, the ritual values of Pascua culture are not closely related to the necessities of the economic life. The societies, however, have important economic functions. They, like the kinship and *padrino* groups, in some measure insure their members against starvation in times of economic stress. They help support members who are ill or jobless and constitute an ultimate insurance group with village-wide resources which may operate in the case of failure of *padrino* or kin groups. This economic function is unquestionably important in a society in which individual economic surpluses do not exist.

The ceremonial societies, then, share the insuring function of the other groups in Yaqui society, and this gives them relevance to the present economic situation; but they also have the function of defining and maintaining the ritual symbols and values of Yaqui culture. In this combination of functions they become the focus of what are perhaps the most significant conflicts in Arizona Yaqui culture today. To understand these conflicts we must proceed to an examination of the relation of the societies to the village as a whole and to a definition of the ritual values in terms of which they are organized.

CHAPTER VI

THE CHURCH AND THE PUEBLO

THE newspapers of Tucson, the chamber of commerce, the Catholic church, and the white Americans who do not have economic relations with the village are accustomed to speak of a "chief" of the Yaquis in Pascua. In their view the "chief" is a man who has been elected or appointed by the people of Pascua and who has authority from them to deal with Tucson whites in all matters affecting Yaqui interests. The "chief" is sought by the chamber of commerce when it wishes to give assistance to the annual Easter ceremonies. The newspapers refer as "chief" to the man who acts as spokesman for the village when the health department orders a round-up of all Pascua dogs. The Society of St. Anthony of the Catholic church regards as chief the Pascuan who takes charge of the distribution of "holy bread" or charity clothing in the village. The whites of Tucson believe that there is a single chief who is the political head of the village. They do not realize that the man regarded as chief by the chamber of commerce is a different person from the one regarded as such by the Catholic church. They do not know that authority in the village changes hands at different seasons of the year or that what authority exists derives entirely from the holding of a ceremonial office.

There is no separation of religious and civil functions in in Pascua at present, although this has not always been the case. From Ash Wednesday in February until the Day of the Finding of the Holy Cross on May 3, there is one recognized head of the village—the leader of the *fariseo* society. The chief function of this man is the organization of the Easter ceremonies, but he has the incidental duty of maintaining order in the village and, in so far, is a "civil" functionary. During the rest of the year there is some difference of opinion as to the proper head of the village, but in fact, if not nominally, the responsible person is the leader of the *matachín* society. What authority either of these men has derives from his ceremonial position. They are the leaders of the male dancing societies primarily, but as such they find themselves looked to by the villagers as the only constituted leaders of the community.

In discussing the realms of authority in the village, it is useful to attempt to make a distinction between the "civil" and the ceremonial. As the impossibility of making a satisfactory distinction becomes more clear, the nature of the village organization will also become clear. We may begin by distinguishing between the church and the community, or village. The Yaquis themselves have words for these two entities. They call the church the '*teopo*. The word means literally the church building where the permanent altar is maintained and the ceremonial paraphernalia stored, but it is used in a wider sense to refer to the ceremonial organizations whose activities center about the church. The '*teopo* as an organization will be discussed below. Meanwhile we shall consider the concept of the "pueblo," which is the term applied to the village as a whole. There is no equivalent Yaqui word.

THE PUEBLO

In sermons a *maestro* or a dance society leader or a *pascola* frequently refers to '*itom* '*pweplum* ("our pueblo"). He may say, for example, that he wishes to thank all participants in a ceremony on behalf of the pueblo. By "pueblo" he means all the people living in Pascua, and he regards himself as in the role of spokesman for all these people. The leader of the *matachinis* or the captain of the *fariseos*, after making a *limosna*, presents the proceeds to the givers of the *fiesta* and states that it is the contribution of the pueblo to the ceremony, referring thus to all the people of the different households which he has visited in the course of the *limosna*. The village of Pascua is thus thought of as a definite entity, distinct from other sections of Tucson and from other Yaqui villages. Its inhabitants constitute the "pueblo." The village is regarded, moreover, as a social unit equivalent to any of the "eight pueblos" on the lower Yaqui River and is often so referred to in sermons.

The historical connection of the people of Pascua with the *ocho pueblos* is a constant theme not only of sermons but also of ordinary conversation. The characteristics of the eight pueblos are a perennial subject for discussion among the older people, and references to the patron saints and special *fiestas* of the different pueblos are frequent. It is said by some that Pascua was organized as a second Torim, because that was the most centrally located of the eight villages and it was desired to make Pascua the center of the Arizona settlements. There is some evidence for this view in the fact that St. Ignatius of Loyola, who is patron of Torim, was chosen as the patron of Pascua. In addition, several Pascuans in 1924 conceived and made a flag, which is supposed to be modeled on the banner carried by Cajeme in his last wars with the Mexicans. This banner was associated especially with Torim, which was Cajeme's headquarters. The flag and St. Ignatius are still vital parts of Pascua life and are the only symbols of

Pascua as a social unit, or pueblo. The flag is flown each year from the top of the church on Easter Saturday but does not appear at any other time. The church itself is dedicated to St. Ignatius, and the feast day of the saint is celebrated annually as one of the four most important events in the village.

Factions.—While Pascua has these two symbols of unity, it does not have and has not had in the recent past any political or other organization centered about them. The church organization does not concern itself with St. Ignatius, and the flag is not the official emblem of a duly constituted political authority. The fact is that Pascua has been, from its foundation, a center of political discord and factions among Arizona Yaquis.

We have dwelt above on the fact that the families who first came to live in Pascua had their origin in different places in Sonora. There are men and women from each of the eight pueblos, as well as some from other of the less important Yaqui villages. A saying has grown up in Pascua which laments the diverse origins of the people in the village. It runs as follows: "We Yaquis are not all from one pueblo; how, then, can we form one pueblo here?" There are not only persons from different Yaqui pueblos; it is also true that many in the village never lived in a Yaqui pueblo at all. Older persons who spent their childhood in one of the eight pueblos speak sometimes of "Rio Yaqui Yaquis" and distinguish between them and "Hermosillo Yaquis." The latter are descendants of Yaquis who settled near Hermosillo or other places in Sonora. It is maintained that they do not know the real Yaqui customs and will not learn them. It is sometimes held against the present leader of the *matachinis* that he is not a "Rio Yaqui Yaqui," and it is said that, as a result of that fact, he is ignorant of the proper way to manage the *matachín* society. It is true, however, that he goes on managing the society to the apparent satisfaction of most persons, and few are able to point out specific errors in what he does. There is no clear division into articulate parties or groups on a basis of origin, but "Hermosillo Yaqui" can be used at times as a derogatory epithet by a "Rio Yaqui Yaqui."

Other differences are more important. The distinction between Yaquis *broncos* and Yaquis *mansos*, for example, is an old one and one that has played a part in the history of the Tucson Yaquis. The *mansos* (meaning "tame" in Spanish) were the Yaquis in Sonora who did not resist the Mexican government, who did not oppose the Mexicans settling in the Yaqui country, and who sometimes joined forces against the Yaquis with the Mexicans in open warfare. There were many such, even in the 1880's, in the eight river pueblos. The *broncos* (meaning "wild") were the Yaquis who resisted the Mexicans at every turn, who joined with Cajeme in the last battles, and many of whom after Cajeme's defeat scattered into the Bacatete hills. They were the "wild" Yaquis who have carried on guerrilla warfare with the Mexicans frequently even up to the present time. Most of those who first came to Pascua were *broncos*, or at least their sympathies were with the *broncos*. Juan Pistola was a *bronco*, even though he was a Mayo, and the Tucson Yaquis who first supported him were mainly of the same kind. But when Pistola declared himself against gun-running and assistance to insurrectionist Yaquis in Sonora, many of the Tucson *broncos* turned against him and organized an opposition in South Tucson.

The division among Tucson Yaquis then became centered about the leadership of Pistola. Only *Pistoleros* came to settle in Pascua at first, but after Pistola's death some anti-*Pistoleros* began to filter in. Gradually in the last ten years the feeling between the two factions has become less and less strong. At present no one would call himself by either term. Men sometimes talk now of "Yaquis *legítimos*" and "Yaquis *liberales*." What is meant is not altogether clear, but the distinction seems to be somewhat as follows: a man or woman who is a Rio Yaqui Yaqui and has been a *bronco* and a *Pistolero* is certain to be classed as a *legítimo*. The application of the term "liberal" is less clear. One man says that it refers to a person who does not come to the Yaqui church and who wants to be like a Mexican; in other words, it would seem, a sort of *manso*. But the term is not often used, and there is certainly no organized faction in Pascua corresponding to the conception of "liberal."

Political factionalism has never become much organized since Pistola's time. There has been a number of attempts at political organization since Pistola, but the leaders have never obtained popular support, and at present the organizations, though in some cases existing in name, are dead letters. The leaders of one of these recent attempts at political organization were living in Pascua in 1936. Their activities afford an interesting illustration of the operation of a political idea which seems to have had its origin in the time of Pistola. Before we consider them, however, it will be necessary to examine the government which Pistola set up in 1918 and under which Pascua was founded in 1921.

The Pistola government.—We have described the incidents which led to Pistola's prominence among Arizona Yaquis and his founding of a political organization, but we have not discussed the details of the latter. The ideas on which it was based still have a vigorous spokesman in the form of the secretary, Lucas Chavez, of the original Pistola group. So far as the rest of the village is concerned, however, the ideas underlying Pistola's political organization are little more than a vague memory.

There is a good deal of evidence indicating that Pistola was originally inspired by white men in Tucson, but the government which he worked out seems to reflect some features of an older Yaqui political system. Pistola called himself *comandante-general* of all the Yaquis in Arizona. He had an advisory committee of two and a secretary, the latter being the only one of the four who could read and write. These four men were definitely a self-constituted governing body; they were never formally elected to the offices which they created. But that does not mean that they were unsupported by other Yaquis. They had a following composed of the men who were supposed to have been freed from prison as a result of Pistola's activities, the families of these men, and a number of other Yaquis from both north and South Tucson who liked Pistola personally or saw certain advantages in his leadership. No one at present can give an estimate as to how many supporters he had. There may have been more than two hundred and fifty.

One aspect of Pistola's objective was quite definite; it was an aim inspired by the white men of Tucson with whom he had come into contact during the trial of the "*prisioneros*." They wanted a man whom they could regard as the official representative of all the Yaquis in Arizona and whom they could hold responsible for the maintenance of order in the Yaqui communities. They were interested, further, in a means of regulating the immigration of Yaquis from Sonora and also the undercover activities of Yaquis sympathetic with Sonoran revolutionary groups. Pistola tried to attain these objectives. On the painted placard which he carried from house to house of the Tucson Yaquis he stated that he and his committee were the head of a "Yaqui nation" within the United States and that they were charged with keeping order in the Yaqui villages. The placard also stated that all Yaquis entering the United States (there was no United States Immigration Border Patrol operating effectively before 1923) should report to Pistola and keep him informed of their whereabouts in Arizona. What reception the placard met with is difficult to say; it is still remembered, but what it said is not even a memory.

These ostensible aims of the Pistola government were clearly designed to further white interests as much as Yaqui. However, the actual organization which Pistola effected was worked out by himself and his assistants. It is in the conception which they had of political organization that we find some indication of cultural influences from Sonora. According to his secretary, the office which Pistola assumed could be equated with that of war chief (*'wikoijaut*) in a Yaqui River pueblo. Pistola, as *comandante-general* or captain, stood in the position of a leader like Cajeme, who was war chief of Torim and later became such for all the Yaqui pueblos. This official was entirely outside the church organization in Sonora, and similarly Pistola had no ceremonial affiliations in Pascua. When there was no warfare, it was the war chief's duty to maintain order in the pueblo. To this end he recruited a police force of young men, presided over all trial courts, and administered punishments. These duties Pistola attempted to carry out for all the Tucson Yaquis.

He organized a small police force, and, whenever there was a *fiesta* either in north or in South Tucson, he and the police attended, kept drunken disturbers away, and maintained order. On the Yaqui River a *'wikoijaut* could have enforced order with customary punishments, such as the use of stocks and the administering of lashes. In Tucson the Yaquis were not legally permitted to do this. They attempted to assert their authority by staking drunks out on the ground, but this was stopped by whites, and Pistola's police became merely assistants to the sheriff's office in Tucson, where they were required to take all prisoners.

Besides the police duties, Pistola undertook a number of other functions. One of these was also consonant with what he and his assistants believed to be the old Yaqui political system. Each pueblo, according to the secretary, had an official called the pueblo *'kovanau* or, in Spanish, *gobernador* (governor). It was his duty, first, to administer the land of the pueblo and, second, to concern himself in all disputes and difficulties arising in each individual household in the pueblo. The war chief presided over trials; the *'kovanau* gathered witnesses for defense and tried to uncover extenuating circumstances. The best-remembered function of the pueblo *'kovanau* in Pascua today is his fatherly attention to all the needs and troubles of each family of the village. It is said over and over again that the *'kovanau* went from house to house each day, passing the time of day and inquiring into family affairs. He would ask who was sick, how much food the family had, what it needed, if anything, etc. This pattern of the daily visit to all the households Pistola tried to carry out, and he is still remembered for these efforts. He became the intermediary between the Yaquis of north Tucson and all sources of economic aid and charity relief. In 1922, when there were hard times, just before he died, he had got some dozen families in Pascua placed on the relief rolls of the Red Cross and was securing food regularly for them. It is recalled that he obtained medical aid for many persons in the early days of Pascua. Unquestionably, he was modeling his activities in this respect on the remembered office of the Sonora pueblo *'kovanau.*

Pistola also fulfilled another function, one which is not thought of by his secretary as being similar to any that a *'kovanau* or war chief would have fulfilled on the Yaqui River. He secured jobs for all Yaquis who would permit him to act for them. He kept in touch with persons in Tucson who kept him informed of available jobs. He had a plan for organizing the Tucson Yaquis into labor groups; for example, all those who did ranch work would have a leader and would go out to jobs in a group. Their time records and accounts were to be kept by the leader, who would report to Pistola from time to time. The railroad workers, the powder company workers—all were to be organized into groups. The plan of organization remained a little nebulous, but one aspect of it seems to be clear. Pistola did not plan to carry out this part of his activities free of charge. We are told by men for whom he secured jobs that he took from fifty cents to a dollar a week from their pay.

Pistola died about the time that he had perfected his organization. He bequeathed his leadership to one of his assistants, Francisco Matus, and the organization continued—but in name only. Matus himself did not live in Pascua and made no effort to visit the houses, as Pistola had done, or to secure aid of any sort for any family. Moreover, he early antagonized Pascuans by bringing a police force to one of their *fiestas,* which was composed in part of Papagos from South Tucson. After that, Pascua definitely turned against Matus and refused to regard him any longer as a leader. Since Matus' death in 1928 the people of Pascua have made no effort to organize themselves politically. An election was held in 1928, but only under pressure from a Tucson lawyer and the notorious Guadalupe Flores. A Pascuan was elected "captain" of the village, but neither he nor anyone else knows what duties he is supposed to fulfil as such or just why the election was held.

Post-Pistola politics.—The idea of a "Yaqui nation" within the United States, which seems to have originated with Pistola, has persisted more or less up to the present. Yaquis living in Pascua, in South Tucson, and in Guadalupe (near Phoenix) have at various times attempted to rear an organization about the idea. One of the attempts dates from 1928, just after Guadalupe Flores, a recent arrival from Mexico, had begun to promulgate his idea that all Arizona Yaquis should go back to Sonora. A man named Salvador Muñoz, living in Guadalupe at the time, felt much opposed to the Flores plan and had the vague idea that some sort of organization of Yaquis could combat Flores' activities. As in the time of Pistola, a *junta* of a few persons was called, and Muñoz found himself in the position of "chief," with a secretary and two assistants. The plan of organization or its methods of work were never clearly formulated. Even Muñoz himself, who now lives in Pascua, says that he is not sure what he wanted to do. He "tried to do things for the Yaquis" but found them unresponsive to his leadership. He steadily lost heart and eventually turned the "chieftainship" over to one of his assistants, who in turn presented it to one of his assistants. The last, Francisco Valencia, died in Pascua in 1936. Only one or two persons in the village were aware that Valencia was a "chief," and only the Tucson newspapers mentioned it when he died.

This examination of political history gives us some insight into the concept of the "pueblo." In summary, we may say that, although Pascua came into being as a territorial unit as a result of Pistola's political organization, yet the village has not, since Pistola's death at its very foundation, had a political organization. The development has been steadily away from an interest in politics and toward a smoothing-over of factional differences based on leadership loyalties. The political ideas which have developed among Arizona Yaquis have tended to ignore pueblo lines and to emphasize a "national" basis of organization. The people of Pascua, as a community, have not taken part in these occasional efforts to unite Yaquis along political lines. The idea of the pueblo depends evidently upon something other than a political government.

Inter-pueblo relations.—It has been mentioned that there are six other Yaqui villages in southern Arizona. Persons in Pascua know about all of these, and most of them have either relatives, *padrinos*, or *compadres* in each of them. Visits are constantly being made back and forth between the villages, particularly between the Tucson group of Libre, Pascua, and Marana. Only two of the villages do not have a ceremonial organization of their own, and these two are of relatively recent origin. They are Marana and Eloy, composed mainly of former residents of Pascua and Libre but also containing some families from the Phoenix Yaqui settlements. Marana and Eloy clearly regard themselves as dependent on Pascua in ceremonial matters. Eloy, for instance, sent to Pascua for *maestros* for a funeral in 1937, for *matachinis* for the dedication of a Catholic church, and for *fariseos* and *maestros* for a Lenten household *fiesta*.

All the other villages, like Pascua, have resident *maes-*

tros, *matachinis*, and *fariseos*, and consequently organize their own ceremonies. There is, however, an exchange of ceremonial performers between villages which takes place with some frequency. That is, Pascua *matachinis* may dance in Libre or Libre *matachinis* in Pascua; Pascua *maestros* go not only to Marana and Eloy but also to Libre and Mezquitál in South Tucson. The fact is that a ceremonial society has no territorial limits whatever, so far as its ritual functions are concerned. If a man has been confirmed in the *fariseo* society, he may dance as such in any of the Yaqui villages in Arizona. The same is true of members of any of the other ceremonial societies. In 1937 a man who had been a *fariseo* for some years at Guadalupe was working, just prior to the Easter season, at Marana. Instead of going back to Guadalupe to participate in the Easter ceremonies, he came to Pascua because it was nearer and acted as *tʃapa'jeka* there. Another *fariseo* who had served for many years in Pascua had an angry falling-out with the Pascua *fariseo* leader some weeks before Easter. When Holy Week came, he went down to Libre and took part in the ceremonies there instead of in Pascua. Membership in a society, therefore, has nothing to do with pueblo lines, at least as far as the fulfilment of ritual obligations is concerned. A man does not need to be reconfirmed if he goes to another village and wishes to participate.

There is, however, an aspect of membership in a ceremonial society which is connected with village residence. The economic assistance which societies render to members who are in need seems to be regarded as an obligation only of the pueblo in which the member was confirmed. Thus Felipe Gonzales, a *fariseo*, became ill in Guadalupe. He was sent back to Pascua, where he had been confirmed and where he had done most of his dancing as a *fariseo*. The Pascua *fariseos* recognized their obligations to him there. Similarly, Luís Angwamea was brought to Pascua when he was about to die. He had been promised by his father to the *matachín* society in Pascua but had never been confirmed. He was brought to Pascua from Libre, was confirmed there, and the *matachinis* made *limosnas* and took care of him until he died. Although there were *matachinis* in Libre, they made no effort to assist him while he was there.

When members of ceremonial societies go in groups to perform in other villages where there are ceremonial societies of the same kind, they submit to the direction of the leaders in the village visited. Several times during 1936–37 the *matachinis* from Pascua went to Libre to dance at funerals and *novenas*. In one case the dead person was a *maestro*, and the *matachinis* felt obligated to dance for him just as they would have for a dead *maestro* in Pascua. In two other cases the dead persons were *matachinis*. The Pascua *matachinis* not only danced at the funerals and *novenas* of these *matachinis* but also made *limosnas* in Pascua and gave the proceeds as a contribution toward the food and firewood which they consumed while participating in the ceremonies. They were accompanied by their leader when they went to dance, but he did not direct their activities during the ceremony. He turned his men over to the Libre *matachín* leader and remained in the background himself. Similarly, when *matachinis* from Libre came to dance at the funeral and *novena* of a dead *matachini* in Pascua, they danced entirely under the direction of the Pascua society leader.

Besides this exchange of ritual services between the ceremonial societies of the various villages, it is also customary for a society of one village to conduct a *limosna* in another on certain occasions. This may be done for any kind of ceremony during the *matachín* ceremonial season but occurs most often in connection with the death of a member of some ceremonial society, such as a *maestro* or *matachini*. During the Easter season the Pascua *fariseos* also make *limosnas* on behalf of household *fiestas* in Libre, and the Libre *fariseos* do the same in Pascua. The primary purpose of such *limosnas* is said to be not the money and food which is collected but rather the giving of news of the ceremony. It is necessary to give *aviso* as widely as possible, so that all persons of whatever village who might be interested may attend the ceremony.

We see, therefore, two aspects of the ceremonial society system which are important in connection with the concept of the pueblo. In the first place, the societies recognize no territorial limits in their ritual activities. They will perform at any village. Only extreme distance, such as that between Yuma or Phoenix and Pascua, confines their activities. In the second place, however, the economic functions of the societies are in some, but not all, respects confined to particular pueblos. The place of confirmation of a member has the economic responsibility for him. Some economic assistance may be rendered a member of another pueblo by means of the *limosna* at the time of his funeral, but sickness aid is limited to the pueblo where he began to dance or was confirmed. This limitation of economic responsibility is coupled with an internal organization of each society which limits the authority of leaders to particular pueblos. When a village sends ceremonial performers to another village, they must submit to the leaders of the societies in the latter. Their own leader has no authority. The pueblo may thus be defined as coterminous with the ceremonial societies existing within it. It is now the situation in Pascua that the pueblo is organized only in terms of its ceremonial societies.

THE CHURCH

The ceremonial societies, as they exist in Pascua today, do not seem to conform in their relations with one another precisely to an older pattern which is still remembered by by some Pascuans. It will simplify discussion of the present situation if we first make clear the rather definite ideas in regard to church organization which older Pascuans still hold.

The older system.—What we shall describe as an "older system" may never have existed anywhere; it may be simply an ideal held by two or three of the older men in Pascua. It seems, however, to have the ring of reality. Those who hold it are "Rio Yaqui Yaquis" who grew up in Sonora Yaqui pueblos. It is most clearly expressed by the three oldest *maestros* now living in Pascua, all of whom are active in the ceremonial life at present.

They say that all the activities of the ceremonial societies were directed and co-ordinated by the oldest *maestro*. His was the ruling voice of the ceremonial life, just as the war chief's dominated war and police activities, and the pueblo *'kovanau's* controlled nonceremonial civil affairs. The war chief and *'kovanau* both had assistants, and similarly the head *maestro* had his assistants. The latter were chosen from among the other *maestros* and *'temastim*. The principal assistant was the *'teopo 'kovanau* (head of the church), who was ordinarily one of the younger *maestros*. All the *maestros*, other than the eldest, rotated in this office, seeming to have held it for a week at a time, each in turn. The real brunt of the organization of a ceremony fell on the shoulders of the *'teopo 'kovanau*. It was his duty, under the direction of the head *maestro*, to inform the heads of the various ceremonial societies concerning the date and the nature of the ceremony to be held. He was responsible for the smooth running of the ritual, regardless of whether the ceremony took place at the church or at a private household. It fell to him not only to inform the ceremonial society heads but also to get the church or private house in readiness, see that the altar was properly arranged, and then directly supervise the activities of the societies during the whole of the ceremony. He carried a small *carrizo* stick tied with a red ribbon as insignia of his authority.

The heads of the ceremonial societies were responsible to the *'teopo 'kovanau*. We have already described the nature of their duties. They had to inform the members of their societies, see that they appeared for the ceremonies, and then organize and supervise the dance or other ritual which they carried out. If necessary, the head of a dance society concerned in the ceremony had to organize and carry out a *limosna* for the purpose of informing the pueblo and helping defray the expenses of the *fiesta*. He was required to bring to the head *maestro* the proceeds of the *limosna* for any ceremony held in the public plaza and count it in his presence; if for a household *fiesta*, he had to do the same in the presence of the persons sponsoring the event and then present the proceeds with a ritual speech in behalf of the pueblo and the church organizations.

This was the main outline of the "older system" of church organization in so far as anyone in Pascua can now state it. It will be seen that it was a hierarchy at the top of which was the head *maestro*. Beneath him were the *'teopo 'kovanau* and the other *maestros*, and directly responsible to them were the heads of the *matachín*, *fariseo*, and *ki'osti* societies. This system does not obtain now in Pascua.

The present system.—The present system differs from the older one in several important respects. Its most notable feature is the greater importance of the heads of the dance societies and the reduced importance of the head *maestro*. It is further characterized by the absence of a duly appointed *'teopo 'kovanau*, distinct from the persons of the dance society leaders.

At present the duties which the *'teopo 'kovanau* used to have seem to be entirely taken over by the heads of the *matachín* and *fariseo* societies, in their respective seasons. Moreover, the co-ordinating functions of the head *maestro* seem also to be a part of the duties of the heads of the dance societies. The fact is that the oldest *maestro* is somewhat senile and does not bother either to see that people are informed of a ceremony or to take charge of the organization of the necessary activities, even though he is fully aware of his duties in these respects. Two of the younger *maestros* are perfectly capable of taking over the duties, but one of them is not a permanent resident of Pascua and the other finds that they conflict with his job. The result is that the *matachín* leader acts in the capacity of *'teopo 'kovanau* (and is sometimes so referred to by the head *maestro*) for all ceremonies during the *matachín* season, and the *fariseo* leader acts in the same capacity during the Easter season.

It is these men who are pointed to when an outsider asks who is "chief" of the village. It is they, in their respective seasons, who act as representatives of the village with all outsiders. They secure burial permits from the county when a person dies and direct the necessary arrangements which the county requires in connection with a funeral. They obtain permits for *fiestas* and processions from the sheriff's office. (Actually the sheriff does not require that they have permits, but since the days of Juan Pistola it has been the custom to get them; everyone in Pascua believes that a permit insures police protection during a *fiesta*, that is, protection from the numerous drunken Mexicans and Yaquis who flock to nearly every ceremony.) They call the county doctor when someone desires him. They are clearly prominent men in the village, but their positions have more the quality of public servant than of director of village affairs, except in the management of ceremonies. It is only in the latter activity that they are vested with authority from the people of the village.

The nature of leadership in the church.—Conceptions of what constitutes community leadership in Pascua are vague and rarely defined by anyone. It is said by some that Pascua "needs a leader." These persons deplore a lack of what they call *esfuerzo* (strength of spirit or force of character) for talking in public and getting villagers together in *reuniones*, or meetings. Pistola's former secretary, now the third *maestro*, says frequently and vigorously that there is no one in the village suitable to be a *'kovanau*. No one has the *esfuerzo*. He condemned equally all the men most prominent in village affairs in 1936–37, and he was not alone in this condemnation. The present leaders, he and others say, lack the qualities of true leaders. The head *maestro* is dismissed as being too old; the other two prominent figures, the *fariseo* and *matachín* leaders, are condemned for various, and each for different, reasons.

The *fariseo* leader is generally acknowledged in the village to be "backward" in his dealings with whites during the Easter season. He knows personally none of the white officials in Tucson who customarily assist in the Easter ceremonies. When they come out to get in touch with him, his manner is diffident and shy. This backwardness is regarded by almost everyone in the village, young and old, as a fault; it is said that a man in his position should show more "spirit" in dealing with whites. On the other hand, no criticism is made of him for backwardness in his dealings with the villagers during his ceremonial season, and it is quite obvious that he gets things done and the ceremonies organized. Certain minor faults are pointed to, however, in connection with these activities. It is maintained by a few persons that his knowledge of the proper sequence of events in the Easter ceremonies is faulty. Few facts are given to support this view. One of the major criticisms advanced is that he does too much himself; he should sit on a bench somewhere and direct other persons (the *cabos*, *tenientes*, etc.) to do the necessary things at *fiestas*. Instead he does many things himself. Actually, it appears to an outsider that he delegates the greater part of his duties to others. The criticism is, nevertheless, widespread. No other definite instance of faulty knowledge of ceremonial procedure is advanced against him, except a failure to demonstrate properly and carry out all the *fariseo* dance-march steps at the proper times. This, however, seems to be a matter of opinion, and there is no one else in the village who can give any more consistent account of the proper steps than this man. There are, however, two other counts on which the *fariseo* leader is criticized. One is that he is dishonest with the *limosna* and other funds collected by the *fariseos* during Lent and Holy Week. Proof of this is held to be that he kept a record in 1936–37 only of the funds that came in and not of the manner in which they were expended. Yet the only specific charge which was leveled at him in this connection was disproved, and there seems to be evidence that the whole surplus of funds was devoted not to himself but to the purchase of ceremonial paraphernalia which was turned over to the village as communal property.

The final charge against him is the most serious. That is, that he permits his labors on a near-by ranch to interfere with his ceremonial duties. We have already gone into this matter to some extent. This charge unquestionably has a basis in fact. Nevertheless, the *fariseo* leader quit his job for one month during the Easter ceremonial season in 1936–37 in order to devote himself exclusively to ceremonial activities. He was criticized little during this period, but the season extended beyond the month which he took off, that is, after Easter Sunday to May 3. He was therefore remiss in making preparations for the *fiesta* of the Holy Cross, although he had attended to most of his ceremonial duties during Easter. The most vigorous criticism which was directed against him last year was for his failure to organize at the proper time a *limosna* party for Felipe Gonzales, the sick and penniless *fariseo*, who came to Pascua during the *matachín* season. He himself showed a great sense of guilt in this instance and admitted that he had allowed himself to lose touch with events in the village because of the demands of his job.

The *matachín* leader is the most vigorous of the public personages, and yet he is probably the most criticized person in the village. He is not altogether backward in dealing with whites; in fact, he is much relied on for this type of assistance. It is generally admitted that he has no background for the position which he holds. He did not become a *matachini* until he was over forty, and his knowledge of the *matachín* ritual is poor. It is pointed out that he does not know enough to give a sermon at the ceremonies at which the *matachinis* appear, and it is clear that he relies heavily on the more experienced *monarcas* in working out the details of a dance and co-ordinating it with the activities of the other church organizations. The fact remains that he attends to his duties regularly at all times and, with the help of others, manages ceremonies and *limosnas* with considerable efficiency. No one criticizes him for neglecting his ceremonial duties for daily labor.

What is held against him is his past record and general character. He was one of Pistola's assistants when he was a young man and gained a reputation as a leader then. But after Pistola died, he become involved with the unpopular successor of Pistola, Francisco Matus, in the misappropriation of funds during an Easter *fiesta*. His guilt was never proved, but there are few who believe that he was innocent. He led a drunken life after Pistola's death and began to mistreat his wife. These things are held against him, even though at present he does not let drunkenness interfere with his ceremonial position. Moreover, ten years ago he formed a connection with the Catholic church, which he still maintains. It is obvious that he is friendly with a Catholic priest in Tucson, and he has worked as caretaker at the Catholic church on the edge of Pascua. When Francisco Matus died, a Catholic organization in Tucson announced through the newspapers that they would consider this man, the present *matachín* leader, as chief of the village. At that time he held no ceremonial office in the village. At present, as leader of the *matachinis*, he frequently takes the dancers to the Church of Santa Rosa and has them dance there. These activities are regarded with suspicion by most of the older people, although they permit them. All these things tend to make the village generally distrustful of the man as a community leader, but his efficiency in the office which he holds is obvious, and there is no one anxious to displace him.

These facts in connection with the leaders of the church suggest some generalizations regarding leadership in the village. In the first place, leadership develops only out of holding the highest ceremonial offices. Conventionally, such leaders hold their positions as a result of seniority in their organizations and are confirmed in them by election. This condition does not obtain in the case of the present *matachín* leader, who appropriated his office without any due election. This state of affairs was made possible as a result of lack of competition for the office, a condition which we have discussed at a former point as connected with a fundamental conflict between the culture of Pascua and that of the surrounding community.

In the second place, the qualities which are regarded as desirable in a leader are not thought to be possessed by either of the present leaders. These qualities are ability to deal effectively with whites as representative of the village, honesty in the handling of funds, and careful attention to ceremonial duties at all times. The general feeling in the village is that leadership is in a low state, because the heads of the dance societies are not thought to have these qualities. Despite this feeling, the specific duties connected with church functions are carried out regularly, and there is no paralysis of the church organizations due to lack of adequate leadership or any other cause. Nevertheless, each leader carries out his duties in the midst of constant and widespread criticism. The persistence of the criticism seems to indicate a lively interest in the public offices even if competition for them is weak. The criticism does not result in the formation of organized factions within the church, although there is some tendency in this direction. The *matachín* leader, for instance, is personally at odds with the *fariseo* head, and each of these has a small, but apparently inconstant, following who from time to time share their adverse opinions of each other. It happens that the head *maestro* is on good terms with both dance society leaders, and this may hinder the development of clear-cut factions based on this personal antagonism. The church remains a unified organization, or group of cooperating organizations, which dominates the organized social and ritual life of the pueblo.

SOCIAL CONTROL

In the absence of any civil government in the village there is no system of legal control of behavior. Moral and supernatural sanctions are operative, but no legal ones except through the action of outside agencies. This, as we know, has not always been the case. We have discussed the police system organized by Pistola and its subsequent disappearance under Matus. Pistola, his secretary says, had a plan for organizing a village court, but it was not realized. Pistola himself became discouraged in the matter because of the county sheriff's interference in his attempts to punish disturbers of the peace at *fiestas*. Nevertheless, after Pistola's death, a court at which only Yaquis presided was held in Pascua as recently as thirteen years ago. It is a well-remembered event, despite the fact that it was held for the purpose only of settling a trivial dispute as to who was the aggressor in a minor assault charge. The loser, a woman, was dissatisfied with the verdict and attempted unsuccessfully to take the matter to a court in Tucson. No court has been held in the village since.

Villagers say that they do not need any courts, because they are satisfied with the operation of those in Tucson. They do believe that they need a police force, but no effort is made to establish one except during the Easter ceremonies, when the *fariseos* act to some extent in that capacity. Legal sanctions are brought into play only through the sheriff's office and the Tucson courts. Use was made during 1936–37 of the latter in a dispute over the adoption of a child, in an effort of a man to obtain custody of his children after separation from his wife, in an effort of a man to obtain custody of a child whom he had previously given to a relative to keep, and in a case of assault and battery. We shall not go into the details of the cases. It may be said merely that the use of the courts by Yaquis was carried out just as by whites and that the affairs were between individuals and families in which the village institutions played no important part.

The operation of moral sanctions may best be indicated not by an enumeration of all the details of cases but rather by a summary statement of the types of behavior which were considered undesirable. First, we may indicate actions which were always referred to the county sheriff; those recorded were wife-beating (when it was serious enough to result in serious injury), rape, assault resulting in serious injury, and extreme disturbance of ceremonies by drunken persons. Murder and robbery would also be so referred probably, but no cases were recorded of such actions. Behavior which was generally and vigorously denounced, but for which no legal sanctions were invoked, consisted in sexual relations between men and unmarried females, adultery, habitual drinking by young men, smoking marijuana, habitual refusal to perform ceremonial duties for a society of which one was a member, habitual seclusion from ceremonies and *fiestas*, and witchcraft. It should be said also that in one case of witchcraft legal sanctions were invoked. These forms of behavior were the most common source of disapproving talk in the village. Only drinking by young men and refusal to perform ceremonial duties received public denunciation in sermons. The other forms of misbehavior were spoken against privately but called forth no other action.

The operation of supernatural sanctions has already been discussed in connection with the ceremonial societies and will be discussed more fully at a later point.

SUMMARY

What social and cultural unity the village of Pascua has may be said to depend on the institution of the church, that is, on the ceremonial societies which together compose the church. There is a concept in use in the village in the form of the word "pueblo," but there is at present no social institution corresponding to the concept. The history of the village reveals an attempt to construct such an institution, but no vestige of that now remains. Leadership in the community may be achieved only through the channels of the ceremonial institutions.

The continued survival of the ceremonial organization and the disappearance of any purely political organization seems paradoxical in the light of data from other Mexican Indian communities. The rule seems to have been in Mexico that ceremonial functions have been absorbed (when they have not died out) by a village organization which increasingly emphasizes political functions. The conditions in the United States are, however, clearly different. Pascua remains politically dependent on a larger community near by. Pascuans, as noncitizens, have no political significance in that community, and hence there are no political powers which might crystallize around Yaqui individuals. The increasing use by Pascuans of Tucson police facilities is indicative of a recognition of complete dependence on the larger community. The political features of the old village organization have been adequately substituted for by the Tucson sheriff's office. On the other hand, neither the sheriff's office nor the Catholic church of Tucson have assumed ceremonial functions which supply the needs of Pascuans. Accordingly, the Yaquis themselves have had to develop the ceremonial features of the old organization.

With this examination of the relation between the ceremonial societies and the village as a whole we complete our discussion of the organized groups in Pascua. Since these groups function in a milieu of supernatural belief and ceremonial context which is peculiar to Yaqui culture, we can fully understand their operation only after we gain some familiarity with Yaqui ritual. The following three chapters will be devoted to outlining the supernatural aspect of life in the village.

CHAPTER VII

THE *PASCOLA* DANCERS

A GOOD introduction to an understanding of some of the changes that are now going on in Arizona Yaqui culture is a discussion of the *pascola* dancers. The *pascolas* and their associated ceremonial performer, the deer-dancer, constitute an aspect of the ceremonial life in which is revealed the nature of certain adjustments which are taking place between old and new elements in the culture. A consideration of the ritual activities of the *pascolas*, of their place in the socioceremonial organization, and of the ideas and beliefs associated with them throws into clear light the composite character of Pascua ceremony with its fusion of European and aboriginal elements. The *pascolas* appear to have a secure place in the life of the village at present, but they seem also to be a focus of conflicting attitudes. They are seen by some persons as the most distinctive of Yaqui institutions, and their appearances are looked forward to with pleasure; on the other hand, some individuals are "ashamed" of them, feeling, for example, that children should not be allowed to see them perform. They remain, in this conflicting atmosphere, an essential feature of many ceremonies. In 1936–37 they made twenty-five appearances, three of which were at three of the four most important ceremonial occasions on the fixed calendar.

The *pascolas* are not simply dancers; they have a number of different functions besides dancing, one of the most important of which is that of ceremonial host at most public *fiestas*. It is from this function that they derive their name. The word *pascola* has been regarded by some as being derived from the Spanish *pascual* (meaning *fiesta* at Easter).[1] This is highly improbable. Their connection with this occasion is incidental only to their general role in ceremony. The Yaqui word for *fiesta* is *'paχko*, meaning a ceremony at which there is feasting and for which there are special organizers, or *fiesteros*. The term is a general one for this kind of ceremony, regardless of the season of the year. The organizers of such an occasion are called by a number of different terms, two examples of which are *'paχko 'atʃaim*, or "fathers of the *fiesta*," and *paχ'kome*, or "those of the *fiesta*." The same stem *'paχko-* appears in several other compounds, for instance, in *'paχkoʾ'ola*, from which the hispanicized *pascola* comes. In the last compound the first stem, as we have said, means *fiesta* and the *-ola* means "old man" or "anything old." A literal translation of the word *pascola*, therefore, may be given as "old man of the *fiesta*." It is not a Yaqui adaptation of a Spanish word but rather a hispanicized form of an original Yaqui word. The Yaqui form is still sometimes used in Pascua, especially by persons who are making an effort to speak "correct" Yaqui, but it is rarely heard, and the form *pascola* may be regarded as the accepted one.

The *pascola* is the "old man" who calls the people, other than performers, together for a *fiesta*, greets them and keeps them interested during the ceremonies, and gives out, in the name of the *fiesteros*, the cigarettes, drinking water, and food. This seems to be his essential role, but these duties are combined with other ritual activities.

[1] Wendell C. Bennett and Robert M. Zingg, *The Tarahumara* (Chicago: University of Chicago Press, 1935), p. 315.

ORGANIZATION OF THE ACTIVITIES OF THE "PASCOLAS"

The *pascolas* cannot be said to constitute a ceremonial society in the sense that the *matachinis*, *maestros*, or *fariseos* do. They do not have the mutual obligation to assist one another in time of need. When a *pascola* dies, his funeral is not attended by the other *pascolas*, nor is he buried with *pascola* paraphernalia. In other words, there is no *pascola* group, constituting a social structure, as in the case of other ritual dancers. Furthermore, a man does not become a *pascola* as a result of a *manda*, or promise, to any deity. Thus there is no *patrón* of the *pascolas*, corresponding to the Virgin Mary for the *matachinis* or Jesus for the *fariseos*. There is some confusion in the village in this matter, however. Individuals frequently say, when asked, that Jesus is the patron of the *pascolas*. They admit that *pascolas* do not promise themselves to the service of Jesus, that there is no "confirmation" ceremony utilizing a crucifix or other image of Jesus, and that the *pascolas* do not "own" an image corresponding to the *fariseo* society's crucifix or the *matachinis'* Virgin; yet they feel that the *pascolas* are somehow like the other dancers and, therefore, that their dancing ought to be dedicated to some "patron." There is this feeling, but clearly there is no organized relationship between a given god and the *pascolas*. This fact together with the lack of mutual obligations between *pascolas* indicates that they do not constitute a ceremonial society. The only indication of organization is that the eldest *pascola* appearing at any ceremony always leads the ritual in which the *pascolas* take part.

The *pascolas*, however, are closely associated with another group of men who seem to be a remnant of what was once a ceremonial society. These men are called *'morum*, or *moro'jautʃim*. (The name seems clearly to be the Spanish *moro*, meaning Moor.) In Pascua these men do not constitute an organized society, but it is said that their duties in relation to the *pascolas* are the same as duties which members of ceremonial societies called *moros* formerly had on the Yaqui River. A full description of the nature of the *moro* society cannot be given by anyone in Pascua. It is remembered that they took part in an annual ceremonial battle on San Juan's Day in which they fought with the members of the *ka'bajum* society (the present Pascua *caballeros*). This quite probably was a form of the dramatization of the war between the Moors and the Christians, widespread among Mexican Indians. The *moros* in Pascua have no such ceremony. The nature of the organization of the society is not remembered by anyone in Pascua, but it is said that the *moros* had certain other duties throughout the year, such as directing the activities of the *pascolas* and preparing dance places for the latter. These duties are the ones carried out at present in Pascua by the *moros*. There are three such men. They have no ceremonial organization and have not been promised to the service that they perform; they merely are called by the term and customarily fulfil the duties.

The duties of a *moro'jaut* are few. When *pascolas* are to appear at a *fiesta*, the *fiesteros* notify one of the *moro'jautʃim*. He goes to the house where the *fiesta* is to be held, prepares a space for the *pascolas* to dance in, informs the *pascolas* and their musicians of the *fiesta*, and remains with the *pascolas* throughout the *fiesta*. His duties in connection with the *pascola* ritual will be described below. He wears no costume and has no insignia of office.

The *pascola* cannot perform without special musicians.

These men are not called *pascolas* but are given the usual general names by which musicians are known in Pascua. A harpist (*ar'pero*), a violinist (*lava'leo*), and a drummer-flutist (*tampa'leo*) are necessary. Like the *pascolas* and the *moros*, they form no organization. There are three men who can play the harp, a dozen or more who can play the violin, and two who can play the drum and whistle for the *pascolas*. Any of these may be called on when *pascola* musicians are necessary.

An individual becomes a *pascola* simply through the apprentice method. He learns the dance and the ritual from an established *pascola*, beginning either as a boy or as an adult. When he has acquired proficiency and the necessary paraphernalia, he is asked to dance somewhere and from that time on may appear as *pascola* at any ceremony requiring *pascolas*. He may or may not dance, as he pleases, when asked by a *fiestero*. He has no obligation of the sort that characterizes *matachín* or *fariseo* participation.

In Pascua in 1936–37 there were five resident *pascolas* and one who lived in Marana but appeared occasionally in Pascua ceremonies. The five who lived in Pascua were adults, over thirty, and the Marana *pascola* was a boy of thirteen.

CEREMONIES IN WHICH "PASCOLAS" APPEAR

It has been said that *pascolas* appear in ceremonies at which there is feasting. They do not, however, appear at all ceremonies at which food is served. At funerals of adults and at funeral *novenas*, for example, it is not customary to have *pascola* dancing. It is said that they might appear at such ceremonies, but no cases are on record in Pascua, and it seems to be an established custom to carry such ceremonies through without *pascolas*. At the third type of death ceremony, the *cumpleaño*, or anniversary, however, it is usual to have them.

Besides the death *cumpleaño*, *pascolas* appear at child funerals, saint's-day *fiestas*, the Holy Saturday and Palm Sunday *fiestas* opening and closing the Holy Week ceremonies, *fiestas de promesa*, and weddings. It is said that they are proper at baptisms, and examples are cited of their appearance at baptisms among Yaquis in Sonora, but no instance of *pascola* dancing at a baptism in Pascua is known. In addition, *pascolas* dance more frequently than any other Yaqui performers outside the village at Papago and white functions. Groups in Tucson, such as the University of Arizona, churches, and schools, have frequently had *pascolas* at various of their meetings or parties, paying them small sums to dance. Regularly each year the Papagos also call at Pascua and hire *pascola* dancers to appear at a New Year celebration on the Reservation. There is only one instance in the last twenty years of the *matachinis* having danced outside the village at a white secular function.

Unlike the *matachinis*, the *pascolas* never appear at the ordinary Sunday services at the Yaqui church, and they have no part in the death *novenas* during October or at the ceremonies centering about All Souls' Day in November. The ceremonies at which they appear are always all-night or all-day *fiestas*, characterized by elaborate preparations, feasting, and large attendance. It is the *fiesta*, or large public gathering, with which they are intimately connected, not the routine church observance of comparatively unimportant dates in the Catholic calendar. They are essential at the kind of *fiesta* which is conceived as the fulfilment of a long-established obligation and to which everyone in the village is supposed to come and enjoy themselves, as well as to witness the fulfilment of the obligation.

For example, *pascolas* are absolutely essential at a child funeral. The funeral of such a person is thought of as the fulfilment of the obligation of *padrinos* to the parents of the child. The obligation was established when the parents gave a feast to the *padrinos* at the time of baptism of their child. The obligation is fulfilled, if the child dies, by the *padrinos'* giving a feast. It is as an official host at this feast that the *pascola* serves. He is not host to the parents and relatives but to the public at large who are expected to come and see that the obligation has been fulfilled. Similarly, the death anniversary is a *fiesta* which is regarded as closing the period of mourning for relatives. They give a public feast at this time announcing the fulfilment of their obligation as mourners, and the *pascola* is an essential part of it. The same sort of interpretation might be put on the saint's-day *fiesta;* it is the annual fulfilment of the obligation of the village to the saint, just as also are the *fiestas de promesa.* Weddings cannot quite be fitted into this interpretation, except as a time of the establishment of obligations between families inaugurated by reciprocal feasts.

THE DANCERS AND THEIR DANCE

The *pascolas* combine very strikingly elements of Western culture with what must be aboriginal Yaqui elements in their costume, their dance, and their ritual functions. It is probably not possible to allocate all these elements precisely to the cultures in which they originated, but the origins of certain of them are obvious and will be clear from a general description of the *pascolas* and their activities.

Costume.—There are two types of costume in which the *pascolas* appear, depending upon the character of the ceremony. In their most usual roles they always wear masks made of wood and painted black. The mask may be decorated in various ways, but it has certain essential features. These are a cross painted in white on the forehead, a long white beard made of horsehair or manila rope, and long white eyebrows of the same material. Common additions are flower designs painted in white and clumps of long white hair affixed to the cheeks.

When he appears as a masked dancer, the *pascola* wears nothing above the waist or on the feet. From the waist to the knees a blanket, which it is said must be of wool (but rarely is), is wrapped, covering the thighs and the lower part of the torso. The blanket is tied in a special way with a black sash around the waist and above each knee. Also around the waist is worn a heavy leather belt which has six or more metal bells attached to it by long strings. These jingle constantly while the dancer is in motion.

The hair is always tied into a topknot with a red ribbon. Around the neck is worn a string of black and white beads, and a small white cross of mother-of-pearl, or other material, is attached to the necklace. Around each ankle is wrapped a string of cocoon rattles called *'teneboim* which sound whenever the feet are moved. An instrument called a *se'nasum* is carried and rattled during certain dances; at other times it is stuck into the leather bell-belt. The *se'nasum* is made of wood and resembles a section of the side of a tambourine, having two or more metal disks which may be shaken up and down to give a tinkling sound.

This is the costume and paraphernalia made use of by

the *pascola* at most of the ceremonies at which he appears. But at a wedding and, it is said, also at a baptism, the costume is very different. No mask is worn at this time. Ordinary shirt and pants and broad-brimmed hat are the only costume. The *se'nasum*, the cocoon rattles on the ankles, and the belt with the bells are, however, always used. The *pascola* may or may not dance with shoes on at a wedding. The hair is not tied in a topknot, but a red ribbon is worn around the hat or sometimes tied around either arm.

The dance.—The dances of the *pascola* all have animal names, such as "badger," "wolf," "canary," "turtle," etc. In some of these, as, for instance, the "badger," the *pascola* prances around on all fours, more or less in time to the music, in imitation of the animal. For most of the others, the dance seems to have no relation to the movements of the animals. The step is a simple shuffle with the weight borne mainly by the toes, but with a constant thumping of the heels on the ground in time to the music. There are variations, such as the swinging of one foot in an arc to the side, dragging the toes, and making the cocoon rattles sound in a special way. The general effect is that of a rather quiet and monotonous tap dance. When there are more than one *pascola* present, each dances in turn. A dance lasts for ten minutes, then there is a rest of ten or fifteen minutes, then another dance, and so on, throughout the night.

The dances go on with little variation all night, but the music changes constantly. At the beginning of the dance the music is always that of the violin and Mexican harp. This alternates through the night with the music of the drum and whistle. The drum is a simple, double-headed hide drum beaten with a special wooden drumstick. The whistle is made of *carrizo* and has four holes. The two instruments are played simultaneously by a single man, the *tampa'leo.*

The harpist and violinist sit at one end of the dance *ramada.* The music which they play is Mexican "creole" or *mestizo.* When the *pascola* is dancing to this music, he does not wear his mask over his face but keeps it pushed to one side over one ear. He does not use his *se'nasum.* The *tampa'leo* sits at the other end of the *ramada,* facing the violinist and harpist. The music which he plays is aboriginal Yaqui. When the *pascola* is dancing to it, he always wears the mask over his face. He also makes use of the *se'nasum,* holding it in one hand and beating it against the palm of the other hand.

RITUAL FUNCTIONS OF THE "PASCOLAS"

We have mentioned thus far the ritual dance and ceremonial host functions of the *pascola.* The latter might be taken to include the other important function, that of ceremonial clowning, but it is better considered as a distinct sort of activity. These three kinds of activities—dancing, acting as ritual host, and clowning—are combined in all that the *pascolas* do during a ceremony.

The dance.—At a ceremony held in the public plaza the *matachinis* dance in front of the church, facing the church altar. Similarly, at a household *fiesta* the *matachinis* always dance facing the altar which has been set up temporarily in a *ramada* beside the house. They dance at the same time that the *maestros* and *cantoras* are chanting prayers or *alabanzas.* The place and the time of the dance of the *pascolas* are quite different. They do not, except at the beginning or end of a procession, dance in front of the altar, whether at the church in the plaza or at a household *fiesta*. In the public plaza there is a structure at the opposite end of the plaza from the church which is called the *pascola ramada*. It is here that the *pascolas* dance. The *ramada* is divided into two parts: on one side is set up a small altar which becomes the repository for a few of the images from the church altar which are taken there in procession during the course of a ceremony; on the other side of the *ramada* sit the *pascola* musicians, and here the *pascolas* dance. Their dance is not co-ordinated, as the *matachinis*' is, with the ritual activities of the *maestros* and other altar groups. Their activities go on independently of the others, throughout the night, except during processions. Similarly, at household *fiestas* the temporary *ramada* is divided into two parts, one half for the altar and church organizations and one half for the *pascolas*. The temporary household *ramada* is, in fact, a duplicate of the *pascola ramada* in the plaza.

Only in processions do the *pascolas* co-ordinate their activities with those of the church groups. The kinds of processions and their functions will be described below. Here it will be sufficient to point out that a constant feature of most ceremonies is a procession from the church to the *pascola ramada*, or, if it is a household ceremony, from the church to the household *ramada*. The processions are composed of the participating church organizations, but they are met at the household *patio* cross by the *pascolas* and the *fiesteros* of the household, and the *pascolas* dance ahead of the church groups from the cross back to the household *ramada*. At the conclusion of a ceremony the *pascolas* again dance at the head of the procession. If it is a household ceremony, they dance only as far as the household *patio* cross with the church organizations; if it is a ceremony in the public plaza, they dance all the way from the *pascola ramada* back to the church, but they do not dance into the church, as do the *matachinis*.

There are other special kinds of processions, such as that during a child funeral and those on Palm Sunday and Easter Sunday morning, in which the *pascolas'* dance is an essential feature.

The dance of the *pascolas* obviously plays a different part in ceremony from those of the other dancers. It will become clear as we proceed that the *pascolas* may be characterized to some extent as profane performers, in contrast with the sacred members of the ceremonial societies, from whose activities their dance is kept somewhat apart. In this connection we may emphasize the following points. Their dance is kept separate from the dancing and other activities of the church groups during the greater part of any ceremony; it follows its own sequence with only slight regard for the prayers of the *maestros* or the dances of the *matachinis* or *fariseos*. This separation is maintained except when the church organizations first appear at the household and when they leave. At these times the *pascolas* join in procession with them, leading the church groups to the house or escorting them away. At a ceremony in the public plaza there is the same procedure of welcoming and escorting-away of the church groups. Whenever in processions the *pascolas* join the church groups, they bring their own musician (the *tampa'leo*) to play for them while they dance; they do not make use of the *matachín* or *fariseo* musicians.

The "pascolas" as ceremonial hosts.—During a ceremony the *pascolas* are constantly addressing themselves to and being addressed by the crowd. There is always a crowd of persons sitting or standing in front of the *pascola* side of the *ramada*, watching, laughing, and exchanging words with the *pascolas*. If *matachinis* and *pascolas* both are present at the ceremony, it usually happens that the *matachinis* dance with hardly an interested spectator to watch them; but it is rare for the *pascolas* to dance unwatched. The *matachinis* pay no attention to the crowd, but the crowd is the chief concern of the *pascolas*.

This situation is a result of the fact that a part of the ritual duties of the *pascolas* consists frankly in keeping spectators interested. The other ceremonial participants, the *matachinis*, the *maestros*, the *fariseos*, and the *cantoras* address themselves in their ritual always and only to God, Jesus, and Mary, never to living persons. But the *pascolas* address themselves to gods only for a brief few minutes at the beginning of their ritual. The rest of the time they are concerned with the crowd and deal directly with them.

It is said in so many words by some of the more thoughtful Pascuans that the *pascolas*' duties consist in "calling the people" to the *fiesta* and in keeping them "awake and active" during its progress. The methods by which they accomplish this are numerous. The dance itself is interesting to people and is watched carefully and frequently criticized, but the dance is less interesting than other things which the *pascolas* do. These activities consist mainly in what we shall discuss below as clowning. Here we shall go into their activities as hosts.

We have mentioned the fact that at a household *fiesta* the *pascolas* do not come from the church to the household. They are already there when the church organizations arrive. They go out to the *patio* cross ahead of the *fiesteros* and bring back the church organizations, dancing ahead of them to the house *ramada*. At the beginning of the ceremony the oldest *pascola* makes a speech, addressing himself to the crowd. He describes the purpose of the ceremony and urges everyone to come to it and see it carried out. He explains that it is a time for rejoicing (this applies to a child funeral as well as to other kinds of *fiestas*) and says that the *fiesteros* want people to enjoy themselves. A little later he greets in a fixed ritual manner the musicians who are to play for the *pascolas*, asking them about the state of health of themselves and their families. Then he greets all the nearest members of the crowd, touching their hands in the standard Yaqui greeting and speaking to them. Then he greets the leading members of the church organizations, welcoming them to the *fiesta;* and, finally, he faces the crowd and shouts the standard Yaqui greeting, '*Dios em tʃani'abu*, to all.

Before the *pascolas* begin to dance, they hand out cigarettes, which the *fiesteros* have provided and the *moros* have prepared, to ceremonial participants and to members of the crowd. The giving of cigarettes continues throughout the ceremony. A *pascola*, it is said, may not refuse to give cigarettes to anyone who asks. Men and women smoke the *fiesteros'* cigarettes all night. When the tables are set and food is served to members of the church organizations, a table is reserved for the *pascolas*. They ask members of the crowd to come and eat with them, and they pass out bowls of food and cups of coffee to all who will accept them. They also give out drinking water to members of the crowd during the ceremony.

In addition to these activities, the *pascolas* make an effort during the night, between their dances, to draw members of the crowd into conversations. The conversations are not serious. They are part of the clowning activities. They discuss at great length the state of health of imaginary relatives of persons in the crowd and make jokes about anything they can think of. They carry on absurd conversations with drunken persons, and the crowd laughs.

The *pascolas'* part in a ceremony is closed with a long speech by the oldest dancer, explaining again why the ceremony was held and expressing the hope that everyone has enjoyed himself and has spent a pleasant night.

The "pascolas" as clowns.—The *pascolas* are most frequently described by Pascuans as *payasos* (Spanish for clowns). The greater part of their activities, aside from the dancing, is devoted to clowning. As a part of the standard sequence in the opening ritual, they perform certain antics which are invariably laughed at by the crowd. One such series is that during which they are supposed to be "warming up" for the dance. In this they have long struggles with various parts of their bodies in an effort to "catch" them and make them co-operate in the dance. In the badger dance they imitate animal movements and cries, and these, too, are funny to the crowd. They carry on horseplay with one another and sometimes with persons in the crowd at various times during the night.

Another aspect of their clowning consists in the misuse of words and ideas. In the greeting ritual described above they use the proper words for a Yaqui greeting, but they always address the person spoken to by a wrong title. They never use a proper name but call a *matachini* a *maestro*, a *maestro* a *caballero*, a person with no ceremonial affiliation a *matachín* *'kovanau*, etc. This misuse of village titles is a source of extreme amusement to the crowd. *Pascolas* have a fairly well-established system of words, phrases, and ideas wrongly used but of which they and the crowd understand the meaning. For instance, if someone asks for a cigarette, a *pascola* will inform another *pascola* that a man in the crowd wants a woman with her hair tied up in a red ribbon. Or if a person asks for a drink of water, a *pascola* will discuss at length the nature of a certain lake or river and finally say that someone in the crowd wants to take a walk beside the lake. There is a set of words which have no meaning outside the *pascolas'* usage, such as a nonsense word used instead of the usual Yaqui expression for "thank you."

The greater part of the *pascola* clowning consists in long stories told jointly by two or more *pascolas* or in monologue or in co-operation with someone in the crowd. The stories may describe a ridiculous situation which the *pascola* claims to have gotten into or they may be pure extemporaneous nonsense. A frequent element in such stories is the indelicate description of a love affair or an obscene reference of some kind.

One of the most frequently used of the *pascolas'* sources of humor is that of burlesque, and particularly burlesque of other dancers. *Pascolas* sometimes imitate in a ridiculous manner the dancing of the *matachinis*. But the most usual burlesque of this type is in connection with the deer-dancer, a performer who, when he appears, dances in the *pascola ramada*. The nature of the deer-dance burlesque will be described below when that performer is discussed. The clowning activities of *pascolas* at weddings may be considered under this head of burlesque. At a wedding there are two *pascolas*, one who represents the bride and one who represents the groom. While the serious ceremony of marriage is taking place on one side of the household *ramada*, the two *pascolas* carry on an absurd burlesque of the marriage ceremony and the marriage relationship. The burlesque is charged with obscenity at times, but consists mainly of a simple farce. The *pascola* representing the groom places a comb in the other *pascola*'s hair and puts a necklace about his neck. The man's *pascola* sits on a blanket and the bride's *pascola* sits on his lap. They talk at length, after a little obscene horseplay. The bride's *pascola* points out all the faults in the house and *patio* of the groom and says that she will clean it up and make things look better. Then she intimates that the well is dirty and that the drinking water is full of mud. The groom's *pascola* insists that it is not and says that he will prove it. He pretends to be getting water, but actually fills a glass with whiskey and hands it to the bride's *pascola*. The latter looks for dirt in it, holding it up to the light, and then drinks it. Then both *pascolas* give out whiskey to the crowd, to their musicians, and to themselves. They and the crowd get drunk. Meanwhile the crowd has been laughing uproariously at the *pascolas'* burlesque.

The *pascolas*, then, have an important clowning function in the carrying-out of which they make use of grotesque gestures and postures, misuse of words, funny stories, obscenity, and burlesque of serious performers and ceremonies.

Other functions.—The *pascolas* also perform other ritual functions. One of these is the throwing of flowers at the *fariseos* in the climax of the Easter ceremonies on Holy Saturday, the implications of which will be discussed below. They also perform exorcism rites at the beginning of a *fiesta*. These can best be taken up as part of a detailed analysis of the opening ritual carried out by *pascolas* just before they begin their dance at any *fiesta*.

The "pascola" opening ritual.—An examination of the opening ritual used by the *pascolas* reveals the manner in which their various functions are combined, their relationship to the other ceremonial performers, and the interesting combination of Christian and aboriginal ritual in their activities. It is worth while, therefore, to discuss the sequence of ritual acts in detail. The sequence which will be described is that which the *pascolas* go through at the beginning of a household or public plaza *fiesta*, other than a wedding or a baptism. It is used by the *pascolas* to introduce their dance at all such *fiestas* outside of the Easter ceremonial season. During the latter season only a few parts of it are used.

The ritual entrance may be broken up into twelve distinct parts. The first five parts are carried out with the assistance of the *moro;* after that the *moro* has nothing more to do with the ritual activities of the *pascolas*, although he frequently stays in the *pascola ramada* and makes cigarettes for the *pascola* to give out and also conducts the *pascolas* to and from the dining-table and when they have to answer calls of nature.

The *pascola*, fully costumed and with his mask over his face, is led to the dancing *ramada* by the *moro*. For this purpose the *moro* has a small wooden stick; he holds one end of it, and the *pascola* holds the other. If there is more than one *pascola*, the others hold onto the belts of the *pascolas* in front of them. The musicians are already in the *pascola ramada*. The *moro* leads the *pascola* around between the *tampa'leo* and the *ar'pero*, making three circles. The *pascola* makes shrill cries from time to time, an action which is carried out at irregular intervals during the rest of the entrance sequence. The cries are said to be in imitation of coyotes.

The *moro* places his end of the stick on the sounding box of the harp, and the *pascola*, with his mask still over his face, leans on the stick. He speaks in Yaqui, addressing his remarks to the village at large, but facing the *ar'pero*.

He announces the occasion of ceremony and asks all well-disposed people to come and enjoy themselves. At intervals in the speech he shakes his hips, tinkling the belt bells, and crosses himself in an unorthodox way, by bringing his thumb up high above his mask to the topknot on his head instead of only to his forehead in the proper manner. This is regarded as funny. After three such crossings have been made, the speech is continued.

The *moro* picks up his end of the stick and leads the *pascola* from the harpist over into the altar side of the *ramada*. Immediately the *pascola* pushes his mask from in front of his face to one side. He and the *moro* kneel before the altar, cross themselves, and say the usual Yaqui prayer, the *'santa 'kusta im 'hunak te'akame*, which it is proper to say before the altar. The *pascola* crosses himself in the proper way.

When the prayer is finished, the *pascola* and *moro* rise, and the *moro* takes hold of his end of the stick and leads the *pascola* out to the *patio* cross and shoots off one or more *cohetes*. He slips the mask to the side of his head again, says a prayer and crosses himself, then puts the mask over his face. The *moro* leads him back to the dancing side of the *ramada*. More shrill cries are uttered on the way.

Again the *moro* leads the masked *pascola* around in three circles between the *tampa'leo* and the *ar'pero*. At the completion of the last circle, he places his end of the stick on the harp and leaves the *pascola* there. The *moro*'s part in the sequence is over. He has conducted the *pascola* through the ritual involving the altar and the *patio* cross. From this point on the *pascola*'s actions have nothing to do with Christian ritual.

The *pascola* leans against the stick and begins to talk. He recites mock prayers, calling on various animals to help him in the dancing that is to follow. The animals which he addresses are "small ones," such as horned toad, lizard, turtle, frog, and small animals which live in the ground. He addresses each one as "saint," such as *'santo 'vovok* ("Saint Frog"). These entreaties for assistance and the use of the term "saint" in connection with the animals are regarded by Pascuans as funny. They do not laugh much during the speeches, but they explain their meaning with grins and sometimes with laughter. At the conclusion of the "prayers" to the animals, the *pascola* begins an exorcism rite. Standing facing the harpist and with his mask over his face, he draws three lines on the ground with the end of the stick by which he was led out by the *moro*. The lines all cross in the center, forming an asterisk-shaped figure. If there is another *pascola* present, he makes a similar figure in the air with his forefinger. As this is done, the *pascola* says that all evil spirits living in the direction in which he is facing (usually west) must keep away from the *fiesta*. Then he turns to his right and makes the same sign and repeats the same words, then toward the *tampa'leo*, and then to his right again, completing the circuit of the four directions.

The *pascola* takes the stick and begins to walk around aimlessly between the *tampa'leo* and the other musicians in the area prepared for the dance. He carries on a monologue in which he explains that he has to get his feet "warmed up" for the dance. Sometimes he continues to call on the animals to help him. He may, however, talk of anything at all and wander into long stories which make the crowd laugh.

Then he goes gack to the harpist and stands facing him,

still talking. The harpist and violinist have meanwhile begun to play the *canário* piece. The *pascola* talks at length about the difficulty of getting himself ready to dance. Suddenly, at a certain point in the music, he grasps a leg, an arm, or his head, and jumps up and down holding on to it. This is the "catching" ceremony mentioned above, in which the *pascola* catches various parts of his body in an effort to prepare them for the dance.

When he has finished the struggle with the various parts of his body, the *pascola* leaves the harpist and goes to the other end of the *ramada*. Here he stands facing the *tampa'leo* and the crowd. He takes out his *se'nasum* and begins to shake it. The *tampa'leo* is playing his drum and whistle now, and the *pascola* may break into a few steps of a dance as he rattles his *se'nasum*. He speaks from time to time about his difficulties in getting started and explains that he has to warm up his *se'nasum*. He keeps the mask over his face.

Finally, the *pascola* puts the *se'nasum* back in his belt and reaches over and touches hands with the *tampa'leo* in the standard Yaqui greeting. He acts as though he has just met the *tampa'leo* and inquires as to the health of his family, what he has been doing, etc. After a lengthy conversation about nothing in particular, the *pascola* turns and greets the harpist and violinist in the same way. Then he greets the members of the crowd in the same way, but carefully calling each one by some title or name which is not his. The *maestros* and members of the participating ceremonial societies are also greeted. When this is done, the *pascola* places the stick, by which the *moro* led him out, in the thatch of the *ramada* roof.

Cigarettes are given out to performers and to the crowd, and the dance begins. The first dance is always to the harp and violin and the second to the drum and whistle. The type of music then alternates throughout the rest of the night.

THE DEER-DANCER

The deer-dancer is a colorful figure in Yaqui ceremony, but his appearances in Pascua are infrequent. He appears only in conjunction with the *pascolas* and dances at the same time the latter do in their side of the *pascola ramada*, but he is by no means necessary at any ceremony in which *pascolas* appear. While the *pascolas* danced at twenty-five ceremonies in 1936–37, the deer-dancer appeared only four times. The deer-dancer is neither a clown nor a ceremonial host. His activities are confined to his dance.

The nature of the deer dance.—The deer-dancer (*'maso* in Yaqui), like the *pascola*, wears nothing above the waist or on the feet when he dances. From his waist to his knees is a skirtlike garment, under which at present in Pascua is usually worn a pair of trousers rolled up above the knees. *'Teneboim* (cocoon rattles) and belt rattles are also worn. The deer-dancer does not wear a mask but dances with a stuffed deer's head tied to the top of his own head. As he dances, he holds a large gourd rattle in each hand and shakes them constantly.

The dance is vigorous, wholly unlike that of the *pascola*. The body is sometimes bent over so that the rattles in the hands nearly touch the ground; the head, with the deer head protruding in front of it, is twisted about during the whole dance. The hands nearly touching the ground and the moving head are regarded as an imitation of a deer walking on all fours, constantly looking about for pursuers. The deer-dancer dances only when the *pascola* is performing to the music of the *tampa'leo*.

The deer-dancer has his own musicians. They are called *maso'wikame*, or deer-singers. There are three of them. Two play wooden rasps, one end of which is supported by a half-gourd resonator. The third beats a half-gourd which is floating in a pan of water. As they play, they sing. The music is entirely non-Spanish. The words are Yaqui, many of them being obsolescent and not now in daily use. They have to do with the life of the deer and other animals and birds, including descriptions of the trees and flowers among which they live. There are no references to Christian gods or ritual.

The deer-dancer has no elaborate opening ritual like that of the *pascola*. He goes immediately to the altar in the *ramada*, prays briefly, then goes to the *patio* cross and shoots off one or more *cohetes*. He returns immediately and begins his dance, which is continued throughout the night until after dawn. The deer-dancer has no connection with any ceremonial society, and his activities are not co-ordinated with other ritual groups, except in processions, when he joins the *pascolas* and *tampa'leo*.

The deer-dancer is the constant butt of the *pascolas'* jokes. It is a customary part of the *pascolas'* activities to stumble over the deer-dancer, interfere with his dance, imitate all his movements, and attempt to make him laugh. It is also part of the deer-dancer's role not to laugh and always to ignore, in so far as he can, the actions of the *pascolas*. The mock conflict between the *pascolas* and the deer-dancer is one of the greatest sources of amusement for the *fiesta* crowd.

History of the deer dance in Pascua.—The deer dance as it now exists is evidently a pruned and modified version of a more elaborate dance ritual. Middle-aged and older persons in Pascua describe aspects of the deer dance of which there was no trace in the 1936–37 performances. They speak of a mock deer hunt which took place at dawn or shortly after, in which the *pascolas* acted as hunters and went through an elaborate hunting scene, eventually catching the deer-dancer, pretending to skin him, and carrying him home to their wives. This hunt with most of the described details seems to have taken place as a regular feature of the *pascola* dance as recently as five years ago. It is admitted that it is no longer carried out, although it is often said that it should be. Another feature of the dance which is not now carried out, but which is spoken of as having occurred at deer dances in Pascua, is the throwing of water at dawn by the deer-dancer. At the first show of light, it is said, the deer-dancer went to the gourd drum and began scattering water at persons in the crowd. If it fell on a woman, it would help her to have children. No trace of this ritual was seen at the deer dances in 1936–37.

The four appearances of the deer-dancer during 1936–37 were at a household *fiesta*, at the *fiesta* of St. Ignatius, on Palm Sunday, and on Easter Sunday. It was said frequently during the year that there would be a deer dance at other *fiestas*, at *fiestas de promesa*, at *cumpleaño* death ceremonies, and at other saint's-day *fiestas*. The predictions, however, did not materialize. This seems to indicate that the deer-dancer is not now appearing at all ceremonies at which he might appear—in other words, that he is going out of vogue in Pascua.

NATIVE INTERPRETATIONS

There are a number of stories current in Pascua which say that the *pascolas* came originally from the devil. A typical one is as follows:

Once the *fiesteros* of Guadalupana (the Virgin of Guadalupe) were planning to have a very big *fiesta*. They wanted to have a lot of *pascolas*, but there were no *pascolas* anywhere, so they started looking everywhere. Finally the *fiesteros* went to see *El Diablo*. They asked him whether he had any *pascolas*, and he said that he had quite a number. They asked him if he wouldn't order them to come up and dance at the *fiesta* that they were going to have. The devil said he couldn't do that because he needed the *pascolas* himself. Then he said that he might lend them to the *fiesteros* if they would promise him that the *pascolas* would come back right away as soon as they were through. The *fiesteros* said that they would see to that. The devil still didn't want to let the *pascolas* go because he said he was afraid that they would remain with the Yaquis after the *fiesta*. But finally he agreed to let them go. The *pascolas* came up and danced at the *fiesta*, but before they danced they crossed themselves and took a *bendición* in the name of Jesus Christ. As soon as this happened, the devil began to be worried. He said, "What a fool I was. I knew this was going to happen. I shouldn't have let the *pascolas* come up and dance. They can't come back any more now." But there was nothing the devil could do, and the *pascolas* never went back but stayed with the Yaquis. That is why the *pascolas* always cross themselves before they put on their masks now. That is the same reason why the *ʧapa'jekam* also cross themselves and put rosaries in their mouths before they put their masks on.

Other stories are more vague but have the essential idea that the Yaquis first obtained the *pascolas* from the devil and that they have stayed with the Yaquis because they performed certain Christian ritual and could not go back to the devil.

There are other stories which have to do with the origins of the *pascolas* and their ritual. One of these says that the *pascolas* first came to the Yaquis because people from "the country" came to the pueblos for *fiestas* and they were not interested in the ceremonies, so the *fiesteros* had to get someone to keep them amused while they were at the *fiesta*. It was the *pascolas* who were secured to fill this function. They have performed it ever since, and the dances which they do are *puros diversiones*, "just entertainment."

But the dances are not interpreted by everyone as pure entertainment, even though the second *maestro*, among others, draws a sharp distinction between the character of the *pascolas'* dances and those of the *matachinis* and *fariseos*. He says that he would not say that the *pascola* dance is *'tekipanoa* as is the *matachín* dance. It is not work for the Virgin, and he does not think that it is work even for Jesus; it is something altogether different. It is true that it amuses people at a *fiesta*, but there is something more about it. The *pascolas* and the deer-dancer have the power of all kinds of animals (*la virtúd de cada animal*); they get this power, according to myth, from streams of water in the mountains or out in the country somewhere. Each *pascola* does not get it there now, but that is where it came from originally. This is where their musicians get their power also. It comes from the animals. This is different from the *matachinis* and from the *fariseos*, too. They are connected not with animals but with the Virgin and Jesus. It is because they are connected with the wild animals that the *pascolas* and deer-dancer dance in the *ramada* and not in the church. But, nevertheless, says a *'temasti*, they are part of "our religion," too.

These statements by no means cover all the interpretations of the *pascolas* current in the village, but they seem to represent the general conception of what the *pascolas* mean. There is, however, a *maestro* who has been much interested in the *pascolas* and has thought out, possibly by himself, a number of interpretations of *pascola* paraphernalia and ritual. He has made use of Christian doctrine in his interpretations, and his statements seem to be attempts to reconcile the *pascolas* with Christian ritual. He believes that the *pascolas* and deer-dancer are the "oldest" of the Yaqui ceremonial performers. This is because they have to do with the nativity, the earliest part of the life, of Christ. Jesus was born in a manger among animals, and it is for this reason that the *pascolas* do animal dances. They do not wear shirts because Jesus did not wear a shirt. He wore only a cloth around his waist, as is evident on all the crucifixes. The blanket worn by the *pascola* represents the cloth worn on the crucifix. The beard on the mask represents the beards of the Apostles, and the dance indicates the joy of the Apostles at the Resurrection. It is possible also that the *pascolas* are connected with Noah's ark and represent the animals that were in the ark. One of these ideas, that of the *pascolas*' blanket being a symbol of the cloth worn by Jesus on the crucifix, has currency throughout the village. The other ideas do not seem to be held by others, although there may be some who are familiar with them.

ATTITUDES TOWARD THE "PASCOLAS"

The third *maestro*, whose interpretations of *pascola* ritual and costume we have just noted, has a great interest in the *pascolas*. He enjoys talking about then, explaining their functions, and speculating about their origins. He takes not only pleasure but also pride in them. He believes that the *pascolas* are the most distinctively Yaqui of all ritual performers in Pascua. He says that other Indians, and even Mexicans, have *matachinis* and *fariseos;* they also have *maestros* and *cantoras*, but they do not have *pascolas*. Wherever you have *pascolas*, there you have Yaquis. When it was pointed out to him that other peoples do have *pascolas* in northern Mexico, he said immediately that they borrowed them from the Yaquis. "The Yaquis taught the Papagos about the *pascolas*." The *pascolas* are a symbol to him of Yaqui culture, and he is very proud of them.

He thinks, however, that the *pascolas* are somewhat degenerate in Pascua. He claims that they speak "imprudently" sometimes and that no Pascua *pascola* has the proper voice or knows the proper things to say. His criticisms are not specific. They do not seem in any way to interfere with his pleasure in a *pascola* performance, nor do they indicate any opposition on his part to the general institution of the *pascola*.

The third *maestro's* attitude of delight and pride in the *pascolas* is shared by many others, including all the leading men in the village. But there is current also another attitude, best exemplified in another *maestro*, named Salvador Muñoz. Muñoz was born and brought up in the United States and has had many intimate contacts with white Americans since his early schooldays. This man believes with conviction that children should be kept away from the *pascola* performances. He says that the obscenity and the jokes dealing with sex relations are bad for anyone, and particularly for children, to hear. He himself does not go to *fiestas* and watch the *pascolas*. He says that he does not understand what the *pascolas* do or why they do it. He cannot understand why they should want to address animals as "saints." Muñoz's most intimate friend in the village was Pascua's leading *pascola* dancer in 1936–37, and the son of the dancer is also a good friend of Muñoz's. The son agrees with Muñoz in his opinion of *pascola* dancing and says often that he is "ashamed" of the fact that his father is a *pascola*.

The attitudes of the third *maestro* and Muñoz probably represent the extremes of opinion in regard to the *pascolas* in the village. Other persons enjoy the dances and ritual and speak with interest and pleasure of them but have no very definite convictions about their goodness or badness. Some combine an enjoyment of the dance and jokes with a tendency to disapprove of the obscenity.

SUMMARY

The *pascolas* may be distinguished from other ritual dancers in Pascua in a number of different ways. They do not constitute a ceremonial society and their activities are not integrated with those of the church organizations in the same way as are those of other dancers, like the *matachinis* and *fariseos*. They have the distinctive function of ceremonial host, which gives their ritual activity the character of being directed not to a deity but to the profane nonparticipants at a ceremony.

The *pascolas* combine obviously Christian with obviously non-Christian elements in their ritual. They dance to European music played on the harp and violin and they cross themselves at the altar, but most of their paraphernalia and actions seem to be non-European in origin. The deer-dancer, with whom they are closely associated in ceremony, seems an almost wholly aboriginal figure. The *pascolas* are intimately connected with animals in many ways and make it a point to address certain animals as their "saints." Their ritual evidently appears contradictory to some Pascuans, and efforts are made in myth and story to reconcile their combination of sacred and profane features.

Some of the results of these efforts have been set forth. In them it is possible to see myth-making in process. The second *maestro* sees clearly the distinction between *pascolas* and other dancers when he refuses to call the dance of the former *'tekipanoa*. He seems to be aware of the historic differences of origin between *pascolas* and, for example, *matachinis*, or at least to recognize that the former derive from a tradition which is at variance with the Christian. He is sufficiently immersed in Christian viewpoints to feel that the "power of animals" is not a Christian power. This kind of feeling, it may be suggested, has given rise to the myth of their origin which is most widespread in the village, namely, that which derives them from the devil and thereby explains their profane and non-Christian nature as a result of their earliest profane contacts.

It is evident, however, that a diabolic origin does not explain away all their contradictions. The third *maestro* has been thinking about the *pascolas* in quite a different way from that of whoever produced the myth linking them with the devil. This man feels that they have (or perhaps ought to have) a more intimate connection with present-day Yaqui religious belief than the myth suggests. He is interested in relating in detail their actions and paraphernalia to orthodox Christian tradition. He has, for example, let his fancy play over the animal affiliations of the *pascolas* and has found an explanation for them in the story of Noah's ark. Following the same approach, he has been able to explain many other details in Christian terms. In doing this, he is discarding completely the tradition from which the *pascolas* actually derive. As yet his speculations have been accorded no general acceptance in the village, but the tendency which he expresses in intellectual ways is, nevertheless, apparent in the vaguer feelings of the villagers.

Their reaction to the ambiguity of the *pascolas* is expressed most clearly in the feeling that they ought to be, even though they actually are not, dedicated to Jesus. They are equating them as ceremonial performers with the *fariseos* and the *matachinis*. There is the feeling that they must somehow be, like the other dancers, devotees of one of the important functioning Christian deities. If they could be so interpreted, then it would not be necessary to explain the details of their ritual. If other factors remained the same (which, of course, they will not), we might expect that the *pascolas* would in the course of time be constituted as a ceremonial society and thus made consistent with the prevailing ceremonial pattern. Meanwhile they remain the object of somewhat conflicting attitudes of approval and disapproval.

CHAPTER VIII

THE CEREMONIAL SYSTEM: EVENTS AND PATTERNS

THE forms of ceremony are a constant source of interest to Pascuans. The tedium which begins to overwhelm a non-Yaqui after hours of witnessing or discussing ceremonial events seems foreign to Yaquis. They may be weary, but they never seem bored. The forms themselves remain fascinating, perhaps because they cannot, for a Yaqui, be separated from their meanings, even though the latter remain somewhere in the regions to which mere verbalisms do not penetrate. An account of ceremony which did not dwell on the minutiae of ritual would be alien to the Yaqui viewpoint, for it is these details which constitute a major aspect of life-activities.

Nearly half the days of a year are wholly or partially occupied with some kind of ceremony. The actual figure is one hundred and seventy-one. This does not include private observances within a household; it refers only to ceremonies of a public character at which members of one or more of the ceremonial societies officiate. By no means everyone in the village or every member of a ceremonial society participates in or even attends each of these ceremonies. The attendance varies greatly. In the autumn, when many families are in the fields picking cotton, a ceremony such as an October *novena* for the dead may go on with perhaps only a single woman as spectator. Or in the winter, when it is cold, a Sunday service may be conducted by only the *maestro mayor*, and there may be no nonparticipants at all. Attendance at the important ceremonies, such as All Souls' Day in November, on the other hand, may include the whole village, even though the majority of the families have to come back from the cotton fields for the occasion. The number of participants and nonparticipants depends both on the character of the ceremony and on the time at which it occurs. But whether or not there is only a single *maestro* in the village, the yearly round goes on. The fact that there were one hundred and seventy-one days on which ceremonies occurred in 1936–37 is an indication of the great interest and great amount of time spent in Pascua in ceremonial observances.

THE CEREMONIAL CALENDAR

The framework of the ceremonial life is the calendar of the Catholic church. All the fixed dates, which constitute about two-thirds of all ceremonial occasions, are Catholic ones. The other third consists of personal crises, which, of course, occur at any time during a year. These latter also, with a few exceptions, have the sanction of the Catholic church. A funeral, a wedding, or a baptism, for instance, all have their counterparts in the ceremonial life of Tucson Catholics. Even the death *novena* (given within nine days after the funeral) and the death *cumpleaño* (given one year after the funeral) are ceremonies carried out in some form by Mexican Catholics. Only the *fiesta de promesa* (which is given in honor of a god in return for assistance in curing) and certain kinds of "confirmation" seem to be distinctively Yaqui. Thus we may say that practically all occasions for ceremony in Pascua have Catholic sanction.

The ceremonial calendar is by no means a rigid pattern. Its chief characteristic seems to be an easy flexibility. If the name day of St. Ignatius of Loyola falls on a Thursday, there will be an observance in the Yaqui church on that day, but the important *fiesta* for the saint will be postponed until the following Saturday, when more people can attend without interference with their jobs. Or if the Day of the Finding of the Holy Cross (Santa Cruz) falls on Monday, the observance of the date will be carried out on the Saturday and Sunday preceding. It is, in fact, the usual practice to hold important ceremonies on the week ends which are nearest to the proper date. That is, the *fiesta* or elaborate public observance of the date is so shifted, while a smaller ceremony involving fewer people is carried out on the proper day. Personal crisis ceremonies are adjusted in a similar manner to the work calendar. A death *novena*, for example, may be held on any day within nine days after death, and the death *cumpleaño* is carried out only approximately one year after the funeral.

The ceremonial seasons.—The year is divided into two ceremonial seasons, the characteristic feature of each being the dominance of a particular men's dance society. Thus from Ash Wednesday in February until the Day of the Finding of the Holy Cross on May 3 the *fariseo* society is in the ascendancy. During the rest of the year the *matachin* society is dominant. There is, however, an overlapping of the seasons. Although it is said that the *fariseo* season extends until May 3, the *matachinis* make their appearance on Easter Saturday and dance at all ceremonies from then until May 3, as well as after the latter date. The *matachín* *'kovanau*, moreover, assumes the duties of organizing ceremonies immediately after Easter Sunday. The role of the *fariseo jaut* as chief organizer is discontinued, although the *fariseos* continue to appear at ceremonies.

From Ash Wednesday until Easter Sunday the *fariseos*

perform all the duties that a dance society ordinarily performs at ceremonies. They appear not only at the processions during Lent and at the Holy Week ceremonies but also at the *fiestas de promesa* during the Lenten period. If anyone dies during this time, it is said that the *fariseos* would appear at the funeral and the *novena* and that they would make the *limosnas* for the ceremonies. All *limosnas* for whatever purpose are made by the *fariseos*. Besides performing their ritual duties at all ceremonies and organizing the latter, they are also charged with keeping order in the village, particularly at ceremonies. During this period the *matachinis* may not appear at all. It is said that the *fariseos* "don't like flowers," and the *matachinis*, having "flowers" on their headdresses, are therefore distasteful. The *matachinis*, however, at present do make one regular appearance during the season at the Palm Sunday ceremony. And in 1936–37 they also appeared at a *fiesta de promesa* in Lent because the *fiestero* had promised it to both the Virgin and Jesus.

During the rest of the year, from Easter Sunday until Ash Wednesday, the *matachinis* take over the general duties of the *fariseos*, such as organizing *fiestas*, dancing, and making *limosnas*. The *fariseos* make no appearances during this period after May 3, unless one of their number dies, when they appear with some of their paraphernalia at his funeral and other death ceremonies, or unless one of their number is in need of economic assistance, when they conduct a *limosna* for him. The interest which the *fariseos* show in maintaining order at ceremonies during their season is not shown by the *matachinis*. They seem to have no such civil duties at present.

Regardless of the season, the *maestros*, *cantoras*, and *ki'ostim* have the same duties and appear at all ceremonies.

Only the *caballeros*, of the other ceremonial societies, are affected by the season. Their activities are intimately associated with the *fariseos*, and consequently they make their appearances only in conjunction with the latter. They have no duties from May 3 until Ash Wednesday.

The kinds of ceremonies.—Strictly speaking, every ceremony has a different form for the reasons that each occasion of the calendar celebrates a different event and also that there is permitted a wide latitude in the ways in which the constituent ritual acts may be combined. The ceremony for St. Ignatius of Loyola requires frequent mention of that saint and, if possible, that a picture or image of him be on the altar; and St. Ignatius will not be mentioned perhaps at any other ceremony during the year. Similarly, on other dates in the fixed calendar there are special rituals proper to those dates and to none other. These differences, of course, give the ceremonies what individuality they have. They vary, however, in other ways. One *maestro* may conduct a funeral in a slightly different manner from that in which another *maestro* would conduct it. A portion of the ritual may be omitted or the order of events may be varied, owing to differences in training, knowledge, or specific circumstances of the event.

It is, nevertheless, possible to consider ceremonies in Pascua as conforming to two general types. The Yaquis themselves have many names for what they consider different kinds of ceremonies. Thus a saint's-day *fiesta* and a *fiesta de promesa* are both *'paχko*. A Sunday service in the Yaqui church goes by the Spanish name *rezar*, which is used as a noun. A funeral is a *ve'larowa* (from Spanish, *velación*, "wake"). A death *cumpleaño* is a *'lutupaχko*, which is a combination of the Spanish *luto* (mourning cloth) and the Yaqui word. There are many other names which serve in some measure to classify the ceremonies. But most of the terms have reference to the function of the ceremonies or to a combination of function and forms. It seems possible to discuss the ceremonies under two categories which have reference primarily to the forms. These two general forms are to some extent recognized in the Yaqui usage of the words *'paχko* and *rezar*. The *'paχko* is a *fiesta grande*, and the *rezar* is a simple offering of prayers before an altar. The distinction is that between a ceremony attended by many people for which extensive preparations of many kinds are necessary and a ceremony which may be carried out with no preparation by a few persons who do not expect a large attendance. We might make use of the Spanish word *fiesta* in speaking of the former and the English word "service" in speaking of the latter. The general pattern of Yaqui ceremony can be described with the use of these two terms, if special description is made of the major variations from the two principal forms.

The "service" takes place in the church in the public plaza, never at a private household. Its essential feature is a single altar before which prayers are offered and ritual dances performed. The latter may be dispensed with. If they are, then the only ritual performers necessary are *maestros* and *cantoras*. The service may last from one to four or five hours, never longer. Weekly Sunday observances, as well as many other ceremonies on the fixed calendar, take the form of the simple service.

The *fiesta* is a much more elaborate affair. Its essential characteristics are the following. (1) It lasts from the afternoon of one day throughout the night until the late morning or afternoon of the next day. (2) The initiative for its organization is taken by a group of persons, called the *fiesteros* or *paχ'kome*. The *fiesteros* may be of several different kinds. They may be the heads of a household, that is, a man and his wife and relatives of theirs, in which case the *fiesta* would be held at their house. They may be the owners of an image representing the god for whom the *fiesta* is being given. Or they may be acting as *fiesteros* in their capacity as members of some ceremonial society, in which case the *fiesta* would usually be held in the public plaza. (3) An essential feature of all the ceremonies which we are classing as *fiestas* is the presence of *pascolas*. (4) It is also necessary to have the co-operation of two or more of the ceremonial societies, the *maestros* and *cantoras*. The dance societies usually take part in their proper seasons, but they are not essential at every *fiesta*. At certain ones, most notably the *Fiesta de la Santa Cruz* in May, the *matachinis* are necessary; at others, for instance, the *fiestas de promesa* in Lent, the *fariseos* are necessary. But *maestros* and *cantoras* are always present. The *fiesta* may take place either at a private household or in the public plaza. (5) In any case, it is always a public ceremony, and it is considered important to have a large attendance, and preparations, such as the gathering of plenty of food and firewood, are made in this expectation.

The more specific elements of the *fiesta* are a procession participated in by the ceremonial societies from the church to the household (or to the *pascola ramada* if it is held in the public plaza), the *pascola* dances and ritual, services throughout the night by the *maestros* and *cantoras*, closing prayers and sermons by the *maestro*, and a final procession by the ceremonial societies back to the church. In other words, whether or not the *fiesta* takes place at a private household, the church is important as a base of operations for the ceremonial societies, and two altars, one in the church and one at the household (or *pascola ramada*), are essential in the ceremony. Other ritual acts may be introduced and usually are, but the features mentioned remain constant in all *fiestas*.

Some of the ceremonies which can be classed neither as *fiestas* nor as simple services will be indicated in the discussion of the ceremonial calendar which follows.

The major calendrical ceremonies.—Four ceremonies stand out as of greater importance during each year than any others. That is, the number of persons participating in them is larger than that in any others, they are attended by many more persons, and the interest in them is greater than that shown in any others. It is these four ceremonies which are not only extensively participated in by all persons present in the village when they occur but which also draw back to the village all or nearly all those persons whose jobs have taken them elsewhere. These four ceremonies are as follows:

1. Holy Week, or Easter, in March or April, called Semana Santa.
2. The Day of the Finding of the Holy Cross on May 3, called Día de la Santa Cruz.
3. Name day of St. Ignatius of Loyola on July 31, called Día de San Ignacio.
4. Day of All Saints on November 1 and Day of All Souls on November 2, called Días de los Muertos.

Of these, Holy Week and the Day of All Souls command the greatest interest and have the largest attendance. The latter occurs in the middle of the cotton-picking season, but every family which is a part of any household in Pascua comes back for the ceremonies. At Holy Week not only all Pascuans but also Yaquis from other villages, such as Marana and Eloy, are invariably present.

These four occasions are not celebrated in the same way. The days of St. Ignatius and of Santa Cruz are observed with *fiestas* of the general kind described above. The St. Ignatius *fiesta* takes place in the public plaza and is organized at present by those men in the village who are named Ignacio. It follows very closely the standard *fiesta* form. The Santa Cruz *fiesta* shows a number of variations from the pattern, although in most respects it is orthodox. Organized by the owners of the image of "Santa Cruz," it invariably requires *matachinis*, because the Santa Cruz is regarded as an image of the Virgin and must be honored, therefore, with a dance by her devotees. The Día de la Santa Cruz draws by far the largest number of participating *matachinis* of any *fiesta* during the year. In addition, there is a special ceremony in connection with the "Santa Cruz" which takes place neither at the church nor at the household of the *fiesteros* but at "Calvary," the highest point in the village where three wooden crosses are erected for the occasion. On the night of the *fiesta* persons in each household in the village make crosses of willow branches which have just turned green and place them on their houses. They then remove the crosses made the year before and burn them, so that the village is dotted during the evening with small bonfires.

Holy Week, which is by far the most elaborate and important of all, opens and closes with a *fiesta* of the usual form in the public plaza, the opening one occurring on Passion Saturday and Palm Sunday and the closing one on Easter Saturday and Sunday. In the days between these two *fiestas* there is a series of ceremonial events which are in part a Christian passion play and in part other ritual not interpretable as Christian. The ceremonies are continuous from Wednesday in Holy Week through Saturday, when the final *fiesta* begins. They are unique in the round of ceremony and deserve special treatment because of their complexity and importance.

The ceremonies of All Souls' Day are also unique, being similar to nothing else which takes place during a year. Two days, November 1–2, are occupied in ceremonies concerned with the commemoration of the dead. Food is set out on a table in the *patio* of each house in the village, and *maestros* and *cantoras* go from table to table, giving *responsos* for the dead of each family during the first day. The other day is occupied in giving *responsos* over the graves in the cemetery. The food which is set out is regarded as being for the dead, but the *maestros* and *cantoras* take it for themselves and their families. Other features of the occasion are *matachín* dances at the church and the burning of candles in the surrounding fields for persons "who died outside the village."

The ceremonial months.—During two months in the year there are daily services at the church in the plaza. The month of May is spoken of as "the mother of months," and special devotions are paid, during it, to the Virgin Mary. A service, participated in by *maestros* and *cantoras*, is held each evening before an altar containing images of the Virgin. Young girls of the village, wearing white veils, place flowers on a table before the altar at certain points in the service. The flowers are spoken of as "the flowers of May." An almost identical set of daily services is carried out in Tucson Catholic churches during the month.

October is the month of the dead. During this month all dead relatives of Pascuans are believed to be in the village both night and day. The first night of the month water and sometimes food are set out on tables in the *patios* of the various households. It is believed that this is eaten and drunk by the dead of each household. After the first night the food and water is taken away, and none is put out again until All Souls' Day in November, when the dead take their leave of the village. During the whole month of October there is a service each evening in the church. It is carried out by the *maestros* and *cantoras* present in the village. Prayers and chants are given before the altar, on which there is always a crucifix. The essential features of the services are the saying of the Rosary and the recitation by the *maestros* of long lists of the dead of the village. Attendance at such ceremonies, which last from two to three hours, is usually very small, most of the villagers being away in the cotton fields.

Other fixed ceremonies.—There is a service each Sunday throughout the year, except when a *fiesta* ends on Sunday morning. Then the usual service is dispensed with. During their ceremonial season the *matachinis* also dance each Sunday evening for an hour or more at the church, except during the cotton-picking season. These are regarded mainly as practice dances to train the *matachinis*, but they are always accompanied by a service, given by *maestros* and *cantoras* before the church altar, on which crucifixes and images of the Virgin are placed.

The other ceremonies appearing on the fixed calendar take place at the church and are of the same general type, with a few exceptions, as those occurring on Sunday. Some are morning services in which the *maestros*, *cantoras*, and often the *matachinis* take part. These are spoken of as *misas* by the Yaquis, although the orthodox Catholic Mass is carried out only in part. Others are called *vísperas;* they are carried out by *maestros*, *cantoras*, and *matachinis* and usually last from sunset until ten or eleven at night. All *misas* and all *vísperas* follow the same general form. There are two ceremonies which do not conform to these patterns. One is on Christmas Eve, or Noche Buena, which takes place in the church and lasts from dark until some time after midnight. *Maestros*, *cantoras*, and *matachinis* take part. Some families contract to make *tamales*, and these are given out about midnight to everyone in the church. On the eve of St. John's Day in June there is a service during the night at the church at which *maestros* and *cantoras* participate. At dawn the people go from the church to the irrigation ditch and plunge into the water.

In addition to the ceremonies mentioned on the fixed calendar, there are two other ceremonies which are important for Pascuans but which are not organized or carried out by them. One is the Fiesta de Santa Rosa, which is given at the Catholic church neighboring Pascua which is dedicated to Santa Rosa de Lima. Many Pascuans attend the vesper service preceding the day and go to listen to the Mass given by the Tucson priest on the morning of the day. In 1936 also the *matachinis* of Pascua danced both at the vespers and after the Mass. Much more important is the *fiesta* of St. Francis Xavier given at the Papago Mission south of Tucson. Large numbers of Pascuans, as well as Yaquis from all over Arizona, come to the three-day celebration of this saint. They do not participate, but they attend all the services, and it is here that many Pascuans who have been sick during the year carry out, individually, the ceremonies of the *hábito*. In 1936–37 Pascuans did not participate, but Yaqui *matachinis* and *pascolas* from Guadalupe danced in front of the Mission, and it is said that dancers from Pascua have participated in the past.

NONCALENDRICAL CEREMONIES

During 1936–37 there were fifty-six ceremonies held in Pascua which were not on the fixed calendar. By far the greater number of these, a total of forty, were connected with the deaths of individuals. The others were *fiestas de promesa*, weddings, baptisms, and "birthday parties." Other "crisis" ceremonies, such as confirmations and ceremonies of the *hábito*, are not included in these figures; they are always simply added features of calendrical ceremonies.

Death ceremonies.—It has already been pointed out a number of times that every adult death requires three ceremonies. Each of these is an elaborate event, lasting throughout a night or longer, and has many of the features of a *fiesta*. No death ceremony is a private occasion. Not only do the ceremonial societies participate but the whole village is informed, and there may be as many as one hundred and fifty nonparticipants present.

Death ceremonies differ according to whether the dead person is married or unmarried. We have already given some description of the unmarried person's funeral. Three ceremonies are not necessary for an unmarried person. The only ceremony is the *fiesta* which the *padrinos* give for the child and the child's parents. This is given usually the night following the death, although it may be postponed for a few days or even weeks, if the *padrinos* cannot raise sufficient funds to hold it or if it interferes with other things they are doing, such as their jobs. It follows the pattern of the *fiesta* as described above, and *pascolas* are essential to it. *Matachinis* dance at a child funeral if the child or his father or other member of the family is or has been a *matachini*. *Matachinis* may also dance simply if they are requested to, even though no one in the family is a *matachini*. The child funeral is held not at the house of the family of the dead child but at the house of his baptismal *padrinos*. The *padrinos* are considered to be the *fiesteros*. The *padrino* ritual, the services by the *maestros* and *cantoras*, and the *matachín* dance, if there is any, follow, in general, the pattern which will be described below for the adult funeral.

The adult funeral, the first of the three necessary death ceremonies, differs from the child funeral in that *pascolas* do not dance at it, relatives rather than *padrinos* are the *fiesteros*, and the scene of the ceremony is the house of the dead person. It may not be postponed until after burial, as the child funeral may be. The ceremony ordinarily takes place the night after death, and it centers around the body throughout the night and into the next morning, when burial takes place.

There is sometimes a conflict between the conventional pattern of funeral and the requirements of the county authorities in regard to the disposal of the dead. The latter require immediate notification of a death and the preparation of the body by an accredited undertaker in Tucson. The burial must be made within twenty-four hours of death, unless embalmment is paid for, and must take place in an established cemetery. Pascuans, in order to adjust their funeral requirements to those of the county, do not always notify the authorities of a death at the required time. If, for instance, a person dies during the night, notification will be made later in the day so that there will be time for the all-night funeral and the body will not have to be buried until the following morning. Efforts are made to avoid burial in the afternoon, because morning is the traditional time.

A city undertaker calls for the body, takes it into Tucson and prepares it for burial, and then brings it back again to the village, where he leaves it for the night. He calls for it again in the morning, takes it to the Catholic church in Tucson for a brief service by the priest, and then takes it to the city cemetery, where it is buried. The Yaqui funeral takes place during the night between the visits of the undertaker.

As soon as the undertaker returns the body, the top of the coffin is removed, and the body is taken out and placed on a wooden bench. A service, called the *rosario*, is given by *maestros* and *cantoras*. This is followed by the beginning of the ceremonies of preparation of the body for burial by the *padrinos*. Over the clothing which the undertaker has put on the body is placed a burial garment of white or blue voile, or two garments, one of each color. The dead person's clothing is rolled up and carefully placed under the head by *padrinos*. A great deal of attention is paid to the comfort of the head. The body meanwhile has been placed in front of an altar which has been constructed at the *patio* cross. It lies during the remainder of the ceremony in front of this altar, the head close to the latter, the feet pointing away from it. The position may not be altered, even if a rain comes. The next part of the ceremony is extremely important. It consists of the placing of rosaries and *'wikosam* on the body by the *padrino* group.[1] This is followed by a gathering of the *padrinos* and the relatives at the *encampamiento* cross, where a public thanking ceremony takes place, the relatives thanking the *padrinos* for their assistance. Meanwhile, if *matachinis* have come, preparations for their dance may begin, and they may at this time begin to dance, facing the body and

[1] See above, p. 105.

the altar. The services of the *maestros* and *cantoras* continue intermittently throughout the night with the recitation of prayers and the chanting of *alabanzas*. At some time during the night the relatives line up and take leave of the dead person. They go individually to the corpse, one after another, each kneeling and carrying out the Yaqui hand-touching greeting. As they do this they form a circle, and each makes the greeting three times. If the person has been a *matachini*, the *matachinis* dance again, place the *matachín* paraphernalia on the corpse, and finally break off in the midst of their dance and run away, not to return. In the morning the body is carried to the Yaqui church by the *padrinos*, where the *maestros* give another service over it. From here it is taken by the undertaker; as it is carried away, the church bell is tolled and firecrackers or *cohetes* are shot off.

While the body is given last rites in Tucson, at the Catholic church, where it is accompanied by *padrinos*, the relatives and a *maestro* go to the cemetery. When the body arrives at the cemetery, the *maestro* and *'temasti* give another service, using holy water, and the body is lowered into the grave. All present throw a handful of earth into the grave. The relatives are required to hide out of sight of the grave until the coffin is completely covered up. Then they return, and they and the *padrinos* place candles on the grave. The funeral is closed with a brief hand-touching ceremony between the relatives and *padrinos*.

Within nine days of the funeral there must be another ceremony, called the *novena*. This takes place also at the house of the dead person; the *fiesteros* for it are the relatives. It lasts from the afternoon of one day, through the night, until the morning of the next day. The *maestros* again lead the services assisted by the *cantoras;* and *mata-*

chinis or *fariseos*, according to the season, attend and dance or march during the ceremony. The relatives headed by a *maestro* form a procession and march through house and yard, scattering holy water over the places where the dead person most frequently sat or slept. This removes the final traces. The *padrinos* are present and carry out a hand-touching ceremony with the relatives. There is a final procession in the morning from the household back to the church by the ceremonial societies.

The *cumpleaño*, or *'lutupaχko*, is held approximately a year after the funeral. It closes the formal period of mourning for the relatives. It is held at the house of the dead person and extends over two days and two nights. The relatives are the *fiesteros*. The ceremony consists of two parts. The first day and night are taken up with formal mourning rites, the *'temasti* placing black cords about the necks of each of the relatives at the beginning of the ceremony. There are services by *maestros* and *cantoras* in front of the altar, and the mourners do not eat or carry on any kind of work for twenty-four hours. The following day the cords are formally removed by the *'temasti* and later are burned before the *patio* cross. The completion of the mourning obligations is then celebrated with a *fiesta*. The *fiesta* is of the usual pattern, with *pascolas*. *Matachinis* or *fariseos* may be present. The *fiesta* lasts all night and into the next morning.

"*Fiestas de promesa.*"—It has already been mentioned that *fiestas de promesa* are given as the result of a vow to a god. When a person is ill, he may vow that if he recovers he will give a ceremony. He may seek the aid of the Virgin for the cure or he may seek that of Jesus. If then he proceeds to get well, he has to give a series of annual *fiestas*, usually three, which are regarded as payments to the god for the cure. In Pascua the *fiesta de promesa* is usually promised for the Lenten season. Thus a person gives a *fiesta* in three consecutive years during Lent. If the promise has been made to Jesus, as it ordinarily is, then the *fariseos* have to be present at the *fiesta*. If it is made to the Virgin, then *matachinis* have to dance at the *fiesta*. Sometimes the promise is made to both Virgin and Jesus, and both *fariseos* and *matachinis* dance. A person may promise his *fiestas* for a season other than Lent. For instance, a vow was recently made in Pascua by the parents of a sick child to hold three *fiestas* on January 1, the Catholic date of the circumcision of Christ. The promise was made to Jesus, but the *fariseos* did not appear at the *fiesta*. It was enough to have the image of the Christ child on the altar. Whenever a *fiesta de promesa* occurs, it takes the form of the usual *fiesta*, with *pascolas*, and lasts throughout one night.

Weddings.—The wedding is a special type of ceremony which conforms to the pattern of no other. It consists actually of two separately organized *fiestas* which during the course of the events merge with each other. It is the only large-scale public ceremony of the general *fiesta* type which does not take place during the night. The usual *fiesta* is an all-night affair; the wedding is an all-day affair. *Pascolas* are essential at a wedding, but they neither dress nor act as they do at the usual *fiesta*. It has been mentioned that at weddings the *pascolas* do not wear masks. They dress in ordinary clothes. Their dances are about the same, but they do not dance to the music of the *tampa'leo*. Only the harpist and violinist appear. The *pascolas*' clowning takes a special form—burlesque of the bride and groom and their relationships.

A wedding begins as two separate *fiestas*. The family

and marriage *padrino* of the groom secure a *pascola* and orchestra, and the *pascola* begins to dance in the morning at the groom's house, while a feast is being prepared. Similarly, the family and marriage *madrina* of the bride have also organized a *fiesta* at the bride's house. Toward the middle of the day a procession, comprising the relatives and friends of the groom and his *pascola* and orchestra, march in procession to the bride's house, where there is a ceremonial meeting between the families at the *patio* cross. The groom's *pascola* and orchestra join with the bride's and begin to dance and play, and the two families eat at a common table. When the feast is over, a procession forms again, including both families, both *pascolas* and their orchestras, and all the onlookers. The procession marches back to the groom's house, where a second feast is held during which both sets of *pascolas* dance and carry on their burlesque of the marriage. A *maestro* is secured who, toward the end of the *fiesta*, gives a sermon, which is regarded as the ritual confirmation of the marriage. The *maestro* is the only member of a ceremonial society who participates in the ceremony; there are no *matachinis*, *fariseos*, or *cantoras;* there is no altar and consequently no altar services. Ritual hand-touching between the groups of relatives is carried out at the *patio* crosses.

Baptisms.—It is said by many persons in Pascua that it is proper to have *pascolas* at a baptism; it is said that *pascolas* should appear in the same way that they do at a wedding, without costume. But no *pascolas* appeared at any baptism during 1936–37. The tendency of the baptism is, in fact, toward departure from aboriginal Yaqui features. One baptism last year was accompanied by what the Yaquis speak of as a "Mexican dance," that is, dancing by couples in the fashion of the Tucson dance halls to the music of violin, clarinet, bass violin, and accordion. Other baptisms, however, followed a different pattern.

Unlike all the ceremonies mentioned thus far, the baptism in Pascua has a private character. As for the wedding, a single *maestro* is secured for the ceremony, but no other members of ceremonial societies take part. Moreover, attendance is never large, as it is at a wedding, and a baptism frequently takes placed in one part of the village without persons in other parts knowing anything about it. No effort is made to inform anyone except the relatives of the child baptized, the friends of his family, and the relatives of the *padrino* and *madrina*.

The ceremony in the village is preceded, like the marriage ceremony, with the usual baptism rites in the Catholic church in Tucson. The *padrino* and *madrina* bring the child back to the latter's house, where the ceremony takes place. It involves a feast, drinking, a hand-touching ceremony at the *patio* cross, and a sermon by the *maestro*. It lasts from a few hours to a half-day, depending on how much the people are enjoying themselves.

Birthdays.—It is customary to give a small party on the anniversary of one's birth, or saint's name day, in Pascua. These, too, are private in character, and no members of ceremonial societies take part in them, except a *maestro*. A "Mexican dance" may accompany them. There were only two known parties in Pascua in 1936–37. They are regarded as being in honor of the saint for whom one is named, as well as in honor of the person giving the party, hence the presence of the *maestro*.

THE ELEMENTS OF THE RITUAL

Although practically all occasions for ceremony are sanctioned by the Catholic church, the forms which the ceremonies take are by no means Catholic in the sense that they meet the approval of the Catholic church in Tucson. Each ceremony has a distinctive form which is peculiar to the Yaquis. It has many clearly Catholic elements, but it also has many elements which are definitely not Catholic. Even the church service called a *misa*, or Mass, by the Yaquis, although it makes use of the Roman missal, and follows the text for the Mass, does not conform to the Mass as given by priests in Tucson churches. The *maestro* recites from the missal and uses the words which would be used by a priest, but he stands some distance back in the church, facing but never going up to the altar. The way in which the Mass is carried out, in other words, is a variation from the orthodox method. In all other ceremonies the differences between Yaqui and orthodox Catholic ritual are even more pronounced. In some instances there are variations of this simple type, in others there are introductions into the ritual of elements which are entirely non-Catholic, and in others there are only Yaqui elements only. In short, the ritual of Pascua is a composite which shows definite Catholic features combined in intricate ways with features which are non-Catholic. Any attempt to say definitely which are which would unquestionably fail. Many features which appear to be Catholic, such as, for example, the altar, might easily be modifications of aboriginal features.

Every ceremony in Pascua is an organized pattern of numerous ritual elements. It is apparent, after one has watched many, that there are ritual forms which recur again and again in each ceremony. The constituent parts of different ceremonies may be the same. It is the general pattern which they form which varies. We shall now discuss those ritual elements which are combined in such varying forms in the Pascua ceremonies. By ritual elements we mean the smaller patterns of standardized behavior which are carried out as parts of larger wholes in each ceremony. Before we describe these, it will be necessary to give some description of a few of the objects which play an important part in the ritual.

The "patio" cross.—In each yard, usually but not always to the east of the house, there is a small, roughly made, wooden cross. This is called in Yaqui *te'vatpo kus*, or *patio* cross. It may be taken up temporarily if it is in the way of building operations or other activities, or it may be moved from one part of the yard to another; its location is not important. But the cross itself is important for any ceremony which takes place at the household.

Similarly, there is a cross of wood which stands permanently about forty paces to the east of the church. It is variously called *te'vatpo kus* and *cruz mayor*. It, too, figures in various ceremonies. Also there is a wooden cross in front of the *pascola ramada* in the plaza, which is used by the *pascolas* in their ceremonies. These two crosses in the plaza may be equated with the crosses in the yards of the individual houses. They go by the same names and are used largely for the same purposes.

There are other crosses in the plaza which have different uses. They are set at the four corners of the plaza and are used as turning-points in processions during certain ceremonies at Easter time. Also fourteen wooden crosses are set up in the streets surrounding the plaza at Easter and are called the Stations of the Cross. Many different kinds of uses are made of them during Lent and Easter.

The altar.—There are only two kinds of ceremonies which take place in Pascua which do not center around an altar. These are weddings and baptisms, both personal crisis ceremonies. In both, the *patio* cross of the household is important. In all others the *te'vatpo kus* may figure and usually does, but some form of an altar is the base for the ceremony. The activities of *maestros* and *cantoras*, which constitute the core of all ceremonies other than weddings and baptisms, are always linked with an altar and cannot be carried on apart from it.

We may distinguish three general types of altars: the *'teopo*, or church, altar; the *pascola ramada* altar; and the private household altar. The last is not be be confused with the altar set up in one side of the *pascola ramada* for a *fiesta* taking place at a household. Almost every house in Pascua has a small table set up in some part of the room, on which are kept crucifixes, images or pictures of the saints, and the paraphernalia of any members of the family who are *matachinis*. Such a table is regarded as an altar, and private devotions are carried on before it in the house by some families, but it never figures in a public ceremony. The altar which is used for a public *fiesta* is always set up only temporarily in a *ramada* outside the house. It is that which we refer to above as the *pascola ramada* altar.

The church, or *'teopo*, altar is the one which figures in every ceremony taking place in the church. At the west end of the building is a rough board table about three yards long. When no ceremony is in progress, the table remains uncovered. When a ceremony is in progress, it constitutes the altar. Its furnishings are kept in a locked room in the church or at the houses of members of the *ki'osti* society. The necessary furnishings are cloth covers of different kinds, images of the Virgin and saints, crucifixes, and various other paraphernalia which will be described below. The furnishings of the altar vary with the type of ceremony. A purple altar cloth is always used during the Easter season. A green cloth is used during the month of May. White or purple cloths are used during the rest of the year. Crucifixes and images of the Virgin are constant features of the altar at any time during the year, although the dresses of the Virgins and the loincloths of the Christs vary during the Easter season. The altar furnishings for nearly every church service consist of two crucifixes and three Virgins, but these numbers are not essential. During some services, as, for instance, those during October, only a single crucifix may be on the altar. Images or pictures of the various saints are placed on the altar on the days of the saints.

The *pascola ramada* altar is much the same as the church altar. As has been indicated, it is set up in one half of the *ramada*, the *pascolas* dancing in the other half. The character and uses of the *pascola ramada* altar in the plaza are the same as those in the household *ramada* altar. It is always set up by the '*temasti* and always has as an essential feature of its furnishings a small black crucifix, known as the '*temasti* crucifix. For death ceremonies of any kind the altar always has a black cloth; for other kinds of ceremonies it has a purple or white cloth. During the course of a ceremony, images from the church altar are brought in procession and deposited on the *pascola ramada* altar.

At any household ceremony temporary altars of another kind may be used. The *patio* cross, for example, is used by the *matachinis* as a place of deposit for their paraphernalia between dances. In addition to this, another cross is sometimes set up outside the fence surrounding the house. It is called the *encampamiento* cross, and a table is set up in front of it. Here are deposited temporarily the images brought from the church to the ceremony. The images are subsequently carried from the *encampamiento* to the house in procession by the *fiesteros*. These two should perhaps not be called "altars," in a strict use of the term. They serve only partially as such, being temporary places of rest for images. They do not fulfil the other functions of altars, namely, as objects of the devotions of the *maestros* and *cantoras*.

The "arco."—Frequently use is made at *fiestas* of two lengths of *carrizo* stuck in the ground near each other and bent over and tied together to form an arch. Bright-colored cloth is then draped in festoons over the arch. It goes by the Spanish name *arco*. Usually an *arco* is about five feet high, so that a person has to stoop to go under it. One is sometimes set up at the *encampamiento* altar and another between the sacred and profane halves of the *pascola ramada*. The Virgin-bearers and all others in procession, except the *fariseos*, go through the *encampamiento arco* when the church organizations arrive to take part in a household *fiesta*. *Pascolas* go under the *arco* in their *ramada* before beginning to dance. *Arcos* are never used at *fiestas* in the public plaza, although one is set up at an *encampamiento* altar outside the plaza in a ceremony on Palm Sunday. No native interpretations of the *arco* were recorded.

The altar devotions.—The altar is clearly the center of most ceremonies in Pascua. With the exceptions, as mentioned above, of the wedding and the baptism, no ceremony is ever carried on without an altar being set up. There may be and often are two altars at a ceremony, with two sets of devotions going on simultaneously at them. The church service, of course, always has its single altar in the church. The *fiesta*, however, always has two, both the church and the *pascola ramada* altars, and sometimes a third, the *encampamiento* altar. The funeral and death *novena* have the *encampamiento* altar sometimes, but usually in Pascua now there is only one set up at the household, and the church altar proper does not figure in the ceremony.

Devotions before the altar may be carried out by *maestros* and *cantoras*, by the dance societies, or by people not acting in the capacity of members of ceremonial societies. The devotions for these various groups follow certain patterns. The *maestros* offer prayers and chant, always facing the altar. The *cantoras* assist the *maestros* in the chants. The dance societies carry out their ritual dances in front of the altar. And persons who are not acting as ceremonial society members, as well as the latter, carry out the ritual acts called the *'muχti*.

The Latin, Spanish, and Yaqui prayers given by the *maestros* and *'temastim* are always given as the latter face the altar, as are the *alabanzas* which they and the *cantoras* chant. We cannot go into all the forms of the altar ritual which they carry out. It is made up of various combinations of prayers, either in Yaqui or in Spanish, which include the Ave Maria, the Pater Noster, the Credo, and the Salve. With certain of these the ritual acts of crossing one's self, smiting the breast, kneeling and placing the hands before the breast, palms together, are carried out. These acts and prayers in their various combinations punctuate every altar service. The rosary is used. *Maestros* ordinarily use a standard Catholic form of the rosary, but there is a form which is regarded as distinctively Yaqui. It is made simply of wooden beads and has a wooden cross at the end which always has a colored tassel, called the '*sewa* ("flower"), attached to it. The Rosary is said before the altar in the standard Catholic way and is essential in certain services connected with the dead and at the beginning of many other services.

The ritual made up of the above elements is carried out at the beginning or end of services which are read or chanted from the Roman missal, a copy of which is possessed by the head *maestro*. There are also fifty or more chants, called *alabanzas*, which are used at certain times in every service. There are *alabanzas* proper to the evening and others proper to the morning services. Still others are proper only at death ceremonies. The patterns of ritual, making use of the elements described, are standardized. There is, for example, a pattern of forms for a funeral from beginning to end, and the same pattern, with some additions, is used for a *novena* for the dead. Besides *alabanzas* and prayers, the latter patterns include a standard *difunto* service which involves the recitation of long lists of the names of the dead with their village offices. An evening service, or *víspera*, takes one form, the morning service another, and a *flores de mayo* service still another, but all include the same basic elements.

All the ritual elements mentioned are used by the *maestros*, '*temastim*, and *cantoras* at any kind of altar; that is, before the *pascola ramada* altar as well as before the church altar. The other ritual included in any ceremony except that of the *pascolas* is timed and adjusted to the ritual of the *maestros* and *cantoras*.

Detailed discussion of the forms of the ritual dance cannot be gone into here. But it is important to note that the *matachinis* carry out their dance as an altar devotion. An image of the Virgin must be on the altar as they dance, either one of the village images or their own. (There may be a substitution, as there was in 1937. The *matachinis'* image was broken, and an image of Jesus the Child was secured. This appeared on the altar when the *matachinis* were dancing.)

The *fariseos'* march-dance is also carried out as an altar devotion, but it may be carried on also apart from the altar, although within the plaza and near the church.

The '*muχti* is an altar devotion which any person in Pascua may carry out at certain times. There is an informal sort of '*muχti* which anyone makes when he comes to a ceremony, and there is the formal kind made by members of ceremonial societies at the beginning or end of their ritual duties. The '*muχti* consists simply of the acts of walking up to the altar, kneeling in front of it, kissing the ground before it, crossing one's self, rising and kissing each image on the altar and crossing one's self before each one, kneeling again before the altar and crossing one's self again. It is proper for anyone, on his arrival at a ceremony, to go up to the altar by himself and go through these acts. He may at the same time put some money in one of the *limosna* bowls before the images.

The formal '*muχti* takes a somewhat different form. Each person performing it goes through the acts described above, but they go in pairs always and sometimes (during Lent) kneel three times during the approach to the altar and also during the return from it. The formal '*muχti* is a fixed part of certain ceremonies. Every *matachín* dance has to end with the formal '*muχti* of both dancers and musicians. During the Easter season every Friday procession is closed with the formal '*muχti* and every *fiesta de promesa* is opened and closed with it. All the latter '*muχtim* are directed by the *fariseos*, who request first all the men present to go up in pairs and *'muχti*, then all the women, the *fariseos* themselves going last.

The procession.—Every ceremony involves a procession of some sort. We have mentioned the existence of two altars at most kinds of ceremonies. The essential feature of the procession is that members of ceremonial societies carry images of various kinds from one altar to another. Thus in the typical *fiesta* the altar is first set up in the church. If the *matachinis* are taking part in the *fiesta*, they head a procession of *maestros*, *cantoras*, and *ki'ostim* to the house or to the *pascola ramada*, depending on whether the plaza or a household is the scene of the ceremony. The *te'nantʃim* bear images of the Virgin to the *encampamiento* altar, if it is a household *fiesta*. From there the procession continues into the household *ramada*, with members of the household bearing the images. Similar processions are formed at the conclusion of the ceremony for the purpose of returning the images to the church or *encampamiento* altar. Similarly, the crucifixes from the church altar are borne in processions by the *fariseos* and *'temastim* during Lent.

There are processions of other kinds as standard parts of certain ceremonies. We have mentioned the important processions each Friday during Lent, in which almost the whole village takes part and in which all the images from church and from private households are carried about the Via Crucis. Processions headed by dancers and made up of nonparticipants as well as image-bearers take place also within the plaza during Holy Week, going from cross to cross within the plaza. A procession is carried out during the course of a child funeral in which the body of the child is borne by *padrinos* from the household altar to the *patio* cross and back. The processions that take place during weddings have also been mentioned.

The essential features of the procession are the presence of ceremonial societies, the bearing of images from one altar to another, and the participation of persons who, outside of processions, would be simply onlookers. It is a standard and important element in all Yaqui ritual.

The sermon or ritual speech.—It is regarded as important that a *maestro* be able to talk well, for it falls to the oldest *maestro* to close any ceremony with a sermon. Similarly, the head of the *fariseo* society must be a good speaker, for he too must give sermons. The *matachín* '*kovanau* is also supposed to be able to give a sermon, although the present one in Pascua has not this ability. The words of the sermons given by the ceremonial leaders are not fixed, but the ideas which they express follow a customary pattern. Thus the *maestro* closes every ceremony with a speech in which he thanks all participants for the '*tekipanoa* which they have performed, reminds them of the purpose of the work, and mentions the next approaching ceremonies and what will have to be done at them. The *maestro* must be familiar with the duties involved in *padrino* and *compadre* relations and be able to explain them at any ceremony involving ceremonial sponsorship. The *maestro* sometimes, but not often in Pascua, describes good moral behavior, in particular advising all members of ceremonial societies against getting drunk at the time of a ceremony. The sermons of the *fariseo* '*jaut* and *matachín* '*kovanau* are somewhat similar but usually contain more detailed statements concerning the nature of the duties of their respective societies. There is a difference of opinion in Pascua as to what constitutes a good sermon. Younger men favor those of a subordinate *maestro* who talks briefly and to the point and uses few words. Older persons approve the rambling sermons of the *fariseo 'jaut*, which are very wordy and full of moral maxims.

The *maestros'* sermons occur only toward the end of ceremonies. The *fariseo jaut* both opens and closes with sermons the portions of ritual in which the *fariseo* society participates. The former are public, addressed to all persons present; the latter are addressed only to the *fariseos*.

The ritual speech is also a part of the *pascolas'* activities. It will be remembered that the head *pascola* speaks to the crowd both at the beginning and at the conclusion of the *pascola* dance. In these speeches somewhat the same pattern as that in the *maestro*'s speech is followed, with the exception that the *pascola* thanks the crowd for its attendance and not the members of the ceremonial societies for their *'tekipanoa*.

There are ritual speeches also which are made by laymen, as, for instance, the speeches of *fiesteros* to all participants at the conclusion of a household *fiesta* and the speech of a man or woman or both to *padrinos* at a baptism or confirmation or similar ceremony. These are always simple expressions of gratitude. They are usually preceded by speeches by the *padrinos* in which recognition of the obligations established is made and the name of the sponsors is presented to the relatives of the person to be sponsored. The ritual speech is clearly an important and often-recurring element in Pascua ceremonials.

The hand-touching ritual.—In any ceremony in which *padrinos* of any kind take part as such, there is a special ritual which has been mentioned above. Such ceremonies are funerals, death *novenas*, weddings, baptisms, confirmations, and the Holy Week ceremonies. The ritual, except in the case of the confirmation by rosary, always takes place at a *patio* cross. *Padrinos* and relatives, or *padrinos* and persons sponsored (in the case of Holy Week), stand in a circle, and the *padrinos* go in single file, each performing the usual Yaqui greeting of verbal salutation and hand-touching with each of the relatives in turn. The hand-touching is repeated three times. This ritual is a prominent feature of all the ceremonies mentioned and takes place at a definite time during the course of the ceremony.

Eating and drinking in common.—At *fiestas* and at death and other household ceremonies, such as baptisms and weddings, eating in common is a part of the ritual. The members of the various ceremonial societies always eat together during the course of the ceremony; thus the *maestros* and *cantoras* eat together at one table, the *matachinis* at another, and the *fariseos* eat as they sit around the *patio* cross. The *pascolas*, *moros*, and their musicians also eat at the same time at one table, at which they ask members of the crowd to join them. The baptismal sponsorship is sealed by the eating of the relatives and *padrinos* at a single table, and the marriage ceremony requires that the relatives of the couple eat first at the bride's house in common and then at the groom's. In all these feasts the eating is concluded in a special ritual way. A pan of water is passed about at the end of the meal, and each person drinks in turn from it. Then all join in the saying of a standard prayer, and each person throws the edge of the tablecloth, where he has been sitting, up onto the table.

Drinking in common is also a part of certain ceremonies, for instance, at baptisms and weddings and at the conclusion of the Holy Week ceremonies. In these, *padrinos* furnish whiskey or wine for men and women who care to drink it and soda pop for others. The *padrinos* are required to pass out the drinks.

SUMMARY

It is clear that the pattern of ritual which we have passed in review is not to be definitely labeled either Spanish or aboriginal Yaqui. The mingling and mutual modification of the two heritages has been too intricate. As in the case of the *padrino* system, the present pattern is something which is uniquely modern Yaqui, or perhaps even uniquely Pascuan.

From the standpoint of our primary interest—namely, the relationship of the economic to the ceremonial life—the significant aspects of the ritual may be summarized under two heads. In the first place, ceremony is not closely connected with the primary (economic) adaptation. In the second place, it remains a time-consuming activity intimately related to the various social institutions which have been described.

The ceremonial calendar does not concern itself with the major rhythm of Pascua economic life, that is, the removal to the cotton fields in September and the return in January. It maintains a ceremonial rhythm entirely separate from economic activities. It happens that one of the events of the ceremonial calendar interferes with the latter: Pascuans must return, at some expense, from the cotton fields in order to participate in the important ceremonies of All Souls' Day in November. The fact that they do indicates a certain subordination of economic to ceremonial interests. The other dates of the calendar do not conflict, but they have nothing to do with making a living. An accidental harmony might, however, be pointed out. The cotton-picking season happens to end just as the Easter ceremonial season begins. Pascuans return to the village, usually with a surplus of money, and are thus enabled to devote themselves to the Easter ceremonies. The fact that the latter bring into co-operation for an extended period every ceremonial group in the village makes them an extremely important integrating factor for the society as a whole.[2] This accidental harmony between work and ceremonial calendars, therefore, would seem to have a great deal of significance for the maintenance of cultural unity in the village.

The number of fixed calendrical dates, the ceremonial elaboration of nearly all personal crises, the number of ceremonies required in connection with the frequently recurring phenomenon of death, and the all-night character, and large number, of activities necessary for a single *fiesta* justify the characterization of Pascua ceremony as time-consuming. That there are conflicts with the outside work calendar, as a result, has already been suggested. The nature of the ceremonial demands should now be clear. The significance of the conflicts for the society will be dealt with later.

The continuing appeal of the ceremonial system to Pascuans, despite its disharmony with the economic life, can be understood only in the light of its meanings. We have been considering the concrete forms of the relations between men and gods and between men who are associated in the never ending business of maintaining these relations. It is now necessary to discuss the content of the relationships.

[2] For an analysis of the social functions of these ceremonies see Rosamond B. Spicer, "The Easter Fiesta of the Yaqui Indians of Pascua, Arizona" (unpublished manuscript, A.M. thesis, Department of Anthropology, University of Chicago, 1939).

CHAPTER IX

THE CEREMONIAL SYSTEM: ANCESTORS AND DEITIES

THERE is a body of beliefs, and a set of symbols related to these beliefs, which give meaning to the ceremonial life and through that to the *padrino* and kinship customs. The symbols, like the ritual itself, are relatively standardized, but the beliefs associated with them are somewhat varied. Moreover, not everyone in Pascua is interested in the beliefs. There are many who see the ritual, who even take part in it regularly, for whom it seems to have little meaning beyond the acts themselves. The head *'temasti*, for example, whose knowledge of the Easter ceremonials is recognized as more extensive and "accurate" than that of anyone else, is vague and obviously at a loss when discussing the nature of the *'animam*, or spirits of the dead. He not only will admit to no definite ideas regarding their character but even remains doubtful in discussing their relations to the living and the purposes of the various ritual associated with them. He is, further, uninterested in these aspects of the *'animam*. Yet he is deeply interested in talking of the proper acts to be performed on All Souls' Day and can describe in minute detail what each family and the *maestros* must do at this time. His descriptions correspond more closely with what is actually done than do those of some of the *maestros*. This focus of interest is characteristic of the greater number of individuals in Pascua. There are, nevertheless, some persons who are deeply interested in the wider meanings of the ritual and even in attempting to synthesize it into some self-consistent scheme. The third *maestro*, whose Christianized interpretations of the *pascolas* we have dwelt on, is one such person, and the present *fariseo* leader is another. Their viewpoints color the presentation which will be attempted here.

THE CHANNELS OF TRADITION

Purely oral tradition is unquestionably in a state of decay in Pascua and is being supplanted by the written word. There are oral traditions like the deer songs and a few myths, but knowledge of the deer songs is limited to a few specialists (the deer-dancer's musicians), and the myths are imperfectly known, mainly by a few of the older persons.

It would be an error to say that there is any standard mythical tradition in Pascua. Even the Bible stories turn up in surprisingly varied forms. There seem to be no standard versions of the remnants of the aboriginal mythology. There are persons who know the elements of a few myths; there is none who claims to know them as they should be told. The knowledge of anyone who will volunteer to tell a myth is always disparaged by others as soon as they learn of it, but one finds that the disparagers are not able to tell the myth themselves. There is a frequent saying: "We don't know the old stories; no one in Pascua knows those things." And the experiences of the investigators seem to bear this out. Old people say that they do not tell the myths to younger people now, and a canvass of young men and women indicates that their knowledge of myth is indeed very slight. Moreover, the attitudes of young men toward what they have heard is often skeptical. Two young men in their late teens say that they are anxious to go down to Sonora in order to determine whether or not it is true, as the old men say, that there is a coyote there with a light in the middle of his forehead who flashes the light once a year during Lent. On the other hand, one young man of twenty-five regards a myth like that of Jomu'muli as "beautiful" and takes pleasure in writing it out in English. He is obviously moved by it and cares little about its truth.

The myth of Jomu'muli is one of the few of which there is general knowledge in the village. It appears in varying forms; a synthetic version of it is as follows:

Jomu'muli was an old woman, some say simply a wise old Yaqui woman; others say that she was the mother of the sea to whom fishermen prayed. She lived in the Yaqui country a long time ago when the Suris lived there. At this time there was a tree without branches, like a telephone pole, in the middle of the Suri country. This tree kept vibrating all the time. The Suris knew that it was talking in some language, but they could not understand it. Finally they decided to go to Jomu'muli and to get her to translate what it said. She came and listened to the talking tree for a long time. Then she translated all that it had said. All the Suris were standing around in a big crowd listening. Jomu'muli told them that the tree was saying many things. It told about the making of the earth and how plants and animals and men, too, came to live on the earth. It said that some time in the future many strange things would happen. People would talk to each other over long distances without shouting. They would fly through the air and they would travel over the land faster than anything then known. Finally a god would come and show the people how to baptize themselves. When they were shown the secret of baptism, then everyone should be baptized because it was a good thing. When Jomu'muli said these things, there were some who believed her and some who did not. Some said that they would get ready for the things that were to come and others said that they would not. After a time Jomu'muli saw that what the talking stick was saying had caused trouble among the Suris. She decided to go away so that the trouble would end. She made a cigarette out of the tree and went away to the north. No one knows what happened to her, but all that the talking stick said has come true. Some say that the people who didn't believe the talking stick went into the ground and remained Suris. The others were baptized and they are the Yaquis.

This fragment is the most elaborate piece of mythology remaining in Pascua. It is also the most widely known. At least four persons feel able to tell it in detailed form. Everyone in the village knows some elements of it, usually the prophetic parts which are regarded as predictions of the telephone, airplane, and automobile. Even the most irreverent men will mention and discuss it when drunk around the night fires at a *fiesta*. The myth of Jomu'muli, however, is not linked in any way with present-day ritual or beliefs. It is pure folklore and, as such, is linked only with the nearly extinct belief in the wisdom of the ants, who are sometimes said to be the descendants of the Suris.

The myth describing the origin of the *pascolas* and one involving Santiago in the origin of the Milky Way are the only other nearly complete oral traditions that are known in the village. The mythical basis of ceremony is Christian rather than aboriginal Yaqui. There is, however, a considerable number of tales which deal for the most part with animals and which survive entirely through oral tradition. Fragments of them crop up occasionally in conversation, and they are sometimes used by older people to point a moral. There seem to be no well-defined occasions on which they are told, but young and old alike are quite familiar with a dozen or more.

The songs used by the deer-dancer's musicians are known by six men in the village. All these men are over thirty years of age, two of whom were born in the United States. Unlike the myths, the songs are remembered word for word. They are sung only during the deer dance, and no young persons are now learning them, although most persons in the village know a phrase or two from many of them. It is often said that these well-known snatches are very beautiful, despite the fact that, as is insisted, they make use of words which are obsolete and the meanings of which are not clear. There are thirty or more deer songs. An example of one translated may indicate their general nature. It is addressed to the deer:

> Little brother, little brother, go find some flowers.
> We are going to a place in the houseyard
> Where there are three crosses standing.
> As for a little child when it dies,
> Throw the flowers about and let them fall.
> Little brother, little brother, go find some flowers.[1]

The only other sort of thing which may be regarded as oral tradition is the sermon or ritual speech which *maestros*, heads of ceremonial societies, and *pascolas* give at *fiestas* or other ceremonies. The content of the sermon is not, however, fixed, except in a general way. Its words are not memorized, the speaker making up what he has to say as he goes along, suiting his words to the specific occasion. Certain conventional forms, of course, appear in the sermons. Thus it is customary to open a sermon by mentioning the ancestors by means of relationship terms, the form of thanking the participants is more or less set, and there are conventional closing phrases. Other than in these respects the sermon is not a vehicle of oral tradition.

The mythology of which Pascuans make use in their ritual is all obtained from books. Three *maestros* each have one or more books in Spanish containing accounts of the biblical stories of the Creation, the Flood, the Tower of Babel, the Passion of Christ, etc. They read these stories and make use of them in explaining, for example, the Easter ritual to others. In addition, they make use of various books of Catholic devotions containing portions of the lives of the saints and other Christian myths.

[1] In the light of a recent study of the deer songs carried out by Mr. Carleton S. Wilder this appears to be a reinterpreted version of one of the old songs. It follows neither the thought nor the rhythmic pattern of the latter.

The ritual itself, however, is handed from person to person mainly through the medium of the personal notebooks which the *maestros* all keep. The material in these notebooks is written out in longhand. Each such notebook contains prayers, chants, and other materials necessary in the services. The chants (*alabanzas*) are always in Spanish or Latin, never in Yaqui. The most usual of the Catholic prayers, such as the Ave Maria and the Pater Noster, may be in either Spanish or Yaqui, and either form may be used in the service, depending on which happens to come to the *maestro*'s mind. The ritual for the dead is in Latin and was originally taken from the Roman missal. There is extensive corruption of the Latin words, resulting both from attempts to adjust its phonetics to Spanish or Yaqui and the cumulative errors of copying from notebook to notebook. There is a series of prayers in Yaqui which is used to close a *fiesta*. It consists of five parts, each portion ending with the standard ritual series of Ave Maria, Gloria Patri, etc. The first prayer asks a blessing on all persons present at the *fiesta;* the second asks a blessing for those who were unable to attend wherever they may be; the third is a prayer for the dead of the village; the fourth, a prayer for the angel-guardians; and the last, a prayer for rain. These are not word-for-word prayers, but they are written out in Yaqui in various forms in some of the notebooks. Like the sermons, they may be varied to suit occasions.

The head *maestro* at present has a Roman missal from which he frequently reads during services. He and the other *maestros* usually have their books of Catholic devotions with them at a ceremony and read portions of the services from them.

During 1936–37 pamphlets published by Judge Rutherford, an anti-Catholic tractarian, were widely distributed by missionary agents in the village. They are for the most part retold Bible stories, in Spanish, interpreted to indicate a coming world-cataclysm in which all organized religious bodies will be destroyed. All the *maestros*, as well as a number of other persons in the village, possess copies of these tracts, and they are much read and discussed.

Books and the spoken word are, of course, not the only channels of tradition. The images used on the altar, the masks of the *čapa'jekam*, the dances of the *matachinis*, and all the various ritual acts are concrete embodiments of tradition which in every ceremony present anew the symbols around which the beliefs and attitudes of Pascuans center. Each *fiesta*, funeral, or service serves as a reminder to those who attend it of the relationships existing between men and gods, men and the ancestors, and men and men.

It is the ritual and the written tradition which have the greater stability and are relatively unvarying. Each ceremony is a product of group activities, and consequently individual differences tend to be obscured in carrying out the ritual. The interpretations of the ritual are to a much greater extent individual matters. Lacking the books of the *maestros* and lacking spokesmen who try frequently to interpret the ritual publicly, the majority of people have either vague or conflicting conceptions of the meaning of the ritual. Several interpretations of a given article of *matachín* paraphernalia, for example, are to be found current in the village. There are a number of different ideas as to just what the souls of the dead are and what they do. These differences exist side by side with fairly close agreement as to how the *matachín* paraphernalia should be used and what a person or a family must do in connection with the dead.

DEATH AND THE ANCESTORS

Interest in the dead appears in nearly every ceremony. The greater number of ceremonies during 1936–37, including funerals, death *novenas*, death anniversaries, the October *novenas*, and the All Souls' series of ceremonies were directly connected with the dead. In addition to these, however, almost every other ceremony involved references to the dead, as in the sermons by the *maestros* which mention all the ancestors, or included the recitation of a list of dead persons read from some family Book of the Dead. Moreover, the standard form of altar devotion, whether for a Sunday service, a saint's day, or apparently any other occasion, includes a portion of the Catholic Mass for the Dead. The latter occurs repeatedly during a service whether or not the ceremony is directly concerned with a death, recent or past. Also any ceremony at which an altar is set up (this excludes baptisms and weddings) is regarded as an opportunity for having the family Books of the Dead blessed. A member of a family brings the book wrapped in a handkerchief and places it on the altar, where it remains throughout the ceremony. It is taken away at the end and is regarded as having been blessed, even if the *maestro* has not read the names contained in it. Mention has already been made of the closing series of prayers, one of which is always devoted to the dead of the village as a whole.

This interest in the dead is not accompanied by any very clear-cut notions as to just what the dead look like or even what their functions are in relation to the living or vice versa. The latter are, however, more definitely formulated than anything else in connection with the dead. There seems to be no Yaqui word in use for a person who has died. A dead body is called *mu'kila*, but after burial the only word applied is the Spanish *anima*. The '*animam* are invisible. At times they are in the village, as, for instance, throughout the month of October. When they are in the village they remain invisible, but they are listening to all that is said. They stay around the household where they formerly lived and watch and listen to their living relatives to find out what they are doing and thinking. During this month they are "on vacation" from where they have been somewhere in the sky with Jesus and God. They have to go back immediately after All Souls' Day. The rest of the year they do not come to the village.

There seems to be a confusion of the '*animam* with certain other beings. In Pascua in 1936–37, immediately after the deaths of two adults, the houses in which they had lived were torn down by their families and rebuilt in another part of the houseyard. In the case of other adult deaths the houses were not torn down or altered extensively, but other instances were recorded of the rebuilding of houses, the removal of families, or the alteration of the part of the house in which a person had lived prior to death. The individuals who made such changes say that they did so because it made them sad to be reminded continually of the dead person by seeing, day after day, the places which they associated intimately with the latter. Others, however, say that there are definite kinds of beings which remain in the places where dead persons have lived. There are "spirits" or ghosts ('*hweʾnam*) which are not '*animam* but are, nevertheless, a form of the dead person, and there are voices ('*huneram*) which speak from the places where the dead person slept or sat. These work no harm, except to frighten people, especially the relatives. But it is better to destroy the places where they might appear in order to avoid being frightened. These noises and evil spirits appear to be an equivalent of ghosts among Christians; they are similarly associated with and yet distinguished from the souls of the dead.

More important in Yaqui belief are the angel-guardians, or, as they are called in Yaqui-ized Spanish, *'ankelwardam.* These again are and yet are not the dead. The *'animam* are individualized, thought of as relatives with specific kinship relations to the living; they are listed by name in the Books of the Dead and called by name in the ceremonies; their village offices are remembered, and they are labeled with these titles in the books. The angel-guardians are not so individualized. They are persons who have died and are living in the invisible world. There is one who is especially concerned with the welfare of each living individual, but a man does not know who his angel-guardian is. He cannot call him by name nor does he think of him as having a village office. The angel-guardians are present in the village in October and on All Souls' Day because all the dead are present then, but no clear distinction is made between the ritual for the *'animam* and that for the *'ankelwardam.*

The concept of the angel-guardians might be regarded as one aspect of the functions of the *'animam.* They seem to be thought of as the active, protective aspect of the activities of the *'animam.* The latter are not thought of as having any power to work evil. They only watch and listen. It is said that in October especially one must be careful to say prayers and to think of the *'animam* often. If one does not, no harm will come through the *'animam,* but they will be very sad. Everyone should do his best to avoid making them unhappy, by showing that they are remembered. It is for this reason that a family must take its Book of the Dead to a ceremony and have it blessed at the altar. On the other hand, a person does not think of doing certain things to please the angel-guardians. They are working for an individual constantly, no matter what he does. They are always "speaking to Jesus and God" in one's behalf. They do not have power to help their charges directly, but they are always interceding and asking for help.

A recurring symbol in both Yaqui thought and ritual is the "angel." These are by no means identical with the angel-guardians. All unmarried persons become angels when they die. Just how the angel is distinguished from the ordinary soul of the dead or the angel-guardian is again not clear, but there is some sort of distinction. Living children are often referred to as "little angels" (*angelitos*) and as such take certain parts in the ritual. On Holy Saturday at the end of the Easter ceremonies, for example, there are groups of boys and girls dressed in white veils and with crowns of flowers. They carry switches, and when the *tʃapa'jekam*, in their capacity as evil spirits, make their mock attack on the church, the "angels" beat the latter back successfully. They are said to be the chief defense of the church against the evil represented by the *tʃapa'jekam*. During Lent also these *angelitos* and *angelitas* appear in their flower crowns and with their switches. They accompany the Virgins in procession and also march with the groups bearing the crucifixes. They seem in these connections to be symbols of all that is good and (if the Yaquis used such a term) "holy." Only unmarried persons may serve as *angelitos*, and when an unmarried person dies, he is buried in clothes reminiscent of the *angelito*, whether or not he has served as such during his life. The dead *angelito* wears a crown of flowers, and flowers are fastened to the burial dress. The atmosphere of the funeral is one of gaiety, and mourning is regarded as very much out of place. Some persons have a tendency to think of the angel-guardians as the dead *angelitos*, but this conception is by no means general.

The obligations which the living have to the dead are thought of as being directed to the *'animam*, not to the angel-guardians or to the *angelitos*. We have dwelt above on the ritual obligations of the members of ceremonial societies to one another at death, and we have made some mention of the nature of the obligations of relatives and *padrinos*. It will be necessary here only to emphasize some of the features of these ritual obligations. In the first place, the living are obligated to prepare a dead body for life in the invisible world. This requires actions by relatives, by *padrinos*, and by members of any ceremonial society to which the dead person belonged. The preparation of the body consists in the saying of certain prayers, the clothing of the body in a prescribed manner, and the performance of certain ritual acts centering about the body.

In the case of an adult it is the relatives who are charged with organizing the ceremonies at which these various actions can be carried out. All the relatives are spoken of as "mourners" (*dolientes*) and, as such, must express their grief at the time of the funeral and subsequently in certain formal mourning customs. When the body is finally ready for burial, the relatives must formally and publicly take their leave of it. They do this by forming a circle and marching around the body, each relative as he comes by the right hand of the corpse touching the hand and breast and murmuring the conventional Yaqui parting words. The circle of relatives marches around the body three times, and each relative goes through the formal leave-taking three times. Then, when the body is taken to the cemetery, the relatives must express their grief by remaining out of sight of the grave until the body is buried. They also devote a day just preceding the death-anniversary *fiesta* to mourning; for twenty-four hours each relative wears a black cord about his neck and refrains during this period from working, eating, smoking, or sleeping. The other important ritual duty of the relatives consists in marching in procession during the *novena*, each carrying a lighted candle, while a *maestro* marches with them, chanting and sprinkling holy water in an effort to remove all traces of the dead person from his favorite haunts in the household. These leave-taking, mourning, and purification rites occur only in the case of adult dead.

In the case of an unmarried person, it is the *padrinos* who are charged with organizing the ceremony of the funeral. But whether the dead person was married or not, it is the *padrinos* who are required to carry out the actual physical preparation of the body for the next world. If the person has had a village office, the work of the *padrinos* is supplemented by that of the ceremonial society to which the dead person belonged. The body must be outfitted with certain insignia which insure that he will be recognized in the next world as having the social personality which he had in this. In the first place, it must be indicated that he was baptized in the church and, moreover, that he was a Yaqui. This is accomplished by tying a small cross to his right thumb and by placing at least six "Yaqui-type" rosaries about the neck. Care is taken that the rosaries be placed on the body in what is repeatedly spoken of as "the Yaqui manner," that is, with the first bead on the right-hand side of the breast. The type of rosary also indicates marriage status. An unmarried person wears rosaries which have at their ends large paper flowers; the rosaries of married persons have only a simple colored yarn tassel which is, however, called a "flower" (*'sewa*). Position in this world as a ceremonial society member must also be indicated. We have pointed out how *matachinis* are buried with headdress, *pluma*, and rattle and how *fariseos* and *caballeros* are buried with the insignia of their societies. Members of the societies place these insignia on the body at the funeral. The *'wikosam*, or breechclout strings, which the *padrinos* place about the waist of a dead person, are regarded as aids in the passage from this world to the next. It is thought that a group of angel-guardians transport the *anima* to the next world after the funeral. The *'wikosam* are necessary for the angel-guardians to hold on to as they perform this act.

The duties of *padrinos* and ceremonial societies to a dead person end after the *novena*, but those of the relatives continue. As soon as the funeral is over, the name of the dead person together with his village office, if he had any, is entered in the family Book of the Dead. We have already indicated at length how those whose names appear in the books are regarded as members of the living families and how the obligations to have the books blessed are frequently recognized. The importance of these books as symbols of the continuing relationships between dead and living is very great. The third *maestro* tells how a Baptist missionary came to the village some years ago in the time of Juan Pistola and explained that his church did not allow *fiestas* for the dead. He said that people in this world could not help the dead after death, nor could the latter help the living. The Yaquis began to dislike the missionary when he said these things, so the *maestro* says, because they know that it is otherwise: "Each family has its book, and among the Yaquis these cannot be destroyed." Not only the families but also the *maestros* "never forget the dead at any time; this is the custom."

Thus, the remembrance of the dead permeates the whole ritual. And annually on All Souls' Day the relationships of living to dead are publicly reaffirmed not only in spoken prayers but also in the ritual setting-out of food, household by household, where the dead return to eat and drink in the presence of the living.

THE VIRGIN MARY

God (Dios) is little more than a word in Pascua and certainly a word that is vaguely understood. The word appears in prayers, but the being for whom it stands has no definite social personality. There is no set of mutual obligations existing between God and men, or at least none that receives any clear expression. The formal relationships that receive expression and in connection with which exist a definite set of symbols and beliefs are those between men and the Virgin and men and Jesus. That part of the ritual which is not directed specifically to the dead is directed, for the most part, to these two. Certain ceremonies honor saints, and certain saints have important functions in relation to the living, such as San Francisco, whose power to cure disease is widely recognized, but the saints remain distinctly in the background. The ritual that has them as its object is even organized primarily in terms of the relations with the Virgin and Jesus.

The Virgin Mary (María Santísima) is perhaps more prominent in the ritual and consequently in the thought than is Jesus. This is a result of the fact that the ceremonial society which is devoted exclusively to her, the *matachinis*, has a longer ceremonial season than the *fariseo* society, which is devoted to Jesus. The *matachín* ritual is prominent in the village for nine months in the year, while the *fariseo* ritual is performed for only three months. It is true that the *maestros* and *cantoras* are regarded as being primarily devotees of Jesus, but the colorful and impressive ritual is the property of the dance societies, and it is they who define the social personalities of their gods most effectively. The Virgin Mary is always called, except in Spanish prayers, *'itom ai*, the usual kinship expression for "our mother." Her symbols are numerous in Pascua. There are three large images of her (the standard Catholic forms), which are not kept in the church storeroom but are the property of two of the *ki'ostim* and a *cantora* and are brought to the church whenever there is a service there. Each of the Virgins is ordinarily called by the same term, *'itom ai*, but during the Easter ceremonies there is a tendency to distinguish between them, and they are called Madre Dolorosa, Virgen María de Salome, and María Magdalena. Any one of them may serve as the generalized Mary during the rest of the year. It is said that every Yaqui village ought to have three Virgins because of the necessity for three during the Easter ceremonies. There is a fourth image of the Virgin in the village which is also called simply *'itom ai*. It is much smaller than the others and is the special property of the *matachín* society. It is always carried by the *matachinis* when making *limosna* and usually, but not always, is on the altar when they are dancing.

Besides these images there is another form of *'itom ai* which is never called Mary or the Virgin. This is a painted wooden cross resting on a square base and having a semicircular background of artificial flowers. It ordinarily goes by the name of Santa Cruz and is the symbol toward which devotions are directed at the *fiesta* of the Holy Cross on

May 3. At this time a skirt is placed about the bottom of the cross, and necklaces of glass beads are hung over the cross-arm; in this garb it is regarded as a female image and is called *'itom ai*. Its role as the latter is explained by the third *maestro* in a brief story:

> Mary always had flowers about her. Jesus was born because Mary smelled a flower; this is the way that she remained a virgin. In the time when the Jews were going to crucify Jesus, they wanted a carpenter to make a cross on which to crucify him. They found Joseph and told him to make the cross. Joseph was a good carpenter, but when he went to look at the wood which he had for making the cross, it was all too short, and there was no way in which he could cut it to make a cross big enough. While he was standing there puzzling over it, his son Jesus came and talked to him. Jesus told him that he was God and that, if Joseph went out into the hills, he would find a tree which he could cut down and make a cross out of it. Jesus then went away. Joseph stood for a long time in doubt. He didn't know whether or not to believe that Jesus was God or not. Finally he went out into the hills and found a tree and cut it down. The tree which he cut down was really Mary, because Mary had turned herself into a tree. Jesus and God had planned this out long before and had told Mary to turn herself into a tree. So, when Jesus was crucified, he was crucified on a cross made of his mother, Mary. She holds him embraced in her outstretched arms.

Probably under the influence of this story, the third *maestro* and a few others sometimes call the houseyard crosses and the *patio* cross in front of the church *'itom ai*, just as they apply the term to the Santa Cruz. Most persons, however, object strongly to this usage and maintain that the only cross which should be addressed as *'itom ai* is the Santa Cruz itself.

As indicated in the beginning of the third *maestro*'s story, there is a constant association of flowers with the Virgin. Flowers are a recurring symbol throughout all the ritual directly connected with her and appear also in other ritual less clearly connected with her. In season, as during the May ritual, the flowers are sometimes real, but those which figure most prominently are artificial, often not resembling flowers in any way except for brightness of color. The real flowers which are placed by little girls on the altar of the church each evening during May are regarded as offerings exclusively to the Virgin. The *matachinis*, in their dancing devotions to the Virgin, wear headdresses which are surmounted by streamers of colored paper, usually red, which are always called *'sewam* ("flowers"). On Holy Saturday the *pascolas* stand before the church when the *tʃapa'jekam* are making their attacks on the latter and throw confetti at the attackers. The confetti is called "flowers" and is regarded as symbolic of a power against evil. It weakens the evil *tʃapa'jekam* so that they may be finally conquered by the switches of the "little angels." In processions during Lent and also at other times, the *ki'ostim* make use of flowers in the form of confetti, showering it over the images of the Virgins each time they come to a Station of the Cross. Finally, flowers are essential at the death of a child. We have described how the body of a dead child is decked with many-colored paper flowers, how a crown is made of them and placed on the head, and how each rosary has a large paper flower at one end. Also the crosses of fresh willow twigs which are placed new on each house front on the eve of Holy Cross Day are called *se'wamta 'santa kus*, or Holy Cross flowers. Thus, flowers have a close connection with the Virgin and the rites which are associated with her, but they also figure in other ritual, as symbols of the unmarried state and of a generalized power for good.

The Virgin has power only to work good, and certain acts must be performed by men to have this good directed toward them. The powers which she has are of two general kinds. In the first place, it is in her power to bestow good luck and general well-being. When the *matachinis* make a *limosna*, carrying their little image of the Virgin, it is believed that general blessings are brought to each house in the village at which the *matachinis* stop. It is the image of the Virgin which brings the blessing, not the *matachinis* themselves. Also, when the *matachinis* dance, it is believed that blessings of this general sort are brought to the whole village. Specifically, the waving of the *plumas* by the dancers is thought to be a blessing of the land all around, through the power of the Virgin. One or two old persons in the village say rather vaguely that the Virgin sends rain through the *plumas*, but the belief seems to be held by no one else, and the old people are not very clear about the matter.

Nearly everyone, however, is convinced of the other important power of the Virgin, that is, of her power to cure disease. Most of the *matachinis* have become members of the society as a result of this belief. They have been promised to serve her because she is believed to have brought about their recovery from a serious illness. The belief is general that such persons must continue to serve her as payment for her assistance and that, if they do not do so, she will withdraw her power and permit them to get sick and die. Thus the *matachín* society exists and continues to function by virtue of the belief in the curing powers of the Virgin. The *ki'osti* society is likewise based on this belief. The women who function in it have also been promised to her service as the result of an illness.

The general powers for good which the Virgin has are brought to the village as a whole also through the performance of an annual Holy Cross *fiesta*. Images of the Holy Cross are owned by individual families only, not by any societies; there are three of them in the village. Their owners are obligated to organize and finance a large *fiesta* each year. There is an elaborate ritual on the eve of the *fiesta* which symbolizes the coming of the Virgin from the sky down to the earth, bringing with her blessings for the year which is to come.

The rosary, as among orthodox Catholics, is regarded as especially connected with the Virgin. Every tenth bead on it is called Holy Mary (Santa María) and is said by many to be a symbol of the Holy Cross. In Pascua the rosary is especially important as a protection against sickness and against witchcraft in particular. We have mentioned its uses in this connection when describing the relations of *padrinos* of confirmation to their godchildren.

There is some connection between the Virgin and the idea of the "angel." Mention has been made of the use of flowers at the death of a child. Further, an image of "Jesus the Child" was substituted in the early part of 1937 for the *matachín* Virgin, when the latter was broken. The *malinches*, who dance with dresses on in the *matachín* dances, are often spoken of as "angels," and every *matachini* is buried with the *malinche* costume on, whether or not he is an unmarried person. There are conflicting statements as to what the *malinches* represent. They are thought of as "angels," but they are also sometimes said to represent the Holy Family, that is, Mary, Joseph, and the Child Jesus. It should be mentioned in this connection that one of the chants which the *maestros* give while the *matachinis* are dancing has to do with the Holy Family.

JESUS: EL SEÑOR

There is some confusion between Jesus and God. Jesus is frequently called El Señor, but the term is sometimes applied to God. Both are likewise called in Yaqui *'itom 'atʃai* ("our father"). The symbols of Jesus are the crucifixes, of which there are six which are used in public ceremonies. Three of these are kept in the church, one is privately owned by one of the *cantoras*, another is kept by the *'temasti* who has charge of arranging altars for household *fiestas*, and the sixth is the property of the *fariseo* society. There is also an image of Jesus in a red robe which is used to represent him in the Garden of Gethsemane and in other incidents of the Passion Play at Easter. This image is kept in the church, belongs to the pueblo as a whole, and is never used except at Easter. The wooden crosses in both the plaza and houseyards are not referred to as Jesus or El Señor, but they are frequently spoken of by the other term applied to a crucifix, *'itom 'atʃai*. The crosses are definitely said to be representative of Jesus on the cross with his arms outstretched. We have mentioned above the confusion of this usage with that which applies the Yaqui term for Mary to the houseyard crosses.

The powers of Jesus are not so clearly formulated in the village as are those of the Virgin, except in regard to curing. There seems to be no idea of general blessings which come through the power of Jesus. His aid is sought in particular instances, such as in the case of a serious illness, and it is as a result of the belief in his curing powers that persons become members of the *fariseo*, *maestro*, and *cantora* ceremonial societies. Crucifixes are rarely used, however, to ward off illness or witchcraft, as rosaries are. There seems to be less connection between Jesus and health than there is between the Virgin and health.

Jesus is associated more with penance and denials than with blessings and well-being. He is also more closely connected with death and the dead than is the Virgin. The Virgin's flowers are associated only with the dead children.

But in all funerals, whether of child or adult, a ritual with the *'temasti* crucifix closes the ceremony in which the *padrinos* clothe the dead body. Crucifixes are also prominent in the mourning and purification rites for adult dead. It is usually said that the *'animam* are with Jesus or with Jesus and God in the other world, but it is never said that they are with the Virgin, whose connection with the world of the dead is remote, if indeed there may be admitted to be any at all.

Crucifixes appear on the altars throughout the year, occupying a central position, except at the Holy Cross *fiesta* and the month of May ceremonies, when they give place to Virgins. But the Easter ceremonial season, when the *fariseos* have replaced the *matachinis*, is the time most particularly associated with Jesus. Lent and Holy Week are regarded as a period of penance and purification. The Catholic taboos take the form of prohibitions against working on Fridays in Lent and throughout Holy Week until Easter Sunday. The taboo against work is spoken of as including house work, such as washing and ironing clothes, as well as the work of men, but it is not strictly regarded in either respect at present. A purification ceremony involving whipping is carried out on Wednesday night of Holy Week each year. *Fariseos* whip one another and the *maestros* in the darkened church, and the villagers do the same. The whipping is said to "make people clean," to purify them from the bad things they have been doing throughout the year. The whole of the ritual activities during the Easter season is sometimes spoken of as a *penitencia*.

There is a definite idea of opposition between the *fariseos*, who are dedicated to Jesus, and the *matachinis*, who are dedicated to the Virgin. This is expressed in the statement: "The *fariseos* do not like flowers," which is given as a reason for the *matachinis'* not appearing during the Easter season. It will be recalled in this connection that flowers are used to drive back the *fariseos* in their attack on the church. The opposition of the two dance societies is emphasized in a number of other ways during the Easter season. During some of the Lenten processions the crucifixes, accompanied by the *fariseos*, are carried around the Way of the Cross by one group while the Virgins are carried separately by another group; the *matachinis* themselves do not appear, but the symbols with which they are associated are kept distinct from those with which the *fariseos* are associated. In one nighttime procession during Holy Week there is a mock battle between the group carrying the Virgins and that accompanying the crucifixes. In the battle, however, *fariseos* participate on both sides, so that the fundamental opposition would seem to be not between the dance societies as such but between the symbols themselves. The separateness of Virgins and crucifixes in the ritual is indicated also in other ways outside the Easter season. In a *fiesta* in the plaza the crucifixes are always carried in procession to the *pascola ramada*, where they remain throughout the night, while the Virgins are carried to the *ramada* and then brought back to the church, where they remain. It will be recalled in this connection that women are not permitted to handle crucifixes and that men, with the exception of the *matachinis*, do not carry Virgins.

No attempt will be made to give an interpretation of this opposition between Jesus and the Virgin, because none that is satisfactory has been formulated by the writer. The social personality of Jesus is not sufficiently clear from the data at hand to permit an adequate explanation.

THE ANIMALS

It has been said that there is a tendency to regard the *pascolas* as being devotees of Jesus in much the same manner as the *fariseos* are devoted to him. There is, however, no evidence that this tendency is more than an expression of desire to make the *pascolas* consistent with the rest of the ceremonial scheme. Actually the *pascolas* are not organized into a society of which Jesus is the patron. Their patrons, if we may judge from what they say and do, are not anthropomorphic; they are different kinds of animals. They appeal to horned toads, badgers, turtles, and frogs for help in their ritual, and they call these animals *santos* ("saints"). To many Pascuans this application of the term "saint" to animals does not fit into the general ceremonial pattern, and they react by laughing, while others are somewhat indignant and regard the usage as sacrilegious.

This connection of the *pascolas* with animals is by no means a clearly formulated aspect of the ritual. The linkage between the two is perhaps in process of being broken down altogether, but it cannot be denied that ideas in connection with it still have some life. The second *maestro*, who is also leader of the *fariseo* society, believes that the *pascolas* "have the powers of animals" (*pascola tiene la virtúd de cada animál*). He thinks that their ritual originally came from a snake which lived in the water in the mountains. Their music also came from this source. The *maestro* readily admits these beliefs and sees no particular conflict between them and his Christian doctrine. The third *maestro* makes some effort to resolve the contradictions. He admits that he differs from the Catholic priest in Tucson in believing that animals have a place in his theology, but he is often, perhaps unconsciously, engaged in reconciling this belief with what he knows of Catholic teaching. We need only turn back to his interpretations of the *pascola* in terms of Christian mythology to see this.

Odds and ends of beliefs in regard to animals, indicating their former close connection with life in general, turn up at many points in Pascua. The third *maestro* believes that the animals had many "secrets" which the old Yaquis used to know. Another *maestro* speaks of a "language" of the ants which he heard his mother talk about. He believes that the deer songs have something to say about this language of the ants. Another person speaks about the "language of the deer." Many animal stories are remembered and told on occasion. It is said that the friendship of two badgers in a certain story is a relationship which each Yaqui would like to have with every other. The *fariseos'* masks represent rabbits and the bull, and it is said that there used to be many more animals represented. The coyote dance is not carried out any more, but there are still coyote dancers in the village. Ten years ago there was a *matu'pari* (a small water animal) dancer who danced several times in the plaza. Persons describe with pleasure other dances imitating animals which they saw as children in Sonora Yaqui villages. On Wednesday of Holy Week the *fariseos* crawl under the altar in the church and make noises like owls, coyotes, and other animals. The *pascola* dances all have animal names. The deer-dancer wears his stuffed deer's head when he dances.

THE ELEMENT OF BURLESQUE

No discussion of the ceremonial life in Pascua can omit the frequent burlesquing of all things, sacred and otherwise. Few aspects of the ritual or of human relations escape being lampooned by the *pascolas* and the *fariseos*. It is only these performers who have the right to make light of serious things in public ceremonies, but the range of their humor and satire extends throughout the culture. It is part of the *pascolas'* routine to interfere with the solemn dancing of the deer-dancer. They stumble over him and go about aping all his movements. When the *matachinis* come over to the *pascola ramada* to dance before the images on the altar, they may find a *pascola* threading his way between their lines, burlesquing their steps and making the crowd laugh in the midst of their devotionary dance. The *pascolas* do not stop, however, at making light of serious ritual. It is also a part of their business to burlesque human relations: at the very time that a marriage is being solemnly affirmed, the *pascolas* are making the marriage relationship appear ridiculous a few feet away from where the ceremony is going forward, and the pronouncements of the *maestro* are being drowned out by the laughter of the crowd surrounding the *pascolas*. The *tʃapa'jekam* carry the burlesque of the sacred even farther. They leap and shiver and scrape imaginary filth from their legs whenever the names of Mary or God are mentioned during the Easter rituals. They interfere with the *maestros*, perhaps dangling toy monkeys before their faces, in the midst of prayers and sacred chants. They have a drunken, jolly *fiesta* by moonlight to celebrate the crucifixion of Jesus. For the *fariseos* these activities are part of the roles they are playing as evil spirits; for the crowd they are sometimes merely antics to be laughed at and sometimes, as in the interference with the *maestros*, actions which they must not permit themselves to notice.

The element of burlesque is a frequently recurring and important feature of ceremony; an understanding of it is of considerable importance for understanding the whole ritual. The interpretation of it, however, falls outside the scope of this study.

INDIVIDUAL ATTITUDES

The views which the people of Pascua have toward their religious institutions are by no means uniform. Just as there is great variation in the amount of knowledge which individuals have concerning the meaning of a given ritual or symbol and as there is variation in the interpretations which are made of specific parts of the ritual, so there is great difference in the importance of the ritual to different individuals. To all but one of the *maestros*, the whole set of religious institutions is vital and provides the chief object of thought and interest. They spend time not only in the ceremonies themselves but also in going over their books and notebooks, memorizing chants more thoroughly, or reciting portions of the ritual to themselves apparently purely for pleasure. When they are not working, their minds are occupied mainly with the ritual. It seems to be for them a lifelong, never ending study which has meaning in and of itself. The dance leader of the *matachinis* and one of the *monarcas* also are likewise preoccupied with the *matachinis*' activities and their parts in *fiestas* past and to come. On the other hand, the majority of persons do not have such consuming interest in the ritual. Their interest is, nevertheless, strong in specific ceremonies. In general, the lives of most Pascuans might be said to move from one *fiesta* to another. A perennial subject for conversation is a discussion of the *fiesta* just past or the one to come.

One often reiterated statement in regard to ceremony might be regarded as a saying in the village. It runs like this: "This religion of ours is very hard work" ("Es muy trabajoso la religión de nosotros"). This view is one expressed by the participants in a ceremony. It is common to hear it said by a *cantora* or *maestro* in the early morning after an all-night *fiesta*. *Matachinis* also regard their dancing as hard work. Ceremonial '*tekipanoa* is, in other words, not regarded as pure pleasure; it is a duty and often an irksome one at that. If it is regarded as hard work, it is rarely avoided on that account. Those who most often speak of it in these terms are the most regular in performing it.

There are persons in Pascua who have no belief in certain aspects of the ritual. A man of forty, born in the United States and trained as a *maestro* in his youth, says that he neither believes in nor understands much of the ritual now. He is familiar with its forms, but he prefers to attend the Pentecostal church in Tucson to participation in Pascua ceremonies. He nevertheless continues to live in the village and even took part in a funeral and *novena* for a friend who died. A woman of twenty, who had been through fifth grade in the Tucson schools, laughs at the belief that the souls of the dead are present in the village in October. She says she does not know why, but she always "has to laugh" when people put out tables of food for the dead; it seems foolish to her. Yet she took an active part in organizing and directing the funeral and *novena* for her mother when the latter died and for months subsequent to the death participated whenever she could as Virgin-bearer in other ceremonies. Another man of thirty who went to school in Tucson rarely attends ceremonies except as a drunken pleasure-seeker, but when he was sick he promised "to help these Yaquis in their religion." He dedicated himself to the *fariseo* society and served in it for three years.

It would be possible to go on listing differences in attitudes and recounting apparent inconsistencies in expressed views and actual behavior almost indefinitely. The point to be made is that Pascua is not at all a homogeneous community in which a single way of life and a single pattern of thinking hold sway. The outline of religious belief set forth in this chapter has been arrived at only by taking as a point of departure the more uniform aspects of the ritual itself and utilizing for interpretation the most consistent of the statements available.

There is a word, much used in sermons, which expresses in summary an ideal of behavior in Pascua. When a man has never avoided the responsibility of holding a *fiesta* in the capacity of relative or *padrino* and when he has fulfilled duties as a member of a ceremonial society with reasonable regularity, it is said of him that there was *lu'turia* in his life: "Lu'turia ta'taʾak." A literal translation gives us only: "He knew the truth." The full translation in Pascua seems to indicate that *lu'turia* is a way of life in which a man recognizes all his kinship, *padrino*, and ceremonial obligations in such a manner that the whole village is aware of it; in other words, through the established channels of ceremony and ritual at public *fiestas*. It is the opinion of the second and third *maestros*, among others, that there are not many persons in Pascua now who can be said to have *lu'turia* in their lives. Yet to a non-Yaqui this ideal of behavior seems still to be the dominant force in Pascua life, and its influence seems to set Pascua culture off quite clearly as distinct from Mexican or American culture.

SUMMARY

Ceremony in the village has three primary centers. It is concerned chiefly with the dead, the Virgin, and Jesus. In addition, there are vestiges of a concern with kinds of animals. The ritual takes the form of an expression of recognized relationships between the living and the dead and between the living and the two deities. Most of the symbols in use can be assigned to, or interpreted as, aspects of the social personalities of ancestors and gods. The beliefs associated with these symbols are not uniform, but nevertheless a more or less consistent body of doctrine may be extracted from them.

There is notably lacking in this body of doctrine any important connection with the economic life. It is true that the Virgin is thought to be able to influence the community welfare and that Jesus is a deity through contact with whom a kind of community sense of sin may be expiated, but the welfare of the community is not conceived as being bound up with any namable economic factors over which these deities have control. Rain or fertility which would affect the ranch crops, in the production of which Yaquis are engaged, are not regarded as controlled by the Virgin. People do not appeal to her for jobs or good wages. Nor do they appeal to Jesus for these things. If the Virgin brings good luck, she brings it only as might a "charm" which insures that its bearer will be favored by events but does not determine what those events shall be. The Virgin and Jesus are, in short, not in control of any specific elements of the workaday life.

There is, however, a realm of life in which both deities have great power, namely, that of personal health. Both are curers, and the conception of them as such has an important bearing on the social organization. Through the *manda* to the Virgin or Jesus, each of the ceremonial societies builds up its nucleus of membership, and the *manda* provides the sanction which insures that the work of the societies will go on. The belief in the curing powers of the deities, therefore, lies at the foundation of the whole ceremonial organization.

The ancestors do not share the qualities of the other deities. They are not powerful supernatural beings who control important aspects of life. They are, nevertheless, a vital center of ceremonial life. The relations between them (in their varied forms) and the living are like those between a father and son who no longer live together in the same household. Mutual economic obligations are no longer important, but social relations involving respect and a sense of social solidarity remain. Despite their lack of economic function, the ancestors are knit into the society in such a way that it is given a continuity extending back into an indefinite past. The rites in connection with them are an affirmation of the continuity of Yaqui culture and the solidarity of its bearers.

Thus, although there is little or no relation between the supernatural beliefs of the village and its economic life, there is a definite and close relationship between these beliefs and the social structure. The ceremonial and the social systems are all of one piece, and the former provides the ultimate sanctions for the latter.

CHAPTER X

ORGANIZATION AND CONFLICT

PASCUA is a community organized basically along the lines of a primitive society yet having its existence in the setting of a mobile, heterogeneous urban environment. There is a definite incongruity between the village and its setting. Moreover, the primitive, or folk, form of the village organization is the instrument for social co-operation of a rather heterogeneous group of persons. That is to say that diversity in life-experiences of individuals is not confined to the surrounding city but extends also into the village. The people of Pascua, as should be clear from foregoing chapters, have not had that uniformity in life-experience which we associate with the participants in an isolated primitive society. Beginning in different parts of Sonora, lives of both men and women have varied in respect to contact with Mexicans, in experiences after arrival in the United States, in extent of contact with the values of Mexican Yaqui culture, and, finally, in degree of acceptance of the social values set up in Pascua Village. It should be clear that it would be extremely misleading to attempt to summarize the cultural forms of the village by describing a typical life-cycle. In terms of the details of orientation in social life from birth to death, there is no typical Pascuan, male or female. Yet the formal social structure of the village at present has unmistakable characteristics of a homogeneous primitive community.

The village may be described in much the same terms

in which we describe a primitive society, that is, in terms of interlocking and overlapping social structures which effect a close integration of the individuals composing the village. The basic importance of kinship cannot be overlooked in the society. The ultimate sanctions are supernatural, and these permeate the whole social structure. It can be said with much truth that the society of Pascua constitutes a closely integrated whole. It comprises institutions designed to promote a high degree of that permanence and fixity in the channels of social interaction and consequent personalizing of the individuals in the society which characterizes a primitive community. It is not too much to say this so long as we omit from consideration the economic aspects of life in Pascua. The moment that we consider them we are forced to admit that, although Pascua is perhaps fundamentally organized like a primitive society, there is a feature of life in the village which does not fit with this interpretation. It is the purpose of the present chapter to analyze the relationships that exist between the socioceremonial structure of the village and its economic life.

THE NATURE OF THE SOCIAL ORGANIZATION

The members of the society.—In our study of Pascua we have focused our attention on a number of people who live in a given small area on the outskirts of a southwestern city. We have limited our attention so that it includes not all the people in this area but only those claiming Yaqui blood. We have had no interest in these "Yaquis" as a physical group; we are interested in them only as a social phenomenon. We have assumed that the claim of Yaqui blood defines them as a group not with certain physical but rather with certain social characteristics, and we have proceeded to describe those social characteristics. We have thus defined a "society" for purposes of study—a society which we have referred to (as the group refers to itself) as Pascua Village. The behavior of the 429 individuals composing the village has been the fundamental data which we have observed.

The ultimate definition of the society is not, however, so simple. A full view of any society involves consideration of the total set of interactions between its human members. Thus, the society of Pascua Village must be considered to include not only those individuals who live in the given territory but also others who do not live there but with whom the former interact. Our analysis of Pascua would be incomplete if we failed to take into account the whites and others who employ Pascuans as laborers, who sell them food and other goods, or who have relations of any kind with them. The impossibility of studying in detail all the individuals who compose Pascua society in this sense is at once apparent. Pascuans have contacts, either face to face or indirect, with a host of persons who live in Tucson, elsewhere in Arizona, in Sonora, and even in more distant places. Moreover, Pascuans are to some extent in that "great society" which characterizes Western life and which is almost world-wide in scope. But those individuals with whom Pascuans have more direct contacts, such as employers and storekeepers, could be and were studied. These non-Pascuans, whether American, Yaqui, Mexican, Papago, or Chinese, have therefore also been included in our "society."

The definition of the society cannot stop there. There are beings with whom Pascuans interact, in much the same manner as they interact with one another, who live neither in Pascua nor in any other clearly definable place.

These are the dead relatives of Pascuans, other dead Yaquis, and certain deities, the most important of the latter being Jesus and the Virgin Mary. The dead and the deities are clearly regarded as in the nature of beings as real as other Pascuans. We have pointed out that Pascuans interact with them in almost exactly the same general ways that they interact with visible and tangible individuals. They communicate with them by speech in the form of prayers, they exchange food and other goods for services with them (as, for example, on All Souls' Day), and they maintain the expectation of reciprocal obligations with them and accordingly exchange services and co-operate with them. The deities and the dead are, therefore, members of the society in the sense that there is social interaction between them and the living.

The society of Pascua as we ultimately define it, then, is composed of Pascuans, non-Pascuans with whom the former have direct or face-to-face contacts, dead Yaquis, and gods, between all of whom there are certain observable relations manifest in various forms of behavior. These relations may be considered to fix the individuals in a structure so that they maintain certain definite positions in relation to one another. When we describe these relations, we are defining the social organization of Pascua.

The three systems of social interaction.—Each of the individuals composing the society acts toward others in certain prescribed ways. These defined modes of behavior constitute the social personalities of individuals. We have dwelt at length on the different aspects of social personality in Pascua. That of a given individual will be affected by the following factors: whether or not he is male or female, older or younger in relation to others, married or unmarried, dead or living. These aspects of social personality are expressed within the limits of three distinct systems of social interaction. They may be distinguished as the kinship, the *padrino*, and the ceremonial society systems. Every Pascuan, dead or living, and the gods are involved in one or all of these three types of social relationships. Not everyone, however, is at present related to others through the kinship system, nor is everyone a member of a ceremonial society. Only the *padrino* system is universal in the village, including all within its network. It will be pointed out, however, that the ceremonial society system, despite its noninclusive membership, is a more effective instrument for social unification of the village than is the *padrino* system. This effectiveness rests on the peculiar nature of the Virgin and Jesus as social personalities.

The kinship system is clearly fundamental in the whole social system which constitutes Pascua. It is the primary frame of reference in the social life for every person, whether he has actual kinship relations with other individuals or not. The other two systems are explained ultimately in terms of kinship. We may consider, for example, the terminology of the *padrino* system. The terms used in the latter are in every case modifications of kinship terms. A ceremonial sponsor is a kind of father or mother. The person sponsored is a kind of son or daughter, and ceremonial sponsors are "co-fathers" and "co-mothers" to each other as well as to the parents of the person sponsored. If the terms themselves were not so obviously modified kin terms, it would, nevertheless, be evident, from a consideration of the behavior involved, that sponsorship is a partial extension of kinship. Aspects of child-parent relationships are basic in the system. The *padrino* system is, in other words, constructed very much like the kin system up to a certain point, but the extension of the kinship relations has resulted in the creation of a new type of relationship—that of *compadres* or "co-parents."

The kinship point of departure is evident also in the ceremonial society system, although it is not so explicit. The persons of Jesus and Mary, who are central in the ceremonial society organization, are regularly called *'itom 'atʃai* and *'itom ai* ("our father" and "our mother"). The relationships to these persons are interpreted by the *maestros* as well as by laymen in terms of the parent-child relationship—an interpretation which is, of course, no more characteristic of Yaquis than of other types of Roman Catholics. Moreover, the relationships between members of the same society are explained in kinship terms both formally at times of confirmation in the societies and informally in ordinary conversations. People say that members are "like brothers" to one another.

Evidently, then, the primary relationships of individuals correlated with blood connection constitute a frame of reference for persons in all the other formalized relationships. The basic relations developed in the households in intimate family groups are extended throughout the society, and the values and behavior patterns associated with them are fundamental in the practices as well as in the ideology, or terminology, of the whole social organization. Whatever may have been the nature of wider social groupings among Sonora Yaquis, that organization which has developed in Pascua is built up on a kinship base, and these kinship-oriented organizations stand as the only effective instruments of social co-operation.

We have seen that the kinship system itself has apparently been reduced to a few fundamental relationships. It is narrowed in scope, and the relationships outside the essential elementary family have been generalized, there being evidence that they were once more particular in character. But these basic relations are sufficient to serve as primary instruments of orientation in the society as a whole. It is through the kinship structure that a child is placed in the other social structures. The kinship relations include obligations on the part of parents to fix the position of a child in three or more *padrino* structures. We have seen that the kinship system is fulfilling this function effectively in Pascua at the present time, for no individual is without *padrino* relations. In addition, it is through the kinship structures that individuals are placed in the ceremonial society system. The nucleus of each society consists of persons who have been promised to the society by their parents as a part of the obligations attendant on kinship relations. This function of the kinship system is operative in the village, but we have seen that it is not brought to bear on every individual. Nevertheless, the ceremonial societies continue to exist by virtue of this function of the kinship system. The latter, therefore, appears in another way as basic in the total social structure.

The kinship system breaks the society up into small units—the household or kin groups. Its formalized relations provide means of interaction between only the members of the same groups. Within these groups it links persons in what we might call continuous vertical integration. The relationships are particularized through three generations; beyond that the ascending generations, whether dead or living, are linked in a generalized set of relationships. The kinship system does not, however, provide directly a means of interaction between the various kin groups. We have seen that affinal relations are relatively weak and that they are insufficiently formalized to provide effective channels for the establishment of relations between the discrete family units.

The *padrino* system, on the other hand, is a means whereby interaction between persons in the various family units is formalized. As a member of one or more *padrino* structures, each individual in the village enters into relationships with persons outside his particular kin group. Every household is linked to other households through this system. The relationships between persons in different *padrino* structures are not only of a ritual character; they are economic as well. We have previously described in detail these various relations. They link not only the households of Pascuans but also those of Pascuans to Mexicans outside the village. It even happens that Americans may be brought into the *padrino* system. The *padrino* system thus accomplishes a wider integration than does the kinship system. We might say that it is a means of integrating laterally the social units formed in terms of the kinship system.

The *padrino* system is an effective instrument for vertical integration as well. It differs from the kinship system in that it does not establish relationships between the living and the dead. It operates wholly within the world of the living. Here it accomplishes a vertical integration in a manner somewhat analogous to that of kinship. The *padrino* system formalizes relations between any three given successive living generations. It establishes channels of interaction between persons sponsored and their godparents in the generation next above them. The former are in turn linked to the generation below themselves by sponsoring persons from that generation. Thus both the *padrino* and the kinship systems bring about vertical integration between successive generations.

It is the ceremonial society system which, through its lateral integration of persons, forms the village into a single social unit. Although the system does not link by its formal relations all the persons in the village, it nevertheless provides means whereby all may interact at different times for a common purpose. It is the only social structure in the village through which this ever comes about. It extends the circle of ritual, social, and economic co-operation which the *padrino* system provides for any two given *padrino* structures to all the fundamental social units, that is, all the kin-linked households. It accomplishes this despite the fact that not all persons in the village belong to the ceremonial societies. The living members are chiefly men, those whose contacts with the surrounding culture are most extensive and intimate. The system also includes in its network the two unique social personalities of Jesus and the Virgin, differing in this from each of the other systems. Mary is a member, for example, of the *matachín* society, the latter existing in fact as a structure as much through the mutual obligations between goddess and men as through those between men alone. Similarly, the *fariseo* society has Jesus as a member. The fundamental relationship in any society is that between a man or a woman and a deity. The relationships between men and women in the societies may be considered incidental to the primary man-deity relationships. Relationships may be established between deities and persons not members of societies, as in the occasional offering of a candle to a deity with the expectation of help in curing; but these relationships are casual and temporary, while those existing between society members and deities are formalized and permanent.

The ceremonial societies are intrusted with the maintenance of the physical forms of the two chief gods—their images—and they are the means of defining anew these symbols in each ceremony in which they participate. The ritual forms of interaction between gods and men are the property of the ceremonial societies. The importance of the maintenance of these symbols may be understood when we realize that the structure of the societies themselves is based so completely on supernatural sanctions. The fundamental sanction of the ceremonial society system is a supernatural one which may be defined as the expectation of death if ceremonial *'tekipanoa* is not performed regularly by the members of the societies. The god must continue to exist as a definite being and as a member of a society if the sanction is to persist.

The mutual obligations of members, including the deities, are not the whole content of the ceremonial society system. There are obligations existing between the ceremonial society segments and the society of Pascua as a whole—the pueblo. These, like the others, are both ritual and economic. We have seen that the societies perform certain functions at every ceremony. It is the ceremonial societies which not only act as intermediaries in a direct way between the gods and the givers of the ceremony but also effect economic co-operation of the village as a whole through the *limosna* and other activities. The ceremonial society system thus integrates the society in the widest sense in which it is integrated. It provides a means of interaction between all persons of all kin groups and all *padrino* groups. We might say in summary that the ceremonial society system is itself the society of Pascua. Pascua could not be spoken of as a social unity in the absence of the ceremonial society system.

The "fiesta": periodic reintegration of the society.—The institution through which the ceremonial society system chiefly operates is the *fiesta*, which, it will be recalled, is a type of ceremony which may take many different forms, a funeral being included equally with a saint's day observance in the type. These periodically occurring events are the only occasions on which the village exists as a functioning social unit, but they are frequent, and their frequency is a factor in the preservation of Pascua's cultural unity.

A complete analysis of any *fiesta* constitutes an analysis of Pascua society. The *fiesta* is an easily observable event in which are to be found in operation all the factors which work from within to maintain Pascua as a social and cultural unit. A study of the behavior of individuals in connection with a *fiesta* gives an insight into the mechanism of internal maintenance of the society. The ceremonies at Easter constitute the most complete expression of the society, but any *fiesta* whatever illustrates the chief factors which contribute to its maintenance.

In a *fiesta de promesa* appear quite clearly the operation of the various types of interaction through which Pascua society exists. Any such *fiesta* begins and ends in a fundamental idea of the culture, namely, the belief in the mutual interaction of gods and men. A vow to give such a *fiesta* is made as a result, in all cases recorded, of a crisis in the life of an individual—an individual who is ill and is expected to die. The vow is made to Jesus or to the Virgin or to both that, if assistance in curing is rendered, the *fiesta* will be given in payment. If the individual gets well, the initial actions in fulfilling the vow are carried out by the person himself or by his relatives. The obligations are immediately extended to the whole kinship group. They assume the responsibility of providing food and other necessities for the *fiesta* and for organizing the activities of persons necessary in it. In fulfilling the economic obligations, they enlist aid from the various *padrino* groups of which they are members. But the kinship and associated *padrino* groups cannot by themselves fulfil the vow simply by the provision of food, place, and paraphernalia; they are helpless without the assistance of the persons who are special devotees of the deities—the ceremonial society members. The latter, acting through the means of their formalized system of relationships, first between themselves and the village as a whole, finally between themselves and the deity, produce the *fiesta* and thus fulfil the original obligation. This is the ultimate rhythm of the social life in Pascua: the appearance of an obligation as a result of crisis in an individual life and the fulfilment of that obligation with the co-operation of the whole village through the interaction of its social segments.

Each activity in the *fiesta* is, further, a concrete expression of the forms of social interaction existent in the village. The *fiesta* proceeds through a series of activities which serve to mark off each of the co-operating groups and to define their relationships to one another.

On the afternoon of the *fiesta* its primary sponsors get things in readiness. The sponsoring kin group provides the place at its own household. It provides a *ramada* for an altar and a place for the dance society to dance—the two necessary items for interaction with a god. With the help of *padrino* groups to which its members belong, it provides food for the performers. Through the medium of the dance society's *limósna*, the family group is further assisted by the whole village. Meanwhile the ceremonial societies concerned have also been preparing. A '*temasti* of the male altar group has brought the crucifix which is in his keeping to the altar table at the household and has arranged the altar there. He remains at the house.

In the afternoon the *pascola* dancers and their musicians come to the house, put on their costumes, and begin to dance. The other ceremonial performers, however, begin their part in the ceremony from the church, not the household. The activities which they carry out at the household are only an incident in a series of events which has its base at the church. They start at the church and end there the following morning.

The dance of the *pascolas* has been going on for some time at the household before the ceremonial societies gather at the church. There, beginning about sunset, *maestros* conduct a few prayers or say a few rosaries. The *matachín* society, if the *fiesta* is primarily for the Virgin, gathers and dances briefly before the church, where the altar has been set up with crucifixes and Virgins. At the end of the dance the images of the Virgin are taken up by the *ki'ostim*, and a procession is formed. It is headed by the *matachinis*, followed by the *ki'ostim* with the images, and finally by the *maestros* and *cantoras*. The procession goes from the church to the household, leaving the church altar bare. The *matachinis* dance at the head of the procession through the village to the place of the *fiesta*.

Meanwhile at the household another altar has been set up some distance from the house, usually to the east. The procession stops and deposits its images on this *encampamiento* altar. The *matachinis* stop dancing. From the house to the *encampamiento* come the givers of the *fiesta* (the kin group), bearing the *'temasti* crucifix and whatever household images they may possess. They are preceded by the *pascolas* and their drummer, who dance ahead of them.

At the *encampamiento* a girl *alpes* (flag-bearer) as representative of the church group blesses the *pascolas* and the *fiesteros* (kin group), who kneel before the altar while the flag-bearer waves her flag over them. Then a *fiestera* takes the flag, and a *fiestero* makes a brief speech of welcome and is answered by the *maestro* or *matachín* leader on behalf of the church groups. The sacred organizations have now been properly related to the profane *fiesteros* and *pascolas*. As a single unified group, the procession proceeds to the household altar, headed by the dancing *matachinis* and *pascolas*. The *fiesteros*, together with the *ki'ostim* and the *'temasti*, carry the images back to the household altar. Arrived there, the *fiestera* with the flag of the *alpes* now proceeds to welcome all performers and spectators to her household by blessing them as they come up in pairs and kneel before the altar. She has been temporarily invested with the powers of the church; her kin group has been, as it were, taken into the church for the duration of the *fiesta*.

The *pascolas* go into their profane side of the *ramada* and begin to dance; the *maestros* and *cantoras* take up their places before the altar on the sacred side of the *ramada;* and the *matachinis* begin their dance outside the *ramada*, facing the altar. The *encampamiento* remains the *matachinis'* church, where they deposit their paraphernalia between dances. The *maestros'* chants, the *pascolas'* dances and chatter, and the *matachinis'* dancing go on more or less independently of one another during the rest of the night.

Twice during the ceremony all the performers eat, the altar groups eating first, the *matachinis* next, and finally

FIGURE 9

Plan of a Fiesta de Promesa in Lent

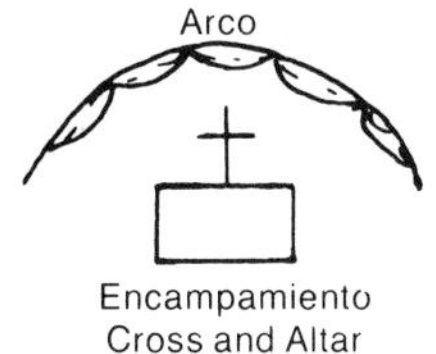

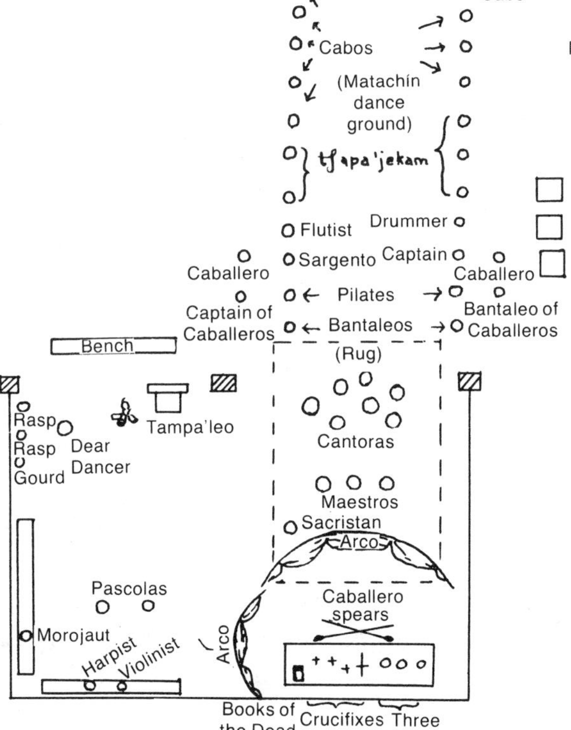

the *pascolas*, each performing group giving out food to their relatives or friends among the nonperformers. At some time during the night, or possibly at the end of the ceremony, the *fiesteros* and *padrinos*, who have assisted in the *fiesta*, line up by the *encampamiento* altar and go through the hand-touching ritual.

In the morning, after breakfast has been eaten by all, the reverse of the welcoming ritual is performed. There is a procession out to the *encampamiento*, where the church organizations take their leave of the *fiesteros* and *pascolas*. The *maestro* delivers a long sermon in which he goes over the reasons for holding the *fiesta*, announces the fulfilment of the obligation, and thanks the performers in behalf of the village as a whole. The church organizations then leave in procession and march back to the church, where they place their images on the altar; the *matachinis* dance once more; and the *fiesta* is over.

This is the general pattern of a *fiesta*. A funeral, a death *novena*, a death anniversary, and a saint's-day *fiesta* all follow approximately the same pattern. The essential features of ritual emphasizing the relationships between *fiesteros*, *pascolas*, *padrinos*, and ceremonial societies, setting them off from one another and indicating their functions in the *fiesta* and thus in the society, are present in all. The nature of the unity which characterizes Pascua society with its three closely interdependent systems of organization, achieving ultimate integration through the supernaturally controlled ceremonial societies, is explicit in the welcoming and departing ritual.

THE NATURE OF THE CONFLICT

Extra-village relations.—The view of Pascua as an organized unity which we have just outlined has been achieved only by omitting from consideration the relationships of Pascuans with non-Pascuans. We have not referred to these relationships as constituting a "system." As a matter of fact, not all non-Pascuans are outside the three systems which we have described. Pascuans are in many kinship and *padrino* structures which extend outside the village into other Yaqui villages in Arizona, with members of which there is constant interaction. It is true also that a number of Mexicans have been brought into the kinship structures of Pascua and that numerous *padrino* structures of which Pascuans are parts include also Mexicans living either in the village or near it. But only Pascuans have roles in the ceremonial society system of the village. Two of the systems which characterize Pascua society do, therefore, serve as means of interaction between Pascuans and non-Pascuans, but one of them does not.

It is, however, generally the case that the relationships of Pascuans with non-Pascuans, other than Yaquis, are not formalized along the lines of any of the three systems discussed. The characteristic of the latter is that any relationship defined by them does not change from time to time. Once established, it is fixed and, throughout the lives of the two individuals recognizing it, remains binding. A godchild and a godfather are such to each other throughout life. Every time they meet, some form of behavior characteristic of their relationship is evident. The same is, of course, true of father and son and other blood relatives. A *matachini* and the Virgin and a *matachini* and a *matachini* have fixed relations throughout life and also as *'animam* after death. This permanency of relationship, with its continuing formalized behavior and its organization of specific individuals in relation to one another, is not characteristic of the relations beween Pascuans and non-Pascuans who are outside the three systems we have described. An American may be in the relationship of employer at one time to a Pascuan, but he does not always remain so. Each relationship is worked out to suit a specific occasion, and the individual non-Pascuan involved is not then fixed in a permanent position in any system of relationships but may move completely outside the society of Pascua within a few days or weeks. Specific relationships are established which at times are effective and at others are inoperative. It is here that we find an important contrast between relationships within the village and those which extend outside the village.

The employer-employee relationships into which Pascuans enter play an important part, as we have seen, in their lives. In these it may be pointed out, in the first place, that the symbols of social personality which run through the other relationships are, with one exception, absent. The idea of the *patrón*, of which some use is made in the ceremonial society system, is the only symbol in evidence; the kinship symbols (terms) and their variants are never applied in these relationships as they are in those of the village. Much as members of a ceremonial society sometimes speak of the deity to whom they are dedicated as their *patrón*, so Pascuans use the term for their employers. The idea is present in the village that an employer ought to remain interested in an employee even though the latter has not worked for him for some time. The older Pascuans, especially, sometimes make the effort, when they are hard up, to seek out a former employer and get financial assistance from him; they personalize the employer as *patrón* and show a definite expectation of a mutual-assistance type of behavior from him. However, during 1936–37 no successful attempts of this kind were recorded, although several were made. In other words, extra-village economic relationships are interpreted to some extent in terms of the familiar ceremonial society system; but this interpretation is only on the part of Pascuans and does not work the other way.

In the second place, the employer-employee relationships provide no basis for interaction of Pascuan with Pascuan. As employees, Pascuans do not, except in the cotton-picking season, act together. Pascuans work and secure jobs on ranches, railroads, and elsewhere as individuals. The Pistola system, which attempted to establish an economic basis of co-operation between Pascuans by the method of group employment, broke down. According to statements of persons who worked under the system, it was abandoned by them because they found that they could get their own jobs as they became more experienced and that they could make more money when they did not have to pay any out to Pistola. The employer-employee relations have, in other words, operated to release persons from group controls in at least that aspect of economic life concerned with production. They have not fostered any sense of group concern over the means of subsistence. Looked at in this way, then, the employer-employee relationships are a disintegrating factor. They do not operate to bring Pascuans together in any activity, and they do operate to make them act without regard to other Pascuans in economic production.

However, the economic relationships cannot all be defined in the same terms. We have seen, for example, that they vary with the season of the year. In the cotton-picking season Pascuans do hire out in groups, that is, in family groups. They are employed by families to a great extent, and, when they leave the village for the cotton fields, they go together and not only live but also work in family groups through the cotton-picking season. In one view, the cotton-picking season, with its scattering of families over southern Arizona, is a factor for disintegration of the society: bringing about the practical desertion of the village, it disrupts the community life. On the other hand, it serves to increase family solidarity. It periodically forces families to become closely co-operating social units, and during this period the families are more isolated from the urban type of environment than they are in Pascua. A survey of cotton-picking families who had moved out of the village to the ranches for the season indicated also that Yaqui families tend to congregate at the same ranches. In general, therefore, it may be said that the production aspect of economic life, although it provides no basis for general co-operation of Pascuans, is nevertheless not wholly a disintegrating factor in the social life.

This somewhat generalized approach does not suffice for an evaluation of the role of economic relationships in the society of Pascua. It is necessary to point out again a very real conflict which exists between activities demanded by making a living and those growing out of the social system which we have described. Before we do this, however, we may pass briefly over the other important extra-village relationships. One of these in the economic field is that of buyer-seller, with the Pascuans always in the buyer situation. Here the sellers are more or less permanent social personalities, a great deal more so than are the employers. The ones whom Pascuans have come to know and deal with as individuals are the Chinese storekeepers of Tucson and the traveling hucksters and butchers who come to the village daily. These are the ones who have specialized in the Yaqui trade. They seek to adjust their stocks to Yaqui (and Mexican, which differ little in the matter of food from Yaqui) wants. In a community where outside trade is a constant necessity, a traveling trader is a force not for change but for stability and conservatism. He assists voluntary segregation, permitting the Yaqui women to remain in their village to do their shopping. Here again, an aspect of economic life, while perhaps in the long run being a factor for assimilation, is nevertheless, when viewed closely in the details of its operation, a factor also making for the maintenance of the society as distinct from the surrounding one, or, in other words, a factor retarding cultural assimilation.

It is possible to view the courts of the county and city also as contributing to conflict within Pascua culture. The basic point of view of the courts is that of individual responsibility for crime, while the older Yaquis still hold to a principle based on a different view. The remembered system of punishment for crimes in Sonora Yaqui villages was based on collective responsibility. A convicted person was lashed three times for his father, three times for his mother, etc. Pascuans do not make a great deal of use of the Tucson legal system, but we have seen that they do go to court of their own accord. They believe, in general, that it is good and do not show any awareness of a contradiction between its principles and their own. These extra-village relations through the courts may be viewed, therefore, not as a source of overt, easily observable culture conflict but as a slow-working factor opposing the present social system and probably striking deeply at the foundations of the kinship system.

Leadership versus the job.—We may now return to a further consideration of the nature of the employer-employee relationships and their conflict with the other social relations of Pascuans. It has been pointed out at length in the chapter on economics that the job pattern of the surrounding culture has by no means been fully accepted. In the first place, the level of subsistence of Pascuans is below even what the charity organizations of Tucson consider the minimum. Moreover, the estimates of villagers tend to be below this minimum; there is, in general, no evidence that it is desired that it be higher. There have grown up no distinctions as to social status between rich and poor. No ideology of saving and future utilization of money has yet developed. All this indicates that Pascuans have not been assimilated to the outside economic life. Something other than the drives at work there operate in determining the place of Pascuans in productive economic life. It is our contention here that these drives have their source in the character of the social system which we have described in the early part of this chapter and that there is a fundamental conflict in the society of Pascua resulting from the play of outside and inside economic motives in the village.

It may be suggested that the system of social relations in which a Pascuan finds himself, which periodically demands *fiestas* which are expensive and thus prohibitive of accumulation, is an important factor working against the acceptance of the surrounding economic patterns. Particularly does this seem important when we consider that social status in the village is related to the proper recognition of the demands of the *fiesta* pattern. Accumulations go to relatives and *compadres* who are faced with the necessity for giving a *fiesta*. In addition, the many activities involved in the *fiesta* system, whether or not one is a member of a ceremonial society, would seem to be important in hindering the adoption of working habits which are regular and in conformity with the patterns to which employers adhere. No doubt these conditions which we have mentioned should be considered in a complete analysis of the relationship between Pascua economic and social life; it seems likely that there should be conflicts along these lines working themselves out in the culture. We have, however, seen that it is possible to accumulate a little property and at the same time maintain active participation in the ceremonial life of the village—even the maintenance of important places in the village life, such as head *'temasti*. We have seen that for the majority of ceremonial society members there is a minimum of conflict between holding a job and performing ceremonial duties. Not all members of a society are necessary for any given *fiesta*. Moreover, *fiestas* are held on the days of the week, whenever possible, which do not conflict with the demands of jobs. Hence these conflicts, although they do exist, are not acute. Accordingly, they are difficult to observe and, in fact, escape all but the most intensive means of investigation. A discussion of their part in Pascua culture will have to await more detailed observation.

A conflict more readily observable and one which seems to strike at the roots of the culture in its present form is, however, connected with the demands of the ceremonial and the job patterns. This is the conflict of leadership in a male ceremonial society with the necessities for maintaining a living for one's family. We have seen that the demands of leadership were not considered compatible with a job by José Robles, the man who was elected *matachín* leader in 1930. He accordingly slipped into the role of an ordinary *matachín* dancer, and his position was taken over by one of the few men in the village who had no family and no interest whatever in economic activity, Teodoro García. Further, it was apparent that the extensive demands on the time of Celso Matus, the leader of the *fariseo* society, conflicted with his desire to hold a steady job for the support of his family. Despite his decision to risk his job by a month's layoff at Easter, he nevertheless incurred the disapproval of the village by his apparent greater attention to his job than to his ceremonial duties at other times. This conflict resulting from the demands of the two patterns of behavior was apparent in the manner and actions of the man himself.

These facts seem to indicate an important conflict. They are not instances of individual maladjustment with small significance for the society as a whole; they are conflicts in the lives of men who hold positions which are vital for the continuance of the society. If those positions cannot be filled, the present character of the ceremonial organization will have to be altered or it will break down altogether. That they are filled only with difficulty is evidenced in the history of the *matachín* leadership. The exacting duties of a ceremonial leader, as they are now formulated, are not compatible with holding a job and supporting a family in the manner set by the surrounding culture. Men may still be sufficiently under the influence of Pascua culture to wish to be leaders in it, but they are then confronted with the physical impossibility of doing the two things at once. The conflict which we are examining here is not a vague and slow-working replacement of one set of cultural values by another; it is rather an acute conflict between specific activities demanded by different types of institutions.

The society itself is not providing a means for resolving this conflict. There is no institution by which a ceremonial leader may be fully supported, so that he can devote full time to his ceremonial duties, although such an institution is reported by Beals among the Sonora Mayos. The compromises which a leader makes are necessarily *ad hoc* and do not follow a pattern or create a tradition. The conflict is recognized only by the individual who finds himself confronted with the insoluble problem of serving the ceremonial interests of the village at the same time that he tries to serve the economic interests of himself and his family. This is true despite the fact that the ceremonial society system, as we have indicated, is the ultimate integrating factor in Pascua society.

The decay of the animal gods.—There is another disharmony in the culture of Pascua which cannot be so readily interpreted as a conflict between activities demanded within one system of relations and those demanded in another. The disharmony which is meant is that between the older animal gods and the developing Christian gods. It has, no doubt, been working for a long time. Our analysis, in view of the lack of detailed comparative data, can be little more than suggestive. But it is worth while undertaking because it has a bearing on the problem of the relation between the economic and other aspects of the culture. The conditions of existence in Pascua are such that no sense of intimate dependence on the natural environment is present. It is suggested here that this condition is closely connected with certain attitudes and practices which are observable in the ceremonial life. Some of the gods are, we might say, changing their social personalities—gods whom we may specifically name as the deer, the horned toad, the snake, and some other small ground-living animals. These gods have not disappeared yet, but there is evidence from the study of Pascua that they are at least suffering profound alterations. As they change, certain institutions connected with them also change. The ones which we shall consider are the *pascolas* and the deer-dancer. An examination of them in the form of a comparison with other ritual dancers, such as the *matachinis*, seems to give some idea of the manner in which the gods change.

If we contrast the deer-dancer, the *pascola*, and the *matachini*, considering them for the moment as "culture traits" in the manner of the anthropologists, it is possible to draw some conclusions as to the nature of the change. It is clear from the data previously given that the deer-dancer is the most thoroughly aboriginal of the three; his costume, the music to which he dances, and the dance itself are all without European influence. He is the only institution, perhaps, about which such a statement may be made. The *pascola*, as we have noted, is a curious combination of aboriginal and European influences; it is sufficient to recall here that he dances half the time to European music and instruments and half to aboriginal. The *matachini*, on the other hand, is predominantly European in character: music, dance figures, and even costume show few characteristics which may confidently be called aboriginal. If we go further in our contrast and attempt to arrange these three types of dancers in the order of their importance in Arizona Yaqui ceremony, we find that the deer-dancer (who is most aboriginal in character) is the least important, while the *matachini* (the least aboriginal) is an important figure and is completely integrated with the rest of the ceremonial life. If we cannot say that the *pascola* is definitely less important than the *matachini*, we can, nevertheless, say that he is more important than the deer-dancer. It must be pointed out, however, that he remains somewhat outside the ceremonial pattern set by the church organizations and that his place in the ritual life shows certain contradictions. These statements require further elaboration.

Although the deer-dancer is a colorful figure in ceremony, he does not appear often. He is, furthermore, not essential in any of the ceremonies in which he does appear. It is entirely optional with him whether or not he dances, since he belongs to no ceremonial society. When he does appear at a ceremony, it is obvious that he has the least connection of any dancer with the church organization, and he remains more aloof even than the *pascolas* from the Catholic ritual which goes on about him during a night of ceremony.

The *pascola*, on the other hand, is absolutely essential at at least one type of ceremony—the child funeral. He also appears at many others. But just as in the music to which he dances there is a dual character, so there is a dual quality in his ceremonial participation. He shows, on the one hand, a certain connection with the church organizations and their activities; on the other, he seems to be a purely secular figure. He is outside the ceremonial organization, but he makes use of Christian doctrine in his ritual speeches. He burlesques the church groups, but he marches with them in processions. He prays, but he serves a *fiesta* crowd rather than a deity. His dual character is recognized in myths current in the village which relate his origin to the devil, although they recognize his importance in Yaqui ritual.

There are no such contradictions in the activities of the *matachinis*. They are essential and important at many ceremonies. As members of a ceremonial society, they have no choice about performing. Everything that they do is co-ordinated with the church groups.

Explanations of the places of these various ritual dancers in the culture are suggested in some of the data which we have thus far used. An explanation can be made in terms of the economic life, the social structure, and the values and symbols in terms of which Arizona Yaqui society is at present organized; in other words, the situation may be explained as a part of a larger whole with which it is consistent. However, an explanation might also be made in terms of the specific historic events which have preceded the present situation. Both types of explanation will be attempted here.

An explanation in terms of function may be briefly indicated. It can be pointed out, for example, that Yaqui life in Arizona goes on independently of any direct connection with the natural environment. Arizona Yaquis never hunt. They do not even practice agriculture except in the capacity of day laborers on ranches. Against this background, it may be seen that a dance concerned with the deer hunt or with animals and their ways would have little relation to the realities of life.

Lack of relationship to the economic life may be an explanation for the small importance of the deer dance, but what relationship does the *matachín* dance bear to the economic life and the rest of the culture? It seems clear that *matachín* dancing has no more direct relation with the economic life than does the deer dance, but it has a number of links with other aspects of the culture. The *matachinis* constitute a ceremonial society. The ritual dance is only one of several functions which the society performs, and the *matachinis* are only one of several other societies. These societies are the only mechanisms for bringing about community and intercommunity co-operation. Evidently, therefore, the *matachinis* and their dance are closely connected with an important aspect of the social organization. They are, moreover, connected with the ritual pattern in a way that the deer-dancer is not. They are devotees of the Virgin, who is important as one of the two major deities in Arizona Yaqui life. The *matachín* dance itself is a recognition of the powers of the Virgin in curing disease; it is connected with an important function of the deity. The dance of the *matachinis* is thus bound up in the details of the social and ritual life and derives its importance in the culture from this whole complex.

The situation of the *pascolas* in relation to the rest of the culture is not so clear as that of the *matachinis*. They are not concerned with curing or with either of the major deities. They are sometimes considered to be dedicated to the other deity, Jesus, but this connection seems rather to be in process of formation and is not yet established. The importance of the *pascolas* seems to be related to their role as ritual intermediaries between ceremonial societies and the households. They are clearly related to the culture at more points than is the deer-dancer, but their relationship is not so extensive as is that of the *matachinis*.

This sort of explanation does not take into consideration certain aspects of the problem which are implicit in our contrast of the dancers in terms of their degree of aboriginality. When we made that contrast, we were thinking of history. If the deer-dancer shows old or aboriginal characters and the *matachini* shows new or European ones, is there any point in relating these facts as to historical origins to the question of relative importance in Yaqui culture? It seems that they suggest a hypothesis as to the course of development of Yaqui culture in recent times. They indicate that the culture has changed in response to certain conditions—that it may be organized at present on a base different from what it formerly was. We can ask certain questions on the basis of our data with reference to the nature of those changes: Does the present position of the deer-dancer represent an adjustment of the culture to a condition of decreased importance of the natural environment in Yaqui life? Does the importance of the *matachini* indicate an increasing importance of curing in the ritual and social life or does it indicate merely a narrowing of the range of interests expressed in ritual and ceremony? Answers to these questions can come only from extended investigations of Yaqui culture in Sonora, but some data are available.

We have pointed out that the deer-dancer does not appear at all the ceremonies at which he might appear in Arizona at present. He seems, in other words, to be losing ground. Moreover, the older Arizona Yaquis recall that, even since their arrival in the United States, the ritual connected with the deer-dancer has decreased in complexity. He was formerly much more intimately associated with the *pascolas* and went through an elaborate mock deer hunt with them at the close of every *fiesta* in which he appeared. This is not the case now in Arizona. A recent observer reports that in Sonora the deer hunt is still carried out in elaborate fashion and that the association between deer-dancer and *pascolas* is still close.[1] In fact, the accounts of observers confuse the types of dancers, referring sometimes to all as deer-dancers.[2] This confusion would be impossible in Arizona. (It might be added that one type of dancer representing an animal, the *matupari*,

[1] Ralph L. Beals, "Present-Day Yaqui-Mayo Culture" (manuscript).

[2] W. C. Holden *et al.*, *Studies of the Yaqui Indians of Sonora, Mexico* ("Texas Technological College Bull.," Vol. XII, No. 1 [Lubbock, Tex., January, 1936]), p. 59; Francisco Dominguez, "Costumbres Yaquis," *Mexican Folkways* (Mexico City, July, 1937), p. 19.

has disappeared within the last ten years among Arizona Yaquis.) These facts would seem to confirm us in positing some relationship between changing economic conditions affecting Yaqui culture as a whole and the forms of the ritual dance.

A minor piece of evidence is available in connection with the *matachinis* in this respect. The older Arizona Yaquis say that the *matachín* dance has rain-making functions, but this is not seriously entertained by American-born Yaquis. Further investigation among Sonora Yaquis would be necessary for satisfactory determination of the older functions of the *matachinis*. Certainly, the *matachinis* in Arizona are now generally considered to be connected only with curing disease.

There is another aspect of the situation which may be dwelt on briefly. Is there any way of describing what is happening in Arizona Yaqui culture, as indicated in our data, in terms which have been used in the description of other specific events involving cultural change? It seems that we might attempt to make use of the concept "secularization" and its opposite. It is suggested that the deer-dancer is undergoing a process of secularization in response to the conditions affecting Yaqui culture in Arizona, that the *matachinis* have incorporated into the culture certain elements which were once not a part of it but which are now sanctified in it as part of the *matachín* complex, and that the *pascola* is at an intermediate stage of sanctification into Yaqui culture in its present form.

We have seen that the deer-dancer, while still a participant in ceremony, is surrounded by secular attitudes. His appearance depends on conditions dictated by personal considerations. A *fiestero* may feel that he does not want to spend the money necessary for the food for the dancer and his musicians, or the deer-dancer himself may not care to dance. Nothing will happen to anyone if the latter does not appear. He is not an essential in the ceremonial pattern. The deer-dancer's activities are, furthermore, gradually being disassociated from those of the *pascolas*. As this happens, his connection with those aspects of the culture which are supernaturally sanctioned—the church organizations—becomes very tenuous. He is gradually becoming simply an entertainer.

The *matachini*, however, is undergoing no such process of secularization. *Matachinis* must dance at certain times. If they do not, both the dead and their patroness, the Virgin, would be displeased, and this would affect the village as a whole as well as specific individuals and families. Whatever may have been the importance of the *matachinis* at a former time, they are now important, and that which is associated with them—European music and types of dance, the Virgin and Catholic doctrine concerning the Holy Family—are important also. We do not know the historical facts in connection with the association of these traits with the *matachinis*, but the result of the fusion is clear. The *matachín* complex contains certain things which were once not a part of Yaqui culture but which are now fully sanctified in it.

The *pascolas* seem to be in process of sanctification as much as the deer-dancer is in process of secularization. It seems to be optional with a *pascola* whether or not he dance, but it is not optional with a *padrino* who is responsible for a child funeral whether or not he have a *pascola*. He must have one, and one is always found. The *pascola* has certain duties to perform which involve Catholic ritual, and there is some association of him with Jesus, in the minds of Pascuans, if not in actual formalized terms. We find a general interest in stories which reconcile the *pascolas'* activities with Christian mythology, and we find also numerous interpretations of the *pascolas'* paraphernalia and functions in Christian terms. In other words, it appears that there are attempts to adjust the *pascola* to the prevailing ceremonial pattern—a process which we might regard as the opposite of secularization.

Perhaps this somewhat labored analysis might be summed up in the following way. Arizona Yaqui ceremonialism is moving from a former system based on intimate connection with the natural environment, indicated in the deer songs and in the animal dances of the *pascolas*, to a pattern which is not closely related to the natural environment. The new basis is primarily concerned with curing, which remains the chief area of existence in which secular techniques do not seem adequate. With weather, crop control, and success in hunting no longer important, ritual and ceremony find their base in the uncertainties of health. Moreover, the purely social functions of the *matachinis*, as a group organized to effect social and economic co-operation in the village, give their ritual and symbols an importance in the society beyond mere curing. While the deer-dancer has no relevance to the new orientation, the *matachinis* exemplify the nature of that orientation. They are supported by the recently adopted symbol of the Virgin and derive their meaning from present ideas in regard to curing. Their modern-looking trappings are not in this case an indication of cultural disintegration; rather, they indicate at least a temporarily successful fusion of old and new.

CHAPTER XI

CONCLUSION: THE HYPOTHESIS OF FUNCTIONAL INCONSISTENCY

THE notion that societies are composed of parts (institutions, customs, social structures, they may be called) which work together in some fashion to produce harmoniously functioning wholes has recently been given currency through the writings of Malinowski and his students.[1] The idea is, of course, not new; it is to be found, for example, in various forms in the conceptions of Spencer,[2] Boas,[3] and Durkheim.[4] Radcliffe-Brown has in the past few years attempted to formulate the idea with some precision. He says, for example:

> Such a view implies that a social system (the total social structure of a society together with the totality of social usages, in which that structure appears and on which it depends for its continued existence) has a certain kind of unity, which we may speak of as a functional unity. We may define it as a condition in which all parts of the social system work together with a sufficient degree of harmony or internal consistency, i.e., without producing persistent conflicts which can neither be resolved nor regulated.[5]

[1] See, e.g., Bronislaw Malinowski, "Culture," *Encyclopedia of the Social Sciences* (New York: Macmillan Co., 1931), IV, 621–45; H. Ian Hogbin, *Law and Order in Polynesia* (New York: Harcourt, Brace & Co., 1934), esp. p. 290.

[2] Herbert Spencer, *The Principles of Sociology* (New York: D. Appleton & Co., 1925), I, 447–62.

[3] It is not easy to find a definite formulation of this view in Boas' writings, but the following is indicative: Franz Boas, *The Mind of Primitive Man* (rev. ed.; New York: Macmillan Co., 1938), pp. 186–89.

[4] Emile Durkheim, *Le Suicide* (2d ed.; Paris, 1911).

[5] A. R. Radcliffe-Brown, "On the Concept of Function in Social Science," *American Anthropologist*, XXXVII, No. 3 (new ser.; 1935), 397.

Following up this conception, he goes on to say:

> A society that is thrown into a condition of functional disunity or inconsistency . . . . will not die, except in such comparatively rare instances as an Australian tribe overwhelmed by the white man's destructive force, but will continue to struggle toward some . . . . kind of social health, and may, in the course of this, change its structural type.[6]

The present study was in part inspired by an interest in the question of functional inconsistency. The situation in Pascua Village was originally seen as one in which functional inconsistencies might be found. The first statement of the problem as an inquiry into the relations between the economic and other aspects of the culture had implicit in it the expectation of discovering an inconsistency between the economic and, for example, the ceremonial life. The study called for some analysis of the conflicts apparent in the behavior of individuals participating in these two aspects of the culture. Some conflicts which were discovered have been outlined in the preceding chapter.

The first of the two major ones which were singled out for analysis—that between the demands of leadership in a ceremonial society and the demands of job-holding—might be classified as a functional inconsistency. The conflicts which we have described in connection with ceremonial leadership are acute instances of conflicts which are to be found in greater or less degree in the lives of most Pascua men. The conflict may be described in broadest terms as one between the job pattern and the ceremonial pattern. The job pattern is one which exists in connection with a complex set of institutions and status-conferring mechanisms characteristic of American society as a whole. The ceremonial pattern is one which exists also in connection with a complex set of institutions and status-confer-

[6] *Ibid.*, p. 398.

ring mechanisms characteristic, however, only of the Yaqui minority in Arizona. The latter can exist only if the men of Pascua continue a measure of participation in the job pattern. It, as much as individuals themselves, requires economic support. Working in the job pattern outside the village, individuals become responsive to it; they come to desire to hold a steady job, to make more money, to purchase more things—in other words, to participate more fully in the job pattern, with its accompanying set of institutions. We find individuals (at least two) who are still living in Pascua who have rejected the claims of the ceremonial pattern almost completely and have done this quite definitely for the purpose of participating more fully in the job pattern. León Valencia, the dairyman-*matachini*, is such an example. He still maintains kinship and *padrino* relations in the village, but he neither participates in nor attends ceremonies. To Pascuans, he is "like a Mexican."

All the adult males of Pascua are classifiable in categories according to the degree of their response to the respective patterns of job and ceremony. At one end of the classification would be León Valencia, the dairyman; at the other end would be Teodoro García, the *matachín* leader. There is little or no conflict for Valencia, who has become responsive only to the job pattern, and there is no conflict for García, who has become completely unresponsive to the job pattern. Acute conflict appears only in the case of individuals, like Celso Matus, the *fariseo* leader, who are considerably responsive to both patterns.

We thus see a condition in Pascua society which is producing "persistent conflicts." We may speak of these conflicts as arising between economic and ceremonial institutions, but we have observed that they are to be studied as a collection of conflicts of varying intensity in the daily activities of specific persons. Radcliffe-Brown suggests that a functional inconsistency exists when the "persistent conflicts . . . . can neither be resolved nor regulated." We have called attention to the fact that the conflict which we have been discussing is not being resolved by regulation proceeding from any of the groups concerned. It is being continually resolved, however, by Yaqui individuals who reduce the amount of their participation in Pascua culture. In the first place, leadership in a society may be avoided, then active participation in a society may be gradually reduced. An individual may drift out of contact with the ceremonial society system yet remain within the *padrino* and kinship systems and also remain as a resident of Pascua. There are individuals whose life is characterized by such partial participation in Pascua culture—individuals who have not gone so far as León Valencia but who are moving in that direction. This process may be carried farther. There are Yaquis who have married Mexicans and moved away into the Mexican community. There is no caste line preventing such voluntary movement out of Pascua society. There is, thus, a kind of resolution of the conflict—a resolution carried out individual by individual. The conflict is not regulated by the society in the sense that there is modification or adjustment of institutions to one another. It is regulated only through the process of all developing foci of conflict removing themselves outside the society into the surrounding one.

The other conflict which we have mentioned may also be classified as a functional inconsistency. It is at the same time a great deal more complex and a great deal less acute than the other. In general, it might be described as an inconsistency between economic production activities and a minor aspect of the ceremonial life. The deer dance and the animal associations of the *pascolas* are no longer relevant to the economic life or to any other aspect of life in Pascua. In response to this situation there are minor conflicts in the culture, observable only in conflicting attitudes toward the ceremonial performers. There is no conflict in daily activities demanded by the two inconsistent aspects of the culture. The animal gods have so far decayed already that they make few demands of those who still maintain relations with them. They are losing their social personalities through the decay of the ceremonies which personalize and define them. They might be said to be passing out of Pascua culture much as are the individuals who become responsive to the job pattern. Their participation becomes only partial and less and less frequent. But, at the same time that they are passing out of the culture, one of the institutions associated with them, the *pascola* dancers, is becoming associated with the new deities and is thus remaining in the culture.

The removal of the *pascolas* from a former, now irrelevant, ceremonial context and their integration into a new and at present vital one seems to be an example of what Radcliffe-Brown meant in saying that, when a functional inconsistency exists in a society, "it [the society] will not die . . . . but will continue to struggle toward some . . . . kind of social health." Elements of the aboriginal ceremonial pattern are being fused effectively with the Christian pattern, and the *pascolas*, a last remnant of the former, are still in process of fusion.

However, if we are to take the "struggle toward some kind of social health" as a part of the hypothesis of functional inconsistency, then how are we to account for the failure of the society of Pascua to adjust its primary conflict—that between leadership and jobs? We have pointed out that the only sort of adjustment that is being carried on is that by individual persons and that it consists chiefly in a process of moving out of Pascua society—a resolution of the conflict which can result ultimately only in the extinction of the culture, not in its reintegration on a new basis. It seems that we might restate the hypothesis: When a society is faced with a functional inconsistency, and a way is presented to resolve the crisis as it is manifest in the lives of the individuals by their withdrawal, either into the old system or out of the society, there need occur no *cultural* resolution of the inconsistency—even though the disappearance of the culture results.

It becomes clear, in the light of this modification of the hypothesis, that we have been dealing with two distinct kinds of functional inconsistencies in Pascua culture. That involving the *pascolas* is being resolved in the manner predicted by the original hypothesis. The irrelevance of the animal associations to the present ceremonial system is resulting in their reformulation in Christian terms. The deer-dancer is passing out of the culture, but the *pascola* is not. His performance has too important a place in the system of *padrino* relations which continue to be vital in the integration of the society. Moreover, as ceremonial host he serves to link the profane crowd with the sacred activities characteristic of the *fiesta*. This aspect of his social function continues, and it becomes necessary merely to reinterpret him in terms of the newer basis of ceremony, namely, to link him by myth and ritual to the functioning Christian deities. This, as we have seen, is being done; he is coming to be associated with Jesus, and even the animals to whom he traditionally appeals are now spoken to as "saints." The resolution of an inconsistency is, in other words, taking place entirely in terms of Yaqui-Christian culture. The latter has moved away from a former base, but, as this happens, it takes with it as an integral feature the *pascola* who is modified to fit the newer system of concepts. This amounts to change within the pattern of determinants of present-day Yaqui culture.

The other functional inconsistency which involves leadership in the ceremonial societies is not being resolved in the same way. Observing from without, we can imagine a solution which would be consonant with Yaqui culture. The leaders of the *matachinis* and the *fariseos*, for example, might be provided with food and clothing by the villagers and thus be free to devote themselves to the work of their respective societies. Such a solution would be in harmony with the values set up by the ceremonial system, but there seems to be no tendency in this direction. The actual history of ceremonial participation and leadership points to an entirely different type of solution. Individual Yaquis react to the inconsistency, but their response is to become, culturally speaking, Mexicans and thus, in greater or less degree, to cease to be Yaquis. There is, therefore, no adjustment of the elements of Yaqui culture to one another in the face of the conflict, that is, no cultural resolution of the inconsistency. It is this consideration which requires modification of the hypothesis.

In conclusion, we may emphasize the difference between the two kinds of changes which are taking place. The distinct character of the phenomena might be made clear by utilizing some such distinction as that between "culture" and "society." The culture of a group of individuals consists in the system of common understandings by which they relate themselves to material objects, to supernatural beings, and to one another. Some of the understandings which Pascuans share with one another in their culture are going through a process of modification in response to a new economic environment, and consequently an old feature of the culture, the *pascola*, is undergoing fundamental change. This takes place with no important disorganization, since the change is guided by already developed concepts with which most Pascuans are familiar. It is an instance of the constant harmonizing of part with part which occurs in any developing culture, through the unceasing interaction of person with person. However, Pascuans do not interact only with Pascuans. They are a part of the society of Tucson; that is, they have social relations with individuals in Tucson and therefore constitute with the latter an aggregate of interacting persons. To some extent they have common understandings with persons of Tucson, but interaction with them does not necessarily mean that the activities have the same meanings for Pascuans as for persons of Tucson. The Pascuan interpretation of an employer as a *patrón*, it will be recalled, was not shared by Tucsonans. Pascuans whose lives reveal the job pattern–ceremonial pattern conflict are members of both Pascua society and Tucson society, but the job may have either Tucson or Pascua meanings for them. To the extent that it has Tucson meanings for an individual, he withdraws from Pascua society. It is in this connection that we find changes taking place in the society, but not in the culture, of Pascua. The society making use of Pascua culture is losing members. The culture continues to exist and even in certain respects to develop, but its existence is definitely threatened by the gradual reduction of the society which finds the culture usable.

BIBLIOGRAPHY

Arizona Daily Star. Tucson, Arizona. Files for the years 1917, 1918, and 1922.

BAERLEIN, H. *Mexico, Land of Unrest.* Philadelphia: J. B. Lippincott Co., n.d.

BANCROFT, H. H. *History of the North Mexican States.* 2 vols. San Francisco: A. L. Bancroft & Co., 1884–89.

BEALS, CARLETON. *Mexican Maze.* Philadelphia: J. B. Lippincott Co., 1931.

BEALS, RALPH L. "Historical Reconstruction of Cahita Culture." Manuscript.

———. "Present-Day Yaqui-Mayo Culture." Manuscript.

BENNETT, WENDELL C., and ZINGG, ROBERT M. *The Tarahumara.* Chicago: University of Chicago Press, 1935.

BOAS, FRANZ. *The Mind of Primitive Man.* Rev. ed. New York: Macmillan Co., 1938.

DOMINGUEZ, FRANCISCO. "Costumbres Yaquis," *Mexican Folkways* (Mexico City), July, 1937, pp. 6–24.

———. "Musica Yaqui," *ibid.*, pp. 32–44.

DURKHEIM, EMILE. *Le Suicide.* 2d ed. Paris, 1911.

HOGBIN, H. IAN. *Law and Order in Polynesia.* New York: Harcourt, Brace & Co., 1934.

HOLDEN, W. C., *et al. Studies of the Yaqui Indians of Sonora, Mexico.* "Texas Technological College Bulletin," Vol. XII, No. 1. Lubbock, Tex., January, 1936.

HRDLIČKA, ALEŠ. "Notes on the Indians of Sonora, Mexico," *American Anthropologist*, VI (new ser.; 1904), 51–89.

KROEBER, A. L. *Uto-Aztecan Languages of Mexico.* "Ibero-Americana," No. 2. Berkeley: University of California Press, 1934.

MALINOWSKI, BRONISLAW. "Culture," *Encyclopedia of the Social Sciences*, Vol. IV. New York: Macmillan Co., 1931.

RADCLIFFE-BROWN, A. R. "On the Concept of Function in Social Science," *American Anthropologist*, XXXVII (new ser.; 1935), 394–402.

RADIN, PAUL. *Mexican Kinship Terms.* "University of California Publications in American Archeology and Ethnology," Vol. XXI, No. 1. Berkeley: University of California Press, 1931.

SAUER, CARL. *Aboriginal Population of Northwestern Mexico.* "Ibero-Americana," No. 10. Berkeley: University of California Press, 1935.

SPENCER, HERBERT. *The Principles of Sociology*, Vol. I. New York: D. Appleton & Co., 1925.

SPICER, E. H. "A Problem in Acculturation To Be Attacked through Field Investigation." Manuscript in Department of Anthropology, University of Chicago.

SPICER, ROSAMOND B. "The Easter Fiesta of the Yaqui Indians of Pascua, Arizona." Unpublished Master's thesis, Department of Anthropology, University of Chicago, 1939.

THOMAS, CYRUS, and SWANTON, JOHN R. *Indian Languages of Mexico and Central America.* Bureau of American Ethnology Bull. 44. Washington: Government Printing Office, 1911.

TURNER, J. K. *Barbarous Mexico.* Chicago: C. H. Kerr & Co., 1911.

PHOTOGRAPHS

Plates II to XIII

PLATE II
A Yaqui Houseyard, looking South over the Mexican Barrio Belén (Photo by D. J. Jones, Jr.)

PLATE III
The House of the *Maestro Mayor* (Photo by D. J. Jones, Jr.)

PLATE IV
Weighing in the Cotton

PLATE V

Making *Tortillas* for a Death Ceremony *(Cumpleaño)*

PLATE VI

The *Fariseos* on *Limosna*

PLATE VII

The Rhythm of the *Matachinis* (before the Church of San Ignacio)

PLATE VIII

ʧapa'jekam

PLATE IX
A Procession on Palm Sunday: *Matachini, Pascolas, Tampa'leo,* Deer-Dancer, and Altar Boys (Photo by D. J. Jones, Jr.)

PLATE X
Before the Altar

PLATE XI
A Stop at a Station of the Cross: Friday Procession in Lent

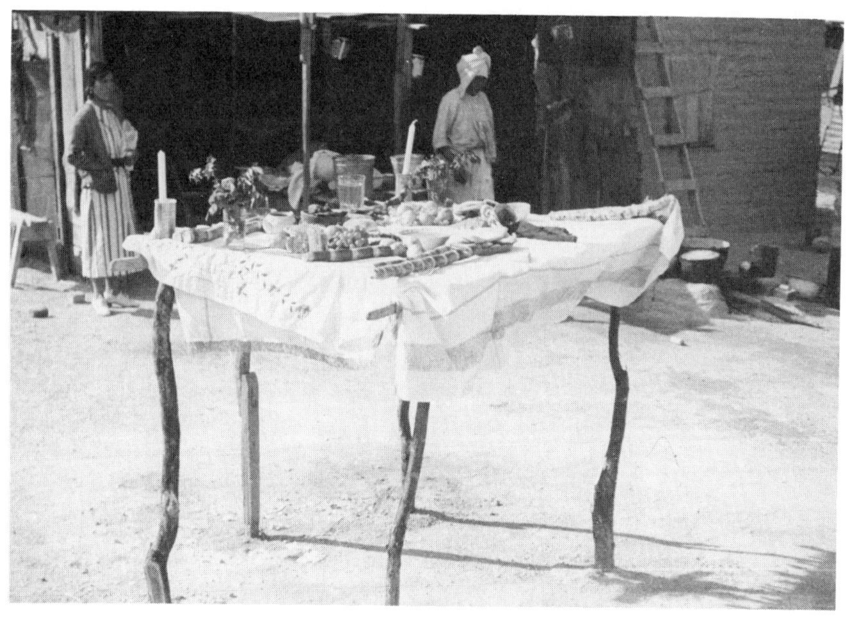

PLATE XII
A Table with Food for the Dead on All Saints' Day

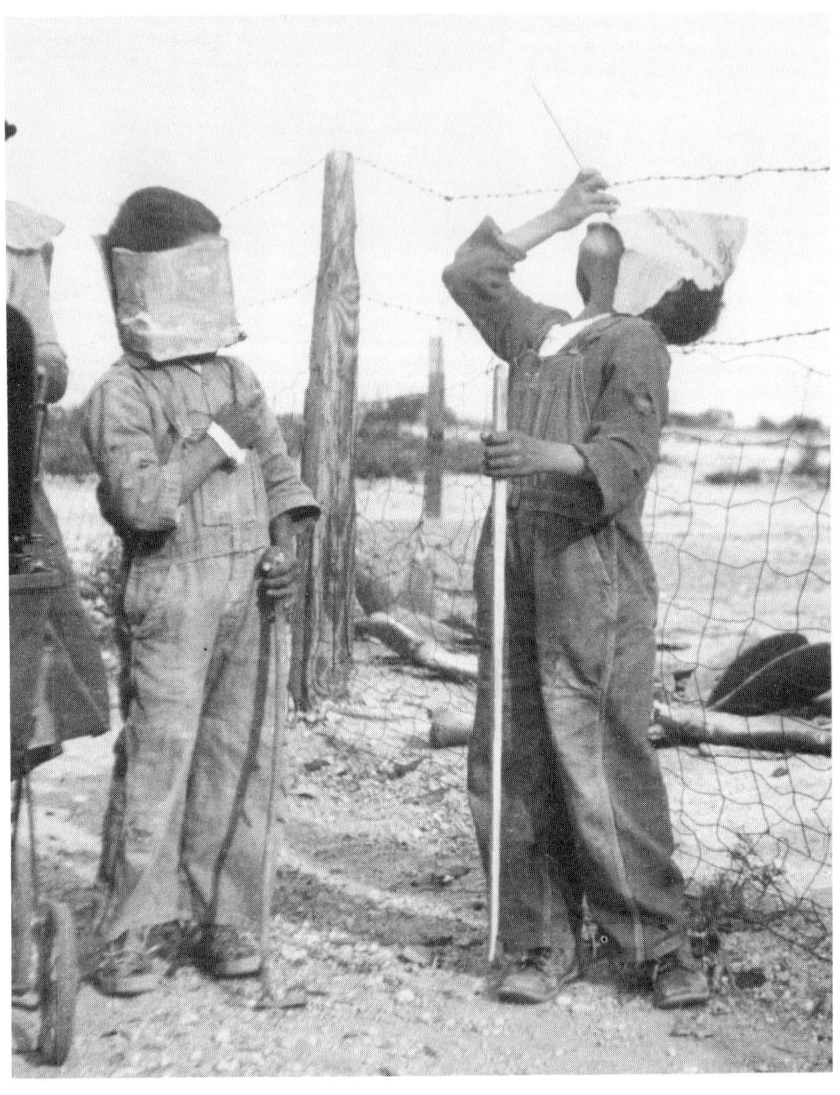

PLATE XIII
Playing *tʃapa'jeka:* Children Learn the Old Ways

INDEX

[PRINTED IN U·S·A]